7003/4002   £12.99   6/11

D1630945

Routledge Revision: Questions &

Employment Law

2011–2012

Routledge Q&A series

Each Routledge Q&A contains approximately 50 questions on topics commonly found on exam papers, with answer plans and comprehensive suggested answers. Each book also offers valuable advice as to how to approach and tackle exam questions and how to focus your revision effectively. New **Aim Higher** and **Common Pitfalls** boxes will also help you to identify how to go that little bit further in order to get the very best marks and highlight areas of confusion. And now there are further opportunities to hone and perfect your exam technique online.

New editions publishing in 2011:

Civil Liberties & Human Rights
Commercial Law
Company Law
Constitutional & Administrative Law
Contract Law
Criminal Law
Employment Law
English Legal System

Equity & Trusts
European Union Law
Evidence
Family Law
Jurisprudence
Land Law
Medical Law
Torts

For a full listing, visit http://www.routledge.com/textbooks/revision

BLACKPOOL AND THE FYLDE COLLEGE

3 8049 00135 915 0

Routledge Revision: Questions & Answers

Employment Law

2011–2012

Deborah Lockton

Professor of Employment Law, De Montfort University

Routledge
Taylor & Francis Group

LONDON AND NEW YORK

Seventh edition published
2011 by Routledge
2 Park Square, Milton Park, Abingdon, Oxon, OX14 4RN

Simultaneously published in the USA and Canada
by Routledge
270 Madison Avenue, New York, NY 10016

Routledge is an imprint of the Taylor & Francis Group, an informa business

© 1996–2011 Deborah Lockton

Previous editions published by Cavendish Publishing Limited
First edition   1996
Second edition   2000
Third edition   2002
Fourth edition   2005

Previous editions published by Routledge-Cavendish
Fifth edition   2007
Sixth edition   2009

The right of Deborah Lockton to be identified as author of this work has been asserted by her in
accordance with sections 77 and 78 of the Copyright, Designs and Patents Act 1988.

Typeset in The Sans by RefineCatch Limited, Bungay, Suffolk
Printed and bound in Great Britain by TJ International Ltd, Padstow, Cornwall

All rights reserved. No part of this book may be reprinted or reproduced or utilised in any form or by any
electronic, mechanical, or other means, now known or hereafter invented, including photocopying and
recording, or in any information storage or retrieval system, without permission in writing from the
publishers.

British Library Cataloguing in Publication Data
A catalogue record for this book is available from the British Library

Library of Congress Cataloging-in-Publication Data
Lockton, Deborah.
    Employment law/Deborah Lockton. — 7th ed.
        p. cm. — (Q&A Routledge questions & answers series)
ISBN 978–0–415–59321–2
1. Labor laws and legislation—Great Britain. 2. Labor laws and legislation—Great Britain—Problems,
exercises, etc. I. Title. II. Title: Q&A Employment Law.
    KD3009.L636 2011
    344.4101076—dc22   2010033206

ISBN13: 978–0–415–59321–2 (pbk)
ISBN13: 978–0–203–83283–7 (ebk)

Contents

Preface

Yet again, since writing the last edition of the Questions & Answers book, employment law has continued to evolve. The complicated statutory dismissal and grievance procedures were abolished in April 2009 after it transpired that, rather than reducing claims to tribunals, they caused claims to increase as parties argued on the interpretation of the regulations. In addition, just before the change of government in May 2010, the Equality Act 2010 received royal assent. This Act repeals all previous anti-discrimination legislation and places it with one statute. Mainly a consolidation Act, it does, however, introduce some new concepts. It overrules the much-criticised *Malcolm* decision relating to disability, by introducing the concept of discrimination arising out of disability and removing the need for a comparator. It puts on a statutory basis the decision in *Coleman*, in relation to discrimination by association, and introduces the concept of indirect discrimination in the area of disability for the first time. It introduces the right to claim for dual-characteristic discrimination – for example, a claim on the basis that someone has been discriminated against because they are black and female – and allows for positive discrimination in certain circumstances. In relation to discrimination on contractual terms, it introduces a right to sue on the basis of a hypothetical comparator in circumscribed situations and also renders void any term in a contract that prohibits employees discussing pay. While all of these are welcome changes, during the writing of this book, the implementation date of October 2010 for the majority of the Act and April 2011 for the right to claim dual-characteristic discrimination was removed from the government website. Panic! The coalition government said that it would implement the Act but would delay some of its more controversial elements. As such, I have written Chapters 5 and 6 using the 2010 Act, but have avoided answers involving the more controversial elements which have been delayed.

While the impact of some the above changes has yet to be seen, judges have not been idle. As a result, a number of questions now have slightly different answers. I have also inserted a number of new questions and answers to take into account some of the recent additions to legislative protection.

This book has always been intended to help students when faced with assessments in employment law. It is meant to be used in conjunction with textbooks in this area and, to this end, I have followed the format I used in my book *Employment Law*

(7th edn, 2010). The questions in each chapter, however, do not cover all the details in individual areas, nor are the answers intended to be the definitive answers. The aim is to give the student an example of the approach to answering questions in each area and to identify the key issues to be learned and understood.

As always, I give my thanks to my colleagues who have kindly given their consent to my use of questions that are not my own. My thanks also to my colleagues and friends who, within the book, have faced some horrendous employment problems, including those friends who, upset at not being in previous editions, I have endeavoured to include in this one! I would also like to thank my students, who show me how students learn and the best way to put across concepts and ideas. My thanks again to Keith for unlimited support and caffeine, and to my son James, who now feels it's cool to be mentioned in a book but is still unappreciative of the amount of time I spend on the computer! Despite all of this help, any mistakes are my own.

The law is stated as I understand it to be on 1 October 2010.

DJ Lockton
Thrussington
October 2010

Table of Cases

Table of Legislation

STATUTES

    Act 1982 145
Theft Act 1968
    s 5(4) 77
Trade Disputes Act 1906 260
Trade Disputes Act 1965 260
Trade Union Act 1871 260
Trade Union Act 1984 260, 261
Trade Union and Labour Relations Act
    1974 260
Trade Union and Labour Relations
    (Amendment) Act 1976 260
Trade Union and Labour Relations
    (Consolidation) Act 1992 135, 195,
    257, 260, 262
    s 10 251
    s 11 252
    s 20(2)(c) 271
    s 46 253
    ss 46–59 253
    s 47 253
    s 47(1) 253
    s 47(2) 253
    s 54(2) 253, 254
    s 55 254
    s 55(5A) 254
    s 56 254
    s 56(4) 254
    s 63(2) 250, 254
    s 65(2) 254, 255
    s 65(2)(a) 255
    s 145A 22
    s 145B 22
    s 152 208
    s 152(1) 208
    s 152(2) 209
    s 154 208
    s 170 141
    s 174 22, 23, 249, 252, 254, 255
    s 174(2) 255
    s 174(4) 254, 255

    s 174(4)(b) 255
    s 174(5) 255
    s 178 56
    s 178(1) 57
    s 178(2) 57
    s 178(3) 243
    s 179 49, 56, 57
    s 188 206, 240, 243
    s 188(1) 244
    s 188(1A) 244
    s 188(2) 244
    s 188(4) 244
    s 188(7A) 244
    s 188(A)(1)(b) 244
    s 188(A)(1)(e) 244
    s 189(1) 244
    s 189(1)(b) 206
    s 189(1B) 244
    s 189(3) 244
    s 189(7) 244
    s 193 240, 244
    s 194(1) 245
    s 207 180
    s 219 210, 258, 269, 270
    s 219(1)(a) 270, 271
    s 224 258
    s 226(1) 271
    s 226A 271, 272
    s 226A(2) 272
    s 226A(2A) and (2B) 272
    s 228 262
    s 228A 262
    s 232B 262
    s 234 271, 272
    s 234A 271, 272
    s 236 160
    s 238 14, 161, 208, 210, 211
    s 238(3)(a) 211
    s 238A 14, 161, 208, 210
    s 238A(1) 210
    s 244(1) 210, 270

STATUTORY INSTRUMENTS

EU LEGISLATION

http://www.routledge.com/textbooks/revision

Visit the Routledge Q&A website to discover even more study tips and advice on getting those top marks.

On the Routledge revision website you'll find the following resources designed to enhance your revision on all areas of undergraduate law.

Good essays are the gateway to top marks. New to this edition, this interactive tutorial provides sample essays together with voice-over commentary and tips for successful exam essays, written by our Q&A authors themselves.

Knowledge is the foundation of every good essay. Focusing on key examination themes, these MCQs have been written to test your knowledge and understanding of each subject in the book.

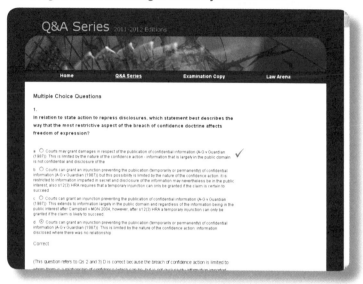

Having studied our exam advice, put your revision into practice and test your essay writing skills with our additional online questions and answers.

Don't forget to check out even more revision guides and exam tools from Routledge!

Lawcards are your complete, pocket-sized guides to key examinable areas of undergraduate law.

Comprehensive selections; clear, easy-to-use layout; alphabetical, chronological, and thematic indexes; and a competitive price make *Routledge Student Statutes* the statute book of choice for the serious law student.

Introduction

This book is intended to help students when faced with assessments in employment law. As the subject tends to build on contract and tort, it is normally taught in the later stages of a degree and thus students will already have been exposed to essay and problem-style questions. As such, this book provides examples of both types of question. It is intended to help students with both coursework and exam questions. It covers the main topics in an employment law syllabus, although it also covers collective employment law, which, in some institutions, is now taught as a separate subject in its own right. The answers in the book are in no way definitive, but show the student an approach to answering the questions and the sort of areas within the questions to emphasise.

PROBLEM AND ESSAY QUESTIONS

Very often, both coursework and examinations will contain a mixture of both essay and problem questions. While the approach to each is different, each answer should contain the three basics – introduction, argument and conclusion. In respect of essay questions, READ WHAT THE QUESTION IS ASKING. Start with a brief introduction to the relevant area. If it is a statement and you are asked to critically evaluate it, do that. Break down the statement into its component parts and critically evaluate each part looking at both sides of the argument. A major mistake that students make in relation to essay questions is that they take what is known in the trade as the 'shovel approach'. In other words, rather than reading what the question is asking, they interpret it as 'write all you know about', which means the answer is unfocused and often goes off at a tangent. Your conclusion should draw together all of your previous arguments and come to an opinion in relation to the question. You should not introduce new material into your conclusion but draw on arguments you have already discussed.

In relation to problem questions, remember that lecturers have to set the scene, so it is useful at the start to separate the wheat from the chaff. Underline all in the problem that you think is relevant and number each relevant point. In your answer make sure you have covered all the points you have numbered. You should write a very brief introduction, just as with essay questions, which identifies the area of law covered by the problem. Then go through the situation of each of the parties in the problem. A major mistake students make is to decide the outcome for each party at the outset. This often has the consequence of the student blithely ignoring any cases that don't fit in with their decided outcome. Have an open mind and pretend that you are arguing for both sides. Discuss the case for and against the party and see if any can be distinguished. Once you have done that, you should have a weight of arguments on one side or the other, which will then lead to a conclusion as to the likely outcome. Repeat the process in relation to all of the parties in the problem.

LENGTH OF ANSWERS

Coursework and examinations are testing different skills. Normally, coursework will have some sort of word limit – often 2,000–3,000 words. The questions are there to test a student's ability to put over all the points within the word limit in addition to research skills. Always read around the topic before you start to do your coursework, including articles on the subject. While textbooks will give you the basic knowledge, articles will go into specific detail on particular issues within the subject and will give you much more of a critical insight. While this is important in essay questions, it is also important in problems because there may be a major case that is relevant and an article may critique that case or criticise it. In examinations, the examiner is testing the student's skill in remembering the area of law and being able to apply it in a time-constrained environment. In both coursework and examination questions, don't write out the facts of the problem or, in most cases, the facts of the cases you are citing, merely the principle from the case. Your lecturer knows the facts and you are wasting words and/or time by repeating them. The only time you should write out the facts of cases is when you wish to distinguish them from the situation in the question to justify why you think it is different and thus would not be applicable. Don't expect to write as many words in an examination as in coursework. Lecturers are aware when writing examination questions that you have a limited amount of time and gear the question to take this into account. It is better to divide your time equally between the number of questions on the paper. Often, students will do a very brief last answer because they have left themselves 10 minutes at the end. This will score few marks.

THE FOOTNOTES

Footnotes in coursework essays are your way of demonstrating your breadth and depth of reading. Learn how to footnote properly and always cite primary sources – for example, don't footnote a statute book when citing statutory sections. Make sure you cite the date and page numbers as well as the citation for the journal when using articles, proper citation and page reference when quoting from a judgment, and the title, publisher, date, edition and page number when referencing a textbook. Make sure all references in your footnotes are included in you bibliography.

EXPRESSING A VIEW

In problem questions, you are being asked to decide what the probable outcome would be in relation to the parties in the problem. You are therefore expressing a view based on the arguments you have already put forward. The same may be true of essay questions. If the question is asking 'How far do you agree with this statement', then go for it! However, don't make generalist comments without supporting evidence. Your reading should lead you to agree in whole, totally disagree or agree with parts of the question. You should state why you agree/disagree, etc after discussing the evidence for and against.

EXAM PAPERS

Most examination papers in this area will contain a mixture of essays and problem questions. Use the same techniques described above. Analyse what an essay question is asking for and cover each point. Underline the relevant points in a problem and make sure you address each point in your answer.

EXAM TECHNIQUES

The suggestions below are intended to help with exam technique and point out common mistakes students make in exams.

(1) Spend five minutes reading the question. (Remember the shovel approach above!) In the case of a problem, underline the relevant parts. In the case of an essay, write a short plan of all the main points you wish to make.

(2) Do not repeat the question in your answer – doing so wastes time.

(3) Always, in any legal writing, use the third person. 'It is suggested', or 'from the discussion above it can be concluded' is better than 'I think'.

(4) Always back up whatever point you are making with a case, an article, a textbook or a statutory section. Never make statements that can't be evidenced.

(5) Unless you wish to distinguish cases do not write out the facts of cases; your examiner knows the facts.

(6) On the other hand, if you forget the name of a case, write down the facts briefly so the examiner knows that you are citing accurate authority.

(7) Don't spend a lot of time on an introduction. Every introduction should merely introduce the topic to which the question relates.

(8) Don't panic! If you feel you don't understand what a question is asking, go to another question and come back to the first when you have calmed down.

(9) Work out how much time you have for each question and stick to it. Leave space at the end of each question so that if you think of any extra points, you can add them in if you have time at the end.

(10) Enjoy! This is your opportunity to show all that you have learned – knowledge and skills – throughout the year. Show off that knowledge!

1 Institutions of Employment Law

INTRODUCTION

Invariably, the first topics studied in employment law are the sources and the institutions. This is because employment law has its own specific adjudicative forums and bodies, which oversee the operation of the law. As such, it is necessary to learn the nature of these institutions to be able to study the subject. General questions may arise on the institutions, or more specific questions may be set, given that the Trade Union Reform and Employment Rights Act (TURERA) 1993 gave to the Secretary of State power to increase the jurisdiction of the employment tribunals and this was introduced by the Employment Tribunals (Extension of Jurisdiction) Order 1994 (now the Employment Tribunals Act 1996). Further changes have been introduced by the Employment Tribunals (Constitution and Rules of Procedure) Regulations 2001 and 2004 and the Employment Tribunals (Constitution and Rules of Procedure) (Amendment) Regulations 2008.

In addition, the House of Lords' decision in *R v Secretary of State for Employment exp EOC* (1994) led to the Employment Protection (Part-time Worker) Regulations 1995, equating the rights of part-time workers with those of full-timers and establishing the basis on which the Commission may seek judicial review. Apart from this, European law has had a major impact in certain areas, particularly sex discrimination, equal pay and transfers of undertakings, in addition to the Human Rights Act (HRA) 1998, implementing the *European Convention on Human Rights*. As such, issues relating to jurisdiction can also arise in questions on other areas, as will be seen in later chapters.

The issues to be considered are:

❖ the role and nature of the institutions;
❖ the relationship between the institutions and the relevant areas of employment law in which they operate;
❖ the legalism in employment tribunals debate; and
❖ the impact of European law in this area.

This will mean that the student must have an in-depth knowledge of a broad area. Remember as well that, unless jurisdiction comes up in other areas, any questions on this topic are likely to be essay questions rather than problems.

Checklist ✔

Students should be familiar with the following areas:

- the jurisdiction of the tribunals and the Employment Appeal Tribunal (EAT);
- changes in jurisdiction, composition and procedure;
- the effect of European Treaty Articles and directives;
- the functions of the Commission for Equality and Human Rights;
- the attack on legalism in employment tribunals; and
- the impact of the **HRA 1998**

QUESTION 1

While employment tribunals can provide a quick and efficient remedy for an aggrieved employee, the restrictions placed upon them created problems for employees who wished to sue their employer. Changes made by the Trade Union Reform and Employment Rights Act (TURERA) 1993 eradicated these problems, and provided tribunals with a comprehensive power to protect employees against infringement of all their rights.

▶ Critically evaluate this statement.

Common Pitfalls ✗

◆ It is important to read what the question is asking for. A list of all the changes made by the Act does not answer the question, which asks you to critically evaluate the statement.

◆ You must identify the problems pre-1993. Note the changes made by TURERA and see which problems have been eradicated but which still exist.

Answer Plan
This question falls nearly into two parts: the first part asks about the problems
facing employees before the TURERA 1993; the second part asks for a discussion of
the changes made by the Act and consideration of whether these changes
eradicated the problems identified.

The issues to be considered are:

    ❖   tribunal jurisdiction before the TURERA 1993;
    ❖   limits on the jurisdiction;
    ❖   the problems that such limits caused;
    ❖   other problems caused by restrictions in making tribunal claims;
    ❖   how the jurisdiction was extended in 1994; and
    ❖   whether the present jurisdiction has met the problems identified earlier.

ANSWER

Employment tribunals were established by the Industrial Training Act 1964 with
limited jurisdiction. Over the years, however, the jurisdiction was extended until, prior
to amendments by the TURERA 1993, tribunals had the jurisdiction to hear almost all
individual disputes based on statutory claims. It is important to note, however, that,
until the 1994 amendments, tribunals only had jurisdiction to hear statutory claims
and, as such, would hear, inter alia, unfair dismissal disputes, redundancy disputes,
sex and race discrimination claims, and equal pay claims. Tribunals had no jurisdiction
to hear common law claims, which had to be heard by the ordinary courts. In addition,
other criticisms have been levelled against tribunals, which jurisdictional changes will
not address. These further criticisms will be discussed below.

Perhaps the major problem facing an employee before the changes made by the 1993
Act was the fact that tribunals could not hear common law claims. While on the face
of things this did not appear to be a major problem, in fact, an unfair dismissal claim
would often also involve a common law claim for damages for breach of contract.
While the employee could sue for the unfair dismissal in the tribunal, the damages
claim could only be heard by the ordinary courts, thus necessitating the employee
taking two actions in different forums in relation to the same act by the employer. For
example, in Treganowan v Robert Knee and Co Ltd (1975), the applicant was instantly
dismissed when the typing pool refused to work with her after she kept discussing
details of an affair she was having with a work colleague. The tribunal found that she
had been fairly dismissed. It further stated that her conduct did not justify instant
dismissal and that she should have received the six weeks' notice she was entitled to

by her contract. The tribunal, however, had no jurisdiction to hear the breach of contract claim or award damages for what the tribunal considered to be a breach of contract. To pursue an action for damages, Ms Treganowan had to take action in the county court. Furthermore, if the notice had been considerable and, therefore, the damages had been outside the county court jurisdiction, Ms Treganowan would have had to pursue her claim in the High Court. Breach of contractual notice provisions are obviously not the only breach of contract an employer can commit: many cases arise over breaches of express or implied terms in the contract. The tribunals, until 1994, had no jurisdiction over these claims, leaving the employee to use the ordinary courts.

While there had been much criticism of the jurisdictional limit placed upon the tribunals, the extent of the restrictions came to the fore with the introduction of the Wages Act 1986 (now the Employment Rights Act (ERA) 1996). This was brought in to remedy the deficiencies in the Truck Acts 1831–1940 and provides that there must be a statutory or contractual right to deduct from wages before any such deductions can be made. Section 13(1) of the 1996 Act states that an employer must not make a deduction from the wages of an employee unless the deduction is:

(a) required or authorised by statute; or
(b) required or authorised by a provision in the contract of employment that has been given to the employee or notified to the employee previously in writing; or
(c) agreed to by the employee in writing before the making of the deduction.

Section 14 then contains a list of exceptions to which s 13(1) does not apply. The Act has been widely criticised and, prior to the changes in tribunal jurisdiction, led to a series of cases on interpretation. The major problem was whether the Act applied to given situations. An illegal deduction gave an employment tribunal jurisdiction, normally within three months of the deduction being made. Any other deduction had to be recovered in the ordinary courts. This led to a series of cases defining the terms 'wages' and 'deduction' for the purposes of s 13(1) to see if the tribunals had jurisdiction in certain situations.

Section 27 of the ERA 1996 lists payments that can be regarded as wages. In particular, s 27(1)(a) refers to 'any fee, bonus, commission, holiday pay, or any other emolument referable to his employment, whether payable under his contract or otherwise'. This definition led to a number of cases discussing whether wages in lieu of notice are 'wages' for the purpose of s 13(1) and therefore whether employment tribunals had the jurisdiction to hear complaints about deductions from such payments. In the House of Lords' decision of *Delaney v Staples t/a De Montfort Recruitment* (1992), their Lordships decided that a payment in lieu was damages for a breach of contract. Such a payment did not arise out of the employment but as a result of the termination of employment and as such was not within the definition in s 27, even if the employer had a contractual right to pay wages in lieu. This decision meant that the tribunals could not hear complaints about deductions from such payments. Such complaints could only be heard by the ordinary courts, a situation acknowledged by the House of Lords, which ended with a plea that the jurisdiction of the tribunals be extended to hear breach of contract claims. Further cases have decided that, while *ex gratia* payments are not wages, it depends on the construction of the contract. In *Kent Management Services Ltd v Butterfield* (1992), an ex-employee complained that on his dismissal his employer had refused to pay him commission that was outstanding. The employer argued that the commission was discretionary as a clause attached to the contract said it would not be paid in exceptional circumstances such as bankruptcy. Wood P in the EAT held that, on interpretation, the anticipation of both parties must have been that, in normal circumstances, commission would be paid. As such, it was wages for the purposes of s 27(1)(a) and the tribunal had the jurisdiction to hear the complaint about the deduction.

The *Kent* case demonstrates another problem of interpretation that arises from the Act. How far is a total non-payment a deduction? The Court of Appeal in the *Delaney* case held that a non-payment was a 100 per cent deduction and, as such, tribunals would have the jurisdiction to hear such complaints. The issue was never raised before the House of Lords, so presumably this is still the law. If the jurisdiction of tribunals had been extended at this time, these problems would not have arisen.

While the limits on the tribunal jurisdiction have raised the major criticisms, other problems can also be identified. The first is the time limits that apply to different claims. These are different depending upon the claim brought. For example, an employee must present a claim for unfair dismissal within three months of the effective date of termination, whereas the time limit is six months on a redundancy claim. While different time limits can be confusing, there are further problems in that the tribunal has the discretion to allow a claim out of time if it was not reasonably practicable for a claim to be made within the three-months period (s 111(2) of the ERA 1996). Given that tribunal decisions are not reported, this can lead to a variation in practice in different tribunals, although some guidelines have been laid down by the courts (see, for example, *London International College v Sen* (1993)). Reporting of tribunal decisions would ensure more consistency.

A further problem lies in the fact that an applicant cannot obtain legal aid for a tribunal claim. Given that a large number of applicants are unemployed at the time of pursuing a case in a tribunal, this can be a major setback. In addition, until changes made in 2001 and 2002, a tribunal had limited powers to award costs where the claim was considered to be frivolous or vexatious and could only award costs of up to £500, a power exercised infrequently. In 1997–98 and 1998–99, they were awarded in fewer than 0.5 per cent of cases. Changes made by the Employment Tribunals (Constitution and Rules of Procedure) Regulations 2004 now give a tribunal the power to award costs where a party or a party's representative has acted improperly. Furthermore, a tribunal must consider awarding costs where a party or its representative has acted 'vexatiously, abusively, disruptively or otherwise unreasonably, or the bringing of the proceedings by the party is misconceived' (reg 14). 'Misconceived' includes having no real prospect of success (reg 2). The amount of costs a tribunal can award has increased to £10,000. While this may benefit a claimant, costs may also be awarded against a claimant and thus the effect of these changes may be to deter potential applicants.

Given the amount of legislation in the past few years in the area of employment law, claims are getting much more complicated and often the applicant will need the skills of a lawyer or other experienced representative to present his or her case. The problem may be exacerbated since the proposals introduced by s 20 of the Employment Act 1989 have come into effect. This section gave the Secretary of State power to make regulations for a pre-hearing review procedure, which would allow the tribunal, after such a review, to order one party to pay a deposit before continuing with the case. The initial amount of the deposit was £150, but this was increased to £500 in 2001. Pre-hearing reviews were introduced by the Employment Tribunals (Rules of Procedure) Regulations 1993. Section 38 of the TURERA 1993 gave the Secretary of State power to extend the jurisdiction of the tribunals to cover claims for damages for breach of contract subject to a financial limit. This extension of jurisdiction was introduced by the Employment Tribunals (Extension of Jurisdiction) Order 1994 (now the Employment Tribunals Act 1996). Personal injury claims are, however, still excluded, as are claims for breach of a term requiring the employer to provide accommodation, breach of a term relating to intellectual property, breach of a term imposing an obligation of confidence and breach of a restraint-of-trade covenant.

In addition, the tribunal jurisdiction applies only where there is a termination of the contract (see Capek v Lincolnshire County Council (2000)) and is subject to a £25,000 limit. The extended jurisdiction means that the situation in Treganowan will not arise again, as the tribunal can now hear both claims as long as the damages claims is within the financial limits set. Furthermore, the problems raised in Delaney relating to wages in lieu of notice are also resolved as, even though such payments are damages for breach of contract, the tribunal has jurisdiction to hear complaints in relation to deductions from such payments. As such, the amendments allowed by the TURERA 1993 have met the problems arising from the restricted tribunal jurisdiction in these types of case, and prevented the duplicity of actions, one in the tribunal and one in the ordinary courts, which used to be necessary.

The other problems identified above were not answered by the 1994 Order. In an area of law that has become increasingly complex over the years, legal aid is still unavailable and, now that the proposals of 1989 in relation to pre-hearing reviews have been enacted, this can only further restrict the number of applicants who can claim. In addition, different time limits in respect of different rights and unreported tribunal decisions, particularly when allowing an applicant to present a claim outside the statutory time limit, emphasise the need for legal aid to be available. Furthermore, the restriction as to the type of breach-of-contract claims that the tribunal can hear, plus the fact that the jurisdiction arises only on termination of the contract, lead one to question whether, in practice, the changes made that much difference. While the changes engendered by the 1993 Act are to be welcomed, the lack of other changes will still mean that not all employees have the opportunity to have their cases heard by an industrial jury.

QUESTION 2

Recent years have seen an attack on legalism in employment tribunals, which has led to both procedural and substantive changes. It can be argued, however, that the changes have gone too far and that there is no longer a balance between flexibility on the one hand and certainty on the other.

▶ Discuss.

Answer Plan

This is a very specific question and calls for a detailed discussion of the literature and the case law. It is not the sort of question that can be answered with a vague knowledge of some of the issues. With this sort of question, if the student has not read the relevant articles and cases, it is best to leave it well alone. On the other hand, if the student has done the required reading, this is a simple question to answer.

The issues to be considered are:

❖   rights of appeal from the tribunals to the EAT;
❖   procedural changes in the tribunals since 1985;
❖   the classification of issues as issues of fact;
❖   the disapproval of appellate courts laying down guidelines for tribunals to follow in recurring cases; and
❖   the narrow approach to what is a 'perverse' decision.

ANSWER

Employment tribunals were first established as an adjudicative forum in 1964. Since then, their jurisdiction has expanded with the increase in employment rights introduced by statute. A tribunal consists of a legally qualified chairperson and two wing members who are not legally qualified, one appointed after consultation with representatives of employers and the other appointed after consultation with representatives of employees. Tribunals were established to provide a method of speedy resolution of industrial disputes and, as such, to a large extent govern their own procedure, which should be flexible. An appeal from an employment tribunal lies to the EAT on a point of law. To appeal, a party must show that the tribunal was wrong in law. The Court of Appeal in *British Telecommunications plc v Sheridan* (1990) has stated that this means either that there is an error of law or that the tribunal's decision was perverse.

While the aim of providing a forum for a speedy and flexible resolution of an industrial dispute is to be applauded, it must be recognised that employment law is not a simple area to administer and that, in recent years, the law in this area has become increasingly complex. As such, employment tribunals have needed to consider more and more legislation, new concepts introduced by European law, and interpretations from the EAT, the ordinary courts and the European Court of Justice. Such considerations have led some commentators to raise concerns that tribunals are getting increasingly legalistic. It is this debate to which the question relates.

To a large extent, tribunal hearings are like those of a court. Both parties present evidence, call witnesses and are often represented. The Rules of Procedure, however, specifically state that a tribunal should seek to avoid formality. This means that a tribunal may hear evidence that would not be admissible in an ordinary court. Wood P, in *Aberdeen Steak Houses Group plc v Ibrahim* (1988), however, has stated that too much informality may itself lead to perceived unfairness, so leading to the conclusion that the EAT wishes to see more formalised hearings. Such increase in legalism has to some extent been prevented by the Rules of Procedure themselves. While the EAT may be concerned about the conduct of the hearings, the Rules allow a tribunal to give reasons for its decision in summary form only. To this rule, however, there are a number of exceptions: first, where the case concerns sex or race discrimination, equal pay, trade union victimisation, the closed shop or unreasonable exclusion or expulsion from a union; second, where it later appears to the tribunal that full reasons should be given; third, where a party orally requests full reasons at the hearing; and, fourth, where a party requests full reasons in writing within 21 days after receiving the summary reasons.

While this means that a party has a right to full reasons in any case, the Court of Appeal, in a series of cases, including *Varndell v Kearney and Trecker Marwin Ltd* (1983), has stated that the tribunals do not have to set out their reasons in full, although a later EAT has said (in *Levy v Marrable and Co Ltd* (1984)) that, where there is a conflict of fact, the tribunal should state that there is a conflict and which version it prefers. In *Yusuf v Aberplace Ltd* (1984), it further stated that a case may be remitted back to a tribunal if the EAT is unable to see why the tribunal reached the decision it did. Furthermore, in *Meek v City of Birmingham District Council* (1987), Bingham LJ emphasised that tribunals should outline their conclusions and reasoning so that an appeal court can see why the decision was made and whether a point of law is involved. This again suggests that later higher courts wish to see more legalism in the tribunals.

To some extent, however, it is how a tribunal's reasons, in whatever form, are used by the appeal courts that is the crux of the matter. Smith and Baker (*Smith and Wood's Employment Law*, 10th edn, 2010, Oxford University Press), while discussing the cases above, argue that there has been an attack against legalism. They quote the procedural changes as an example, but argue that the main attack has been substantive and has occurred on three fronts: the classification of as many issues as possible as questions of fact; the disapproval of appellate courts laying down guidelines for tribunals to follow in recurring cases; and the narrowing of the definition of what constitutes a perverse decision.

In relation to the first point above, Smith and Baker cite many cases in which it has been held that the issue is one of fact and therefore cannot be subject to appeal. For example, in *O'Kelly v Trusthouse Forte plc* (1983), the Court of Appeal held that whether a contract was one of service or for services was a question of fact. Such an interpretation is surely debatable at best and leaves the party with no right of appeal unless he or she can argue that tribunal decision is perverse. This, however, ties in with the third point stated above – that is, the narrowing of what is defined as a perverse decision. In *RSPB v Croucher* (1984), Waite J said that perverse decisions would be exceptional and that the EAT could only call a tribunal decision perverse if the decision was not tenable by any reasonable tribunal properly directed in law. In *Neale v Hereford and Worcester County Council* (1986), May LJ gave this famous definition of perversity when he said that the EAT could only reverse a decision of the tribunal if it could be said, 'My goodness, that must be wrong,' and, although this has had its critics, Wood P, in *East Berkshire Health Authority v Matadeen* (1992), said that a decision can only be called perverse if: it was not a permissible option; it offended reason; it was one that no reasonable tribunal could reach; or it was so clearly wrong that it could not stand. Such an interpretation is much wider than that of Donaldson MR in *Piggot Bros and Co Ltd v Jackson* (1992) and almost appears to be the *Neale* test in a more specified form.

Smith and Baker argue that such an approach demonstrates a policy to return to the tribunals. While commending the policy, they argue that there is a danger it has gone too far and that issues that should be a matter of statutory interpretation and, therefore, questions of law, are being classified as questions of fact by the appeal courts. They give the example of the phrase 'other industrial action' in s 238 of the Trade Union and Labour Relations (Consolidation) Act (TULR(C)A) 1992. This section applies if s 238A does not apply, and removes the jurisdiction of the tribunal to see if a dismissal is fair or unfair in cases in which the employee was dismissed while taking part in a strike or other industrial action, so long as there are no selective dismissals or selective re-engagement. In Coates v Modern Methods and Materials Ltd (1982), the Court of Appeal held that what constitutes 'other industrial action' is a question of fact for the tribunal. This means that a tribunal in one part of the country could come to a totally different conclusion from a tribunal elsewhere, and the decisions could only be appealed if they were perverse. This inconsistency can hardly be said to engender a feeling of fair treatment on the part of complainants.

Smith and Baker's final point is that there has been increasing disapproval of the appellate courts laying down guidelines for tribunals to follow. In the early days of the EAT, that forum laid down guidelines in a variety of cases to establish consistency of approach in the lower tribunals. This was criticised, however, by Lawton LJ in Bailey v BP Oil (Kent Refinery) Ltd (1980) and although later EAT decisions show some guidelines being laid down, this has not been the case recently, although Wood P showed himself to be more accommodating in issuing such guidelines during his presidency. Smith and Baker argue that this relates back to perversity, as without doubt, a tribunal decision that ignored such guidelines would not be a perverse decision within the modern definition and would not be an appealable point of law, so that both (that is, the redefinition of perverse and the restriction on issuing guidelines) together have removed legalism from the employment tribunals. While such an approach does return decision-making to the tribunals and does create flexibility, the danger is that it also creates inconsistency and, with it, the potential for a sense of unfairness on the part of complainants.

QUESTION 3

In the past, employment tribunals were overburdened by the number of claims that were presented. There was little in the way of deterrent to a claimant with a claim that had little hope of success and nothing in the way of an alternative to pursuing that claim in a tribunal. Changes introduced since 2000, however, should go a considerable way to reducing the perceived burdens placed on tribunals.

▶ Critically evaluate this statement.

Answer Plan

This is a good question, asking the student to recount the changes since 2000 and to evaluate the impact of these changes. It is important to note that the question is not just asking about changes to tribunal jurisdiction and powers. It mentions the lack of alternative dispute resolution and therefore also requires a discussion of the introduction of the Advisory, Conciliation and Arbitration Service (ACAS) arbitration scheme and an analysis of its effectiveness.

The issues to be considered are:

❖ the introduction of the ACAS arbitration scheme in 2001;
❖ the changes made by the Employment Tribunals (Constitution and Rules of Procedure) Regulations 2001 and 2004; and
❖ an evaluation as to whether the changes together will reduce the burden on the tribunal system.

ANSWER

Employment tribunals were established in 1964 and, since then, their jurisdiction has been steadily increased. They have jurisdiction in respect of all statutory employment rights such as redundancy, unfair dismissal, discrimination claims, etc, and have limited jurisdiction in respect of breach of contract claims. In 1999–2000, there were 100,000 applications made to employment tribunals although three-quarters of those applications were resolved by a conciliation officer from ACAS or by a privately negotiated settlement. There is no evidence that the number of applications to tribunals is falling.

In 1994, the government looked for alternatives to tribunals to resolve employment disputes and examined ways in which to reduce the number of cases going to a full hearing. This was because of a recognition that the number of applications made to tribunals was increasing and creating an overload. The resultant changes included extending the areas of jurisdiction in which a chairperson could solely hear a claim by the Employment Rights (Dispute Resolution) Act 1998. This complemented changes introduced by the Trade Union Reform and Employment Rights Act (TURERA) 1993, which allowed the question of whether the tribunal had jurisdiction to hear a claim to be determined without a hearing if the parties so agreed and which also introduced the concept of a pre-hearing review, whereby there is a hearing without witnesses (usually conducted by the chairperson alone). If the pre-hearing review determines that there is no reasonable prospect of success, then a party could be ordered to pay a deposit to enable him or her to pursue the claim to a full hearing.

While these measures were intended to reduce the load on tribunals, evidence suggests that in reality this did not happen.

In 2001, the first of a number of reforms was introduced to ease the burden on tribunals. In May of that year, a new ACAS arbitration scheme was introduced as an alternative to a tribunal claim. The scheme only covers unfair dismissal and the right not to be unreasonably refused a request to work flexibly. The scheme is an alternative to a tribunal claim and thus, should parties agree to go to arbitration, they must sign an agreement taking the claim out of the tribunal system. An arbitrator's finding is enforceable in the same way as a tribunal decision and an arbitrator has powers to award reinstatement, re-engagement or financial compensation. In addition, arbitration is quicker and less formal than a tribunal.

In addition to the new arbitration scheme, the Employment Tribunals (Constitution and Rules of Procedure) Regulations 2001 were introduced. These gave employment tribunals more teeth and created a statutory duty for the tribunal to consider awarding costs in some cases. First, the amount of the deposit made after a pre-hearing review (discussed above) was increased from £150 to £500. The new Regulations create an overriding objective that tribunals deal with cases 'justly' (reg 10). This means that tribunals must ensure that parties are on an equal footing, keep down expense, deal with cases in ways that are proportionate to the complexity of the issues, and deal with cases in an expeditious and fair manner. This allows tribunals to move parties on where the issue argued is not difficult and allows parties to argue more fully where issues are more complex. Furthermore, new powers introduced by the 2001 Regulations allow tribunals to strike out any claims or proposed defences on the grounds that they are scandalous, misconceived or vexatious. 'Misconceived' replaces the word 'frivolous' under the old Regulations and appears to give tribunals a much broader category of claims that can be struck out.

The greatest change introduced by the 2001 Regulations is in relation to the costs that can be awarded. Prior to 2001, tribunals had a discretion to award costs of up to £500 where the claim was considered to be frivolous or vexatious. Now tribunals may award costs where either party or the party's representative has acted improperly. In addition, a tribunal must consider awarding costs where parties or their representatives have acted 'vexatiously, abusively, disruptively or otherwise unreasonably, or the bringing of the proceedings by a party has been misconceived' (reg 14). 'Misconceived' includes having no real prospect of success (reg 2). The costs a tribunal can award have been increased to £10,000.

Further changes were made by the Employment Act (EA) 2002. By that Act, the Secretary of State was given the power to issue regulations to cover a number of issues. These changes were introduced by the Employment Tribunals (Constitution and Rules of Procedure) Regulations 2004. First, tribunals have an additional power to award costs against a representative because of the way in which the representative has conducted the case. Representatives for these purposes include only those who charge for their services. Costs are awarded on the same grounds as above and, as above, are subject to a statutory maximum of £10,000. Second, tribunals have powers to determine an extended list of cases without a hearing where both parties consent and waive their rights to a hearing. Third, there is a power for tribunals to strike out weak cases at a pre-hearing review (previously, a tribunal could only require a payment of a deposit if the party continued; it could not prevent the party from continuing).

There have, therefore, been a great many changes since 2000. The question to ask is: what impact have these changes had?

The new ACAS arbitration scheme has limitations, which have led to criticisms. There are no procedural rules and parties cannot cross-examine witnesses. Arbitrators are not bound by existing law or precedent and therefore the provisions of the ERA 1996, which render certain dismissals as automatically unfair, are not binding on an arbitrator. The arbitrator can only find that a dismissal is fair or unfair and cannot decide jurisdictional points, such as whether an applicant is an employee or self-employed. In addition, given that the jurisdiction is limited to unfair dismissal and the right to request flexible working, any claim involving such and another claim can only partially be heard by arbitration. Further, if there is an issue regarding whether a dismissal has actually occurred, this must first be decided by a tribunal before ACAS can arbitrate. It is unlikely in these cases that a party would chose two forums to hear his or her claim, preferring to chose one forum that can hear all of the issues.

A further criticism can be levelled in respect of appeals. There is no right of appeal against an arbitrator's decision except in cases in which there has been a serious irregularity. The logic behind this is that arbitrators are not bound by existing law. It has to be said, however, that such a restriction on an applicant's rights cannot give the users of arbitration much sense of fairness. It is suggested that the restrictions noted may be a reason why, since its inception, the scheme has only dealt with approximately 60 cases. As such, the scheme is unlikely to relieve the existing burden on employment tribunals.

The changes to the tribunals themselves could, however, lessen the number of cases in the system. The power of the tribunals to order a £500 deposit in a pre-hearing review, in addition to the power to strike out a claim, could reduce the number of cases going to a full hearing. The increase in the amount of costs that can be awarded, including the fact that costs can be awarded against representatives who charge for their services, could act as a deterrent to a claimant with a weak case.

A major change relating to tribunal jurisdiction was the ill-fated statutory disciplinary and grievance procedures, which were introduced in April 2004 and abolished in April 2009. The aim of the procedures was to reduce tribunal claims by encouraging more workplace resolution of disputes; however, during their existence, tribunal claims increased. Figures, when released for the year 2009–10, will still not confirm whether the changes noted above have had an impact on tribunal claims, or whether the impact is the result of the abolition of the statutory procedures. As such, it will be some time before an evaluation of the impact of the changes can be made.

> **Aim Higher** ★
>
> ◆ There has been major criticism of the ACAS arbitration scheme and reading relevant articles will give your answer more depth; for example, Baker (2002) 31(1) ILJ 113.

QUESTION 4

Since its introduction in 2000, the Human Rights Act (HRA) 1998 has permeated every aspect of employment law. With reference to decided cases to date, assess the impact of the Act on the law of private employer and employee.

Answer Plan

This question requires a detailed knowledge of the cases since 2000 that have used the HRA 1998. Students need to know how the HRA has an impact on UK law and in particular the relevant Articles of the European Convention on Human Rights. Merely knowing the cases that have used the Act to date is insufficient. Students need to have enough knowledge of the cases to be able to assess the impact of the Act (and therefore the Convention) on employment law. Note also that the question is asking only for the impact in the area of the private not public sector.

The issues to be considered are:

- ❖ how the HRA 1998 introduces Convention rights into employment law;
- ❖ relevant Convention Articles that could impact – in particular, Arts 6, 8, 10, 11 and 14;
- ❖ an analysis of case law alleging breaches of Convention rights and incompatibility of UK legislation; and
- ❖ an assessment of the impact of the HRA 1998 on employment law.

ANSWER

The HRA 1998, which gives effect to the European Convention on Human Rights, came into force on 1 October 2000. Since coming into force, claimants can assert Convention rights in UK courts and tribunals, but only public-sector employees can bring an action against their employers directly by virtue of s 7. Private-sector employees have to rely on ss 2, 3 and 6 of the Act. These sections require tribunals to pay heed to the Convention and Strasbourg jurisprudence.

By s 3 of the HRA 1998:

> so far as it is possible to do so, primary and subordinate legislation must be read and given effect in a way which is compatible with the Convention rights.

Section 6 provides:

> it is unlawful for a public body to act in a way which is incompatible with a Convention right.

Section 6(3) provides that courts and tribunals are included in the definition of 'public authority'. Finally, s 2 provides:

> a court or tribunal determining a question which has arisen in connection with a Convention right must take into account any
>
> (a)   judgment, decision, declaration or advisory opinion of the European Court of Human Rights . . . .

Thus while a private individual (as opposed to the state) has no direct obligations under the Convention, courts and tribunals, under ss 2 and 3, must therefore read and give effect to legislation in a way that is compatible with such rights, taking into account Strasbourg jurisprudence. As such, the Act does not create any free-standing rights for employees, as there must be an existing right that has to be interpreted in line with Convention rights. Thus, prior to the introduction of the Employment Equality (Religion or Belief) Regulations 2003 (now the Equality Act 2010), given there are no free-standing rights to freedom of religion under Art 9 of the Convention, a private employee could only use the Convention to obtain a remedy for religious discrimination if such a claim could be brought under the Race Relations Act 1976 (now the Equality Act 2010) (for example, under the principle in Seide v Gillette Industries (1980)). As such, it is the recent expansion of protection, as required by the UK obligations to Europe, which may increase the impact in the future. In addition, in Whittaker v P and D Watson t/a M Watson Haulage (2002), the Court of Appeal held that neither an employment tribunal nor the EAT has the power to make a declaration that domestic legislation is incompatible with Convention rights.

Many commentators, at the introduction of the HRA 1998, thought that it would significantly impact on employment law. Relevant Convention Articles that were thought to produce such impact were:

❖ Art 6 – the right to a fair trial;
❖ Art 8 – the right to respect for private and family life;
❖ Art 9 – the right to freedom of thought, conscience or religion;
❖ Art 10 – the right to freedom of expression;
❖ Art 11 – the right to freedom of assembly and association; and
❖ Art 14 – the right to freedom of enjoyment of Convention rights without discrimination on any ground such as sex, race, colour, language, religion, political or other opinion, national or social origin, association with a national minority, property, birth or status.

As discussed above, the limitation within the Act that such rights are not free-standing means that the anticipated impact has not been so great. Cases to date indicate that where the Act may have the most impact is in respect of Arts 6 and 8 of the Convention.

Article 6 guarantees the right to a fair and public hearing within a reasonable time by an independent and impartial tribunal established by law. The Article has no effect on employer's disciplinary proceedings as the employee will always have a right to apply to an employment tribunal, which is independent and impartial. The Article has been used, however, in respect of delay in tribunals. In *Kwamin v Abbey National plc* (2004), the EAT held that excessive delay between the tribunal hearing and the decision rendered the decision unsafe (in that case, nearly 15 months after the hearing). The EAT stated that such a proposition was enshrined in the principle of natural justice, which was compatible with Art 6. However, in *Bangs v Connex South Eastern Ltd* (2005), the Court of Appeal held that the question of whether a decision is given without reasonable delay per se was not a question of law but of fact and therefore could not be appealed to the EAT under s 21 of the Employment Tribunals Act 1996. Only where the delay 'could be treated as a serious procedural error or material irregularity giving rise to a question of law in the proceedings before the tribunal' would it fall under s 21. Such cases, however, would be exceptional – for example, where the delay deprived the party complaining of its right to a fair trial. It is submitted that this decision severely limits the right contained in Art 6. In contrast, in *Teinaz v London Borough of Wandsworth* (2002), the Court of Appeal stated that the right under Art 6 entitles a claimant to an adjournment where, without fault on the part of the claimant, he or she is unable to appear. It is, however, for the claimant to prove the need for such an adjournment. Article 6 has also recently been applied in relation to legal representation in disciplinary hearings in the cases of *Kulkarni v Milton Keynes Hospital NHS Trust (2009)* and *R (on the application of G) v The Governors of X School (2009)*. In both cases, the result of the disciplinary would result in a loss of livelihood (in *Kulkarni*, being struck off, and in the second case, being put on the register as unable to work with children). The Court of Appeal, obiter in *Kulkarni*, and the High Court in the second case, said that in such proceedings the employee should be allowed legal representation to protect his or her rights under Art 6.

Article 8 guarantees the right to respect for private and family life, but Art 8(2) places restrictions on the exercise of such rights. This states that there shall be:

> no interference by a public authority with the exercise of this right except such as is in accordance with the law and is necessary in a democratic society in the interests of national security, public safety or the economic well being of the country, for the prevention of disorder and crime, for the protection of health or morals, or for the protection of the rights and freedoms of others.

Thus, in *X v Y (2004)*, it was held that such protection applies only to activity carried out in private, and a dismissal when the employer discovered that the employee had been cautioned by the police in relation to sexual activity in a public toilet was not protected by Art 8 as the activity had taken place in public. In *Whitefield v General Medical Council (2003)*, a doctor argued that the conditions imposed on his registration by the General Medical Council, which banned alcohol consumption and required submission to random testing for alcohol, were an infringement of his rights under Art 8. The Privy Council held, however, that there were no such interference as he could still enjoy private life without drinking alcohol and further, if there were such interference, it was justified on public safety grounds, since the ban was imposed because of his excessive use of alcohol. Likewise, in *Pay v Lancashire Probation Service (2004)*, Pay was a probation officer working with sex offenders and was dismissed when his employer discovered he ran an Internet company selling products relating to sadomasochism and attended fetish clubs. He argued that his dismissal was a breach of Arts 8 and 10, an argument rejected by the EAT. So too in *McGowan v Scottish Water (2005)*, in which McGowan was suspected of falsifying his time sheets over call outs and was dismissed after covert surveillance proved this to be the case. He argued a breach of Art 8. The EAT held that there was a breach but that the employer's actions were justified as it was protecting its assets.

There is an argument that the rights contained in Arts 6 and 8 may conflict, particularly where one party wants to introduce evidence that may be in breach of the other party's Art 8 rights. In cases involving secretly filmed conduct or those involving medical evidence, the courts have upheld that the right to a fair trial takes precedence over the right to respect for family life (*Jones v University of Warwick (2003)*).

Other Convention rights may impact on employment law. Article 9 may be relevant. In *Copsey v WWB Devon Clays Ltd (2005)*, a case before the introduction of protection against discrimination on religious grounds, an employee was dismissed because he refused to work on Sunday because of his religious views. He claimed unfair dismissal, raising Art 9. The Court of Appeal rejected his claim but on different grounds. Mummery LJ held that Art 9 did not apply because of the reasoning of the European Court of Human Rights in *Stedman v UK (1997)* that no one was making Copsey take a job that required him to work on Sundays. Rix LJ thought that Art 9 applied but that the exception in Art 9(2) (justified interference) applied and was covered by the criterion of reasonableness inherent in unfair dismissal. It is submitted that the Employment Equality (Religion or Belief) Regulations 2003 (now Equality Act 2010) may mean that Art 9 will have more of an impact in the future. Rights under Art 10 (freedom of expression) could have implications for dress codes but, in view of Art 14, rights under Art 10 will not be infringed where the dress code is non-discriminatory. One further provision, however, that has had an impact is Art 11 – the right to freedom of association and assembly.

Wilson and others v United Kingdom (2002) is a pre-HRA (1998) case but is important because the European Court of Human Rights (ECtHR) held that, by allowing employers to use financial inducements to persuade employees to come out of collective bargaining, UK law was in breach of Art 11. As a result, the Employment Relations Act 2004 has amended the Trade Union and Labour Relations (Consolidation) Act 1992. New ss 145A and B create rights for workers not to suffer an inducement to prevent them becoming or persuading them to become members of a trade union or to prevent them from taking part in trade union activities (s 145A). Section 145B also gives the worker a right not to be offered an inducement to pull out of collective bargaining. These amendments are a direct result of the *Wilson* case. Likewise, in *ASLEF v UK (2007)*, the ECtHR considered the impact of Art 11. In the case, Lee, who was a train driver and a member of ASLEF, was also a member of the BNP and had stood as a candidate in elections. His activities against anti-Nazi supporters had been reported to the police and the union expelled him. An employment tribunal held that the expulsion was in breach of s 174 of the TULR(C)A 1992, which, at the time, stated that it was unlawful to expel a member from a union on the basis of membership of a political party. ASLEF applied to the ECtHR arguing saying that the Act prevented the union from expelling a member of a political party whose views were contrary to the union's rules and that this was an infringement of Art 11.

The ECtHR stated that the expulsion did not interfere with Lee's freedom of expression (Art 10). It did, however, uphold the union's right to choose its members and held that the balance between competing Convention rights had not been struck and there was a breach of Art 11. As such, s 174 was amended by the Employment Act 2008 and now allows a union lawfully to exclude or expel an individual due to membership or past membership of a political party if such membership is contrary to a rule or objective of the union.

So what has been the impact of the HRA 1998 to date? From the cases so far, it seems to be very little. Apart from Wilson and ASLEF, the cases seem to conclude that the common law reflects the Convention, or that Convention rights do not apply, and thus the tribunal is not required to interpret the law in a way that is compatible. The fact that the Act does not create any free-standing rights has limited its impact, although the recent creation of additional rights, such as protection from discrimination on the grounds of religious belief and sexual orientation, may see more cases reflecting Convention rights. Hardy, in a paper given at the Society of Legal Scholars Conference in 2001, has suggested that the ACAS arbitration scheme could be an infringement of Art 6 rights, and Smith and Baker (*Smith and Wood's Employment Law*, 10th edn, 2010, Oxford University Press) argue that the Article may also be infringed because of the lack of legal aid in employment tribunal claims. Thus, to date, the impact is limited but may become considerably more important in the next few years.

Aim Higher ★

❖ The **HRA 1998** is having more of an impact now and it is important to incorporate recent decisions into your answer for extra marks.

❖ There have been a number of articles written on the impact of the **HRA 1998** on employment law. See, for example, Ewing (1998) 27 ILJ 275, Palmer (2000) 59 CLJ 168 and Skidmore (2003) 32 ILJ 334.

2

Nature of the Relationship

INTRODUCTION

Very often, examination papers on employment law contain a question on the nature of an employment relationship. In other words, the examiner is looking for the distinction between independent contractors and employees, and the various tests that have evolved over the years to determine whether a person works under a contract of service or a contract for services.

The issues to be considered are:

❖ the differences between independent contractors and employees;
❖ the legal consequences of the distinction; and
❖ the tests used to determine whether a person is an employee or an independent contractor.

Questions may be in the form of either essays or problems. Specific issues that students need to be familiar with are:

❖ the different liabilities an employer has for employees compared to independent contractors;
❖ how the status of the person may affect terms in the contract;
❖ how the status of the person affects employment protection rights;
❖ the control test (*Performing Rights Society v Mitchell and Booker* (1924));
❖ the organisation test (*Stevenson, Jordan and Harrison Ltd v Macdonald and Evans* (1952));
❖ the multiple test (*Ready Mixed Concrete (South East) Ltd v MPNI* (1968)); and
❖ the irreducible minimum.

It is also important to remember that if the question is a problem-type question, it may involve other areas, such as whether the person has a right to sue for an unfair dismissal. It is necessary therefore to establish exactly what the question is asking for. With regard to the above example relating to unfair dismissal, a question on whether the person is an employee and therefore can sue for an unfair dismissal is different from a question asking if the employee in the problem has the necessary qualifying criteria to pursue a claim, as will be seen in Chapter 9.

Checklist ✔

Students should be familiar with the following areas:

- the distinction between contracts of service and contracts for services;
- the legal consequences of the distinction;
- the different tests to determine status;
- the 'small businessman' approach; and
- the position of atypical workers.

QUESTION 5

'The tasks which people carry out and the contexts in which they do so daily become so much more numerous, more diverse and more sophisticated that no one test or set of tests is apt to separate contracts of service and contracts for services in all cases.' (May J in *The President of the Methodist Conference v Parfitt* (1984))

▶ To what extent do the courts use one test to determine the nature of the relationship between the parties and what are the consequences of deciding that a person is an employee?

Answer Plan

This question is a fairly standard one in this area and breaks down into two parts:

- ❖ what are the tests to determine whether there is a contract of service or a contract for services?
- ❖ what are the consequences of deciding that a person is an employee?

ANSWER

For a variety of reasons, which will be discussed below, it is important to determine whether a person is employed under a contract of employment. By s 230(2) of the Employment Rights Act (ERA) 1996:

a 'contract of employment' means a contract of service or apprenticeship, whether express or implied, and (if it is express) whether it is oral or in writing.

By s 230(1) of the ERA 1996:

> 'employee' means an individual who has entered into or works under (or, where the employment has ceased, worked under) a contract of employment.

This definition of an employee, although provided by statute, is not, however, helpful as it fails to define what is meant by a 'contract of service'. It is important to note that the definition given by the parties to the relationship is not conclusive, and it is the court that determines the status of the parties within the relationship. Thus, the fact that a person is called an employee does not mean that he or she is employed under a contract of employment. Due to the lack of clarity provided by statute, the courts over the years have devised a series of tests to decide if the relationship is one of employer–employee or employer–independent contractor.

In early cases, when employees were less skilled than they are today, the courts used the single test of control. This test arose in the context of vicarious liability and it seemed logical to look at the control an employer exercised over the employees. In *Performing Rights Society v Mitchell and Booker* (1924), McCardie J said: 'The final test, if there is to be a final test, and certainly the test to be generally applied, lies in the nature and degree of detailed control over the person alleged to be a servant.' The question of control was very simple: it meant that the employer controlled not only when the work was done, but also how it was done. As Bramwell LJ said in *Yewens v Noakes* (1880): 'A servant is a person subject to the command of his master as to the manner in which he shall do his work.' While the control test worked well when workers were unskilled, it became apparent that it became more of a legal fiction as the Industrial Revolution meant that workers became more skilled. In *Hillyer v Governors of St Bartholomew's Hospital* (1909), it was held that nurses were not employees when carrying out operating theatre duties, although a more realistic approach was taken in *Cassidy v Minister of Health* (1951). Cassidy, however, shows that control by itself was an insufficient test in a modern industrial society.

Due to the inadequacies of the control test, the courts looked for another test that would reflect the realities of a modern-day employment relationship. In *Stevenson, Jordan and Harrison Ltd v Macdonald and Evans* (1952), Denning LJ developed what he called the 'integration test'. He said in the case: 'Under a contract of service, a man is employed as part of the business and his work is done as an integral part of the business but, under a contract for services, his work, although done for the business, is not integrated into it but only accessory to it.'

While such a test got round the problems of the control test, Denning LJ never explained what he meant by 'integration', and later judgments regard the question of integration as part of a wider test rather than a test on its own.

The courts realised that, in a modern industrial society, no one factor could be isolated as the determinant of the relationship and, therefore, they developed what is known as the 'multiple test'. This was first propounded by McKenna J in *Ready Mixed Concrete (South East) Ltd v MPNI* (1968). In that case, he looked at a variety of factors, some indicating that the lorry drivers were self-employed, some indicating that they were employees. At the end of this balancing exercise, McKenna J asked himself three questions: (a) Had the employee agreed to provide his skill in consideration of a wage? (b) Was there an element of control exercisable by the employer? (c) Were there any terms in the contract that were inconsistent with it being a contract of service? In the case, the drivers could delegate driving duties and, therefore, although there were factors indicating that they were employees, McKenna J ruled that this term was inconsistent with a contract of service and therefore the drivers were self-employed.

While his decision was later criticised, the basis of it (that is, looking at a multitude of factors) was not, and this is the approach of the courts today. Cooke J summarised the approach of the courts in *Market Investigations Ltd v MSS* (1968) when he said that the question to be determined by the court was whether the person was in business on his own account (the 'small businessman approach'). If so, then there was a contract for services.

This then leads to the question of what factors are considered when adopting the multiple test. It is the court that decides the nature of the relationship and not the parties, although what the parties think is a factor that the court will take into account. In *Ferguson v John Dawson Ltd* (1976), a builder's labourer was self-employed. He was injured when he fell off a roof. The employer was in breach of safety duties owed to employees under the Construction (Working Places) Regulations 1966. The employer argued that, as the labourer was self-employed, no duties were owed to him. The Court of Appeal found that the labourer was, in reality, an employee, despite the label the parties had put on the relationship. If there is ambiguity as to the nature of the relationship, Denning MR suggested in *Massey v Crown Life Insurance* (1978) that the label the parties attach to the relationship will be conclusive. This has been doubted and narrowed in the later case of *Young and Wood Ltd v West* (1980), in which Stephenson LJ said: 'It must be the court's duty to see whether the label correctly represents the true legal relationship between the parties.'

In *Protectacoat Firthglow Ltd v Szilagyi* (2009), Szilagyi was dismissed from Protectacoat and claimed unfair dismissal. The company argued that it did not employ him as he had signed a partnership agreement. Szilagyi argued that, because the company supplied his van and tools, had control over him and he was not free to work elsewhere, he was an employee. The Court of Appeal said that normally the contract is the document that decides on the type of relationship, but if, on the evidence, the agreement was a sham, the court could disregard it when deciding the true nature of the relationship. On the facts the court decided that the agreement intended to conceal the actual relationship and Szilagyi was an employee. Likewise, in *Autoclenz v Belcher* (2009), car valeters had a contract that said they did not have to attend work and could send a substitute but they had to inform the company if they were going to send someone else. The Court of Appeal held that the two terms were inconsistent and did not reflect the true relationship between the parties, as no substitution had ever taken place. As such, the tribunal was entitled to look at the actual relationship between the parties and conclude it was one of employment.

The small businessman approach summarised by Cooke J in *Market Investigations* means that the court looks at a variety of factors such as investment, ownership of tools, who bears the risk of loss and who stands to make a profit. Homeworkers and casual workers are particular groups for which establishing the nature of the relationship may prove difficult. In both *Airfix Footwear Ltd v Cope* (1978) and *Nethemere (St Neots) Ltd v Taverna and Another* (1984), it was decided that homeworkers were employees – in *Cope*, because work was provided on a regular basis and there was a strong element of control, and in *Taverna*, because, in reality, there was a mutuality of obligations due to the length of the relationship.

By contrast, a case involving casual workers was *O'Kelly v Trust House Forte plc* (1983), in which it was held that casual workers were self-employed even though they worked solely for one employer, because there was no obligation for the employer to provide work when they showed up and no obligation on the casuals to offer their services. It was thus the lack of mutuality that led to the decision, despite the clear control exercised by the employer and the fact that it would be difficult to describe a casual worker as being in business on his own account. The House of Lords reached a similar conclusion in *Carmichael and Leese v National Power plc* (1999), in which it was decided that guides employed on a 'casual as required' basis were self-employed. Lack of mutuality of obligations has led to agency workers being classed as self-employed (*Wickens v Champion Employment* (1984), although see *McMeechan v Secretary of State for Employment* (1997)), and trawlermen who entered into separate crew agreements for each voyage were also deemed to be self-employed, despite the fact that they invariably returned to the same employer, again because of the lack of obligation to provide work or services.

The Privy Council highlighted the factors that the court must look to in *Lee v Chung and Shun Chung Construction and Engineering Co Ltd* (1990). The worker was a mason who suffered a back injury while working on a building site. The court looked at whether it could be said that the mason was in business on his own account and said that matters of importance were: whether the worker provides his own equipment;

whether he hires his own helpers; what degree of financial risk he takes; what degree of responsibility he has for investment and management; and whether, and how far, he has the opportunity to profit from sound management in the performance of his task. In *Hall (Inspector of Taxes) v Lorimer* (1992), however, the court stressed that the list of factors should not be gone through mechanically. Upholding a decision of the special commissioners, the court said: 'The whole picture has to be painted and then viewed from a distance to reach an informed and qualitative decision in the circumstances of the particular case.'

More recent cases have talked about the irreducible minimum needed to constitute a contract of employment. In *Carmichael and Leese v National Power plc* (1999), mutuality was seen as the irreducible minimum, while in *Express Echo Publications v Tanton* (1999), the Court of Appeal regarded personal service by the employee to be essential so that the power to delegate job duties was fatal to an employment claim. A later EAT, however, in *Macfarlane v Glasgow City Council* (2001), stated that a limited or occasional power of delegation is not inconsistent with a contract of employment. In *Dacas v Brook Street Bureau* (2004), the Court of Appeal upheld an appeal by the agency that Dacas was not an employee of the agency, but Mummery LJ posited that there may be an implied contract between the end user and the complainant because of the control exercised by the end user and the fact that Dacas had worked for the end user for some time could create mutuality. In *Bunce v Postworth Ltd t/a Skyblue* (2005), the Court of Appeal again held that the complainant was not an employee of the agency because of a lack of control and a lack of mutuality. However, in *Royal National Lifeboat Institution v Bushaway* (2005) and *Muscat v Cable and Wireless plc* (2006), it was held that the agency workers were employees of the end user. Smith LJ in *Muscat* saying that the decision in *Dacas* directs tribunals to consider the possibility of an employment contract between the worker and the end user, although the Court of Appeal in *James v London Borough of Greenwich* (2008) has stated that every case must turn on its own facts.

The question that must now be asked is: why is the distinction between employees and independent contractors important? A variety of rights and liabilities apply in respect of employees that do not apply to independent contractors. The major differences are listed below.

An employee pays insurance contributions, which are a percentage of his or her earnings, and the employer also makes a contribution. This gives the employee certain benefits in respect of unemployment, sickness and industrial injury, as well as State Pension rights. An independent contractor pays a flat-rate National Insurance contribution, irrespective of earnings, and has no rights to the benefits mentioned.

An employer must deduct tax at source for its employees and may be committing a criminal offence should it fail to do so (*Jennings v Westwood Engineering* (1975)). The employer is under no such obligation in relation to independent contractors although, in the building industry, the employer is required to deduct tax as if the workers are employees, and the workers can then claim tax back if they are genuinely self-employed. This was introduced by the Finance Act 1971 to avoid the notorious 'lump' system that was operating at the time. Criticisms have been raised against this as it provides only for the payment of tax and does not give the workers any other protection.

An employer is vicariously liable for its employees if they cause injury during the course of their employment, while, generally, no such liability exists in respect of independent contractors. In addition, while independent contractors and employees are protected by the Health and Safety at Work etc Act 1974, the employer owes more stringent duties to its employees, supplemented by implied terms in the contract of employment.

The law implies a host of terms into the employment contract and other terms come from sources outside the individual parties' negotiations, such as works rules and collective agreements. By contrast, a court is unlikely to imply terms into a contract between an employer and its independent contractor.

Finally, employment protection legislation – in the form of unfair dismissal and redundancy compensation, time-off rights, guaranteed payments and maternity rights – apply only to employees. Independent contractors have no such protection, although *Quinnen v Hovell* (1984) decided that all workers, whatever their status, are protected by the Equality Act 2010 where they are providing personal services, and the rights introduced by the Employment Relations Act 1999 (amending the ERA 1996) apply to workers and not only to employees.

It is therefore possible to say that while the courts use what on the face of it appears to be one test – the multiple test – to decide if a person is an employee, this test involves looking at a whole variety of factors with the aim of deciding whether the person is in business on his or her own account. Of these factors, control, mutuality of obligations and who bears the financial risk appear to be the most important, although the case of *Lorimer* has stressed that the court should not use the list of factors mechanically but should look at the overall picture. More recent cases are now talking about the irreducible minimum, but what the irreducible minimum is remains unclear, although the most recent cases suggest that there must be mutuality of obligations and control. It is important for both parties, however, to know what the legal relationship is. On the part of the employer, it will then know the extent of its liability and, on the part of the worker, he will know what rights he has, both in respect of his employer and in the wider context of welfare benefits and employment protection rights.

QUESTION 6

Arthur, Ian and Ricky are lorry drivers for East End Ltd, a haulage company. They have all been employed for three years. Employees at the company receive both holiday pay and sick pay. The company states in the contracts that the lorry drivers are self-employed. All of the lorry drivers are employed on different terms.

Arthur is paid per delivery although he is guaranteed a minimum of 20 deliveries a week. His lorry is provided by the company, although he must maintain it. He receives no holiday or sick pay. He pays his own tax and National Insurance and may substitute another driver if he wishes.

Ian and Ricky are on identical terms. They are paid a minimum weekly wage (which is the equivalent of 20 deliveries) and, after that, per delivery. They use company lorries, which the company maintains. They may also substitute a driver, but only with written permission from the company. Ian receives no holiday or sick pay and pays his own tax and National Insurance. Ricky used to receive his wages net but, recently, the company told him it would be cheaper for both the company and Ricky if he were to become responsible for his own tax and National Insurance. Ricky agreed to this.

Last week, Arthur was injured when a badly stacked load on the company premises fell on him. Ian was injured when his brakes failed going down a hill and Ricky was made redundant. The company argues that it has no liability towards any of them as they are all self-employed.

▶ Advise Arthur, Ian and Ricky if they are in fact employees and may therefore claim against the company.

Answer Plan

This problem is equivalent to the one addressed in the last question. We have three parties and the issue relating to all three is whether they are, in reality, employees and, in the case of Arthur and Ian, whether they can sue for their injuries and, in the case of Ricky, whether he can claim a redundancy payment.

The issues to be considered are:

❖   a brief discussion of the tests to determine status;

❖ a discussion of the multiple test – in particular, the main cases, such as *Ready Mixed Concrete (South East) Ltd v MPNI* (1968); *Market Investigations Ltd v MSS* (1968); *Lee v Chung and Shun Chung Construction and Engineering Co Ltd* (1990); *Hall (Inspector of Taxes) v Lorimer* (1992);

❖ recent cases talking about the irreducible minimum – *Carmichael and Leese v National Power plc* (1999); *Express Echo Publications v Tanton* (1999); *Macfarlane v Glasgow City Council* (2001); *Dacas v Brook Street Burean* (2004); *Bunce v Postworth Ltd t/a Skyblue* (2005); *Royal National Lifeboat Institution v Busbaway* (2005); *Muscat v Cable and Wireless plc* (2006); and

❖ the effect of tax avoidance on the rights of employees.

ANSWER

The issue to be discussed initially in respect of the three parties is whether they are in fact self-employed, as their contracts say. It will be seen below that while the label that the parties attach to the relationship may be a factor considered by the courts, it is by no means conclusive and, therefore, even though the parties are called self-employed, the law may decide that they are employees and are thus entitled to sue East End Ltd.

The original test used by the courts to determine if the relationship was one of employer–employee was the 'control test'. As employees became more skilled, however, it became apparent that the control test, as a single test to determine whether the person was an employee, was inadequate. Denning LJ, in the case of *Stevenson, Jordan and Harrison Ltd v Macdonald and Evans* (1952), developed what became known as the 'organisation integration test' to overcome the problems with the control test. In the case, he said:

> under a contract of service, a man is employed as part of the business and his work is done as an integral part of the business but under a contract for services his work, although done for the business, is not integrated into it but only accessory to it.

The problem with the test is that Denning LJ did not define 'integration' and the test never won favour in the courts. The case is important, however, in that it showed a move away from control as the sole determinant.

By the 1960s, the courts realised that a variety of factors needed to be examined to see if the relationship between the parties was one of employment. In *Ready Mixed Concrete (South East) Ltd v MPNI* (1968), McKenna J laid down what is now known as the 'multiple test'. This involved looking at a multiplicity of factors and then asking three questions: first, whether the employee agrees to provide his skill in consideration of a wage; second, whether there is an element of control exercisable by the employer; and third, whether there are provisions in the contract that are inconsistent with it being a contract of employment. Whereas the decision was later criticised, the essence of the test was not. Cooke J, in *Market Investigations Ltd v MSS* (1969), summarised the approach taken by the courts by saying that the question to be determined was whether the person was in business on his own account. Later, cases such as *Lee v Chung and Shun Chung Construction and Engineering Co Ltd* (1990) and *Hall (Inspector of Taxes) v Lorimer* (1992) have given us a list of factors the courts have identified as relevant. More recently, cases such as *Carmichael and Leese v National Power plc* (1999), *Express Echo Publications v Tanton* (1999), *MacFarlane v Glasgow City Council* (2001), *Dacas v Brook Street Bureau* (2004) and *Muscat v Cable and Wireless plc* (2006) have laid down the irreducible minimum needed for a relationship to be one of employment.

In all the cases in the problem, the contracts state that the lorry drivers are self-employed. In *Ferguson v John Dawson Ltd* (1976), a builder's labourer agreed to work as self-employed and was injured when he fell off a roof. No guard rail had been provided, in breach of the duty owed to employees under the Construction (Working Places) Regulations 1966. The employer argued that the worker was self-employed and no duty was owed to him. The Court of Appeal held that the worker was an employee and that the statement as to his status was not conclusive. On the basis of *Ferguson*, therefore, it would appear that the statement in the lorry drivers' contracts is not conclusive, but may be a factor the court takes into account.

The Court of Appeal, however, has distinguished *Ferguson* in cases in which there has been an agreed change in status. In *Massey v Crown Life Insurance Co* (1978), the worker had been employed for two years as a branch manager. He then agreed to register himself as John L Massey and Associates and became the branch manager of his one-man business. The reason for the change was that the employer no longer wanted the administrative burden of deducting tax and National Insurance contributions and the Inland Revenue agreed to the change in status. When Massey was sacked, he claimed unfair dismissal. The Court of Appeal said that he had no capacity to claim as he was self-employed. Denning MR distinguished *Ferguson* on the basis that, in *Massey*, there was a genuine agreement entered into from which Massey benefited. The agreement was instigated by Massey himself, and he could not claim the benefits of self-employment and some time afterward say he was an employee in order to claim unfair dismissal. While this case is of no relevance to Arthur and Ian, it may have a bearing on Ricky's claim as Ricky agreed to become self-employed, having originally been an employee. *Massey* may be distinguished from Ricky's case, however.

While Denning MR was prepared to accept that, in *Massey*, an agreement had been made at the instigation of the worker and the agreement should stand, he also stated, 'the parties cannot alter the truth of the relationship by putting a different label on it and use it as a dishonest device to deceive the Revenue'.

Furthermore, in *Young and Wood Ltd v West* (1980), in which a worker chose self-employment for tax reasons, Stephenson LJ distinguished *Massey* on two grounds: first, that Massey had two contracts – one as the manager and another for services under a general agency agreement; and second, there was a deliberate change in status agreed by the parties. On this basis, it may be possible to argue that, in Ricky's case, the court will not accept the label later agreed by the parties for two reasons: first, it appears that the change is to deceive HM Revenue & Customs (HMRC); and second, because there is only one contract and not two, as in *Massey*. Should this be the case, the court can look to see the true status of Ricky.

In Arthur's case, there are a variety of factors that the court will examine. He is paid per delivery but he is guaranteed a minimum of 20 deliveries per week. This means that he has a guaranteed income every week and this may indicate that he is an employee as per the first condition laid down by McKenna J in *Ready Mixed Concrete*. His lorry is owned by the company, although he must maintain it. In the *Lee* case, the court listed a variety of factors to consider when deciding the nature of the relationship. There, the court looked at: whether the worker provided his own equipment; whether he hired his own helpers; what degree of financial risk he took; what degree of responsibility he had for investment and management; and how far he had the opportunity to profit from sound management in the performance of his task. In *Lorimer*, the worker was a vision mixer and used equipment provided by the television company that employed him. He was paid gross for his work; he had no long-term contracts with any company; he was responsible for his own pension and sick provision; and none of his money was used in the programmes he mixed. Nor did he stand to make a profit or loss from any of the programmes with which he was involved. The court held that Lorimer was self-employed. If we apply these cases to Arthur's situation – although he is guaranteed a minimum number of deliveries a week, which would suggest that there is mutuality of obligations, it is up to him whether he does the work and if he goes above the minimum; therefore, to some extent, he controls how little or how much he does and therefore earns. While he does not own the tools, he has to maintain the lorry, so, to a large extent, he controls the way he earns in that, if he does not invest in adequate maintenance, he will be the loser and not the company. He can delegate his driving duties, so, in a way, he can hire his own workers. Looking at all these factors, and the judgments in *Lee* and *Lorimer*, it would appear likely that the court would hold that Arthur is self-employed, since there appears to be little control on the part of the employer.

One other indication that Arthur is self-employed comes from the judgment of McKenna J in *Ready Mixed Concrete*. The third question McKenna J said had to be asked was whether there were any terms in the contract that were inconsistent with it being a contract of employment. Here, Arthur can delegate driving duties when he wishes without any consultation with the company. Such a term is inconsistent with a contract of employment as such a contract is a personal contract under which the employee is taken on for his original skills. Duties cannot be delegated under a contract of employment without the permission of the employer. Furthermore, in *Express Echo Publications v Tanton* (1999), the power to delegate duties was seen as fatal to an employment claim, although the later case of *MacFarlane v Glasgow City Council* stated that a limited power of delegation was not inconsistent with a contract of employment. In Arthur's case, however, there appears to be no limit on his power of delegation, unlike the limit on both Ricky and Ian under which they can delegate only with written permission from the company and thus it would appear that Arthur's situation is more like that in *Tanton*. The term in Arthur's contract is therefore further evidence that he is not an employee but self-employed. As such, he is owed no specific safety duties, but may be able to sue for his injuries under occupier's liability or through the law of negligence.

Ian and Ricky are on identical terms. While their contracts state that they are self-employed, looking at the relevant terms and the judgments in *Lee* and *Ferguson*, it is questionable whether, in reality, this is the case. Both are paid a minimum wage, which they appear to get whether or not they work (unlike Arthur who is only guaranteed a minimum number of deliveries if he wants them). The company both provides and maintains the lorries and, therefore, neither Ian nor Ricky has to put in any financial investment. Both can delegate driving duties, but only with the written permission of the company (that is, a limited power of delegation), which means the company has the ultimate say as to who makes the deliveries. While they pay their own tax and National Insurance, this is only one factor and it is submitted that the factors indicating that they are employees outweigh this fact. As such, Ian is an employee and the employer owes him a duty to provide safe equipment. The employer has broken this duty and Ian can sue.

It has already been stated that, although Ricky agreed to the change in his status, *Massey* could be distinguished and the parties' statement as to status will be a factor for consideration only and not conclusive. If this is the case, following the arguments above in relation to Ian, Ricky is also an employee. On the face of it, therefore, he is entitled to sue for a redundancy payment. It depends, however, on the reason for the change in status. Until recently, if the reason was to defraud HMRC, the contract became void as it was set up for an illegal purpose. As such, no rights could arise out of it and Ricky would have had no right to redundancy pay (*Jennings v Westwood*

Engineering (1975)). Ricky's innocence or guilt would be irrelevant, as the contract was void *ab initio* because its purpose was illegal, rather than it having been established for a valid purpose but illegal in its performance (*Corby v Morrison* (1980)). *Jennings* however, must now be read subject to *Enfield Technical Services v Payne/Grace v BF Components Ltd* (2008). In the joined cases, the Court of Appeal stated that, to defeat an unfair dismissal claim on the grounds of an illegal contract, there must be some misrepresentation or hiding of the true relationship. A mislabelling of the relationship or an arrangement that deprives HMRC of monies is not enough to render the contract illegal. This may suggest that, for the purposes of redundancy as well, if the sole purpose of the change in status was only to prevent money going to HMRC, this in itself will not render the contract illegal, and Ricky may be entitled to a redundancy payment In addition, if Ricky can show that the intention behind the change in status was, for example, administrative convenience for the employer and no other reason, then, as an employee, he is entitled to redundancy pay based on his three years' service.

QUESTION 7

While the law gives some protection to atypical workers, it has not gone far enough, with the result that millions of workers still do not have basic employment protection.

▶ To what extent do you consider this statement an accurate reflection of the law?

Common Pitfalls

❖ There have been a number of recent cases on agency workers but this question is asking about all atypical workers and not only agency workers.

❖ Ensure that you answer all of the question.

Answer Plan

This is a question that picks up on recent Court of Appeal decisions in the area, in particular cases involving agency workers. It is necessary to begin by defining what an atypical worker is, and to look at the protection or otherwise given to each class of such worker.

The issues to be considered are:

❖   what is an atypical worker – that is, homeworkers, casual workers, part-time workers, fixed-term workers and agency workers;
❖   how the tests for determining who is an employee exclude certain groups of workers, concentrating on cases such as *Airfix Footwear Ltd v Cope* (1978); *Nethermere (St Neots) Ltd v Gardiner* (1984); *O'Kelly v Trust House Forte* (1983); *Carmichael v National Power plc* (2000); *Motorola plc v Davidson* (2001); *Dacas v Brook Street Bureau* (2004); *Bunce v Postworth Ltd t/a Skyblue* (2005); *Craigie v London Borough of Haringey* (2007); *James v London Borough of Greenwich* (2008);
❖   any specific statutory protection that exists;
❖   shortfalls in employment protection; and
❖   future developments.

ANSWER

Employment law in Britain gives protection to certain classes of people. While those who come under the definition of worker receive limited protection, full protection, including rights not to be unfairly dismissed and rights to compensation on redundancy, is only given to those who satisfy the definition of employee in s 230 of the Employment Rights Act 1996. While all employees are workers, not all workers are employees. Further, the normal employee is a person who works full-time, at the workplace, under a contract of services. Increasingly, however, the workforce has become more flexible, which reflects government policy stated in *Fairness at Work* (1998). This has led to an increase in workers described as atypical – that is, those falling outside of the normal pattern of working – and in some cases the law has not adapted to give these atypical workers employment protection. Atypical workers for these purposes are part-time workers, fixed-term workers, homeworkers, casual workers and agency workers.

In respect of part-time workers, there is some protection as a result of EU intervention. The Part-Time Workers Directive resulted in the Part-Time Workers (Prevention of Less Favourable Treatment) Regulations 2000. These protect a part time worker against less favourable treatment than a comparable full-time worker, as regards terms of the contract or being subjected to any detriment by an act or deliberate failure to act, unless the treatment is objectively justified. In assessing whether the treatment is less favourable, the pro rata principle is applied – for example, while the same hourly rate should be applied to both full-time and part-time workers, it is legal to pay for the number of hours worked. There is no legal definition of part-time worker; this is assessed 'having regard to the custom and practice of the employer' (reg 2(2)) and the comparison is with a full-time worker who is defined in reg 2(4) as employed by the same employer under the same type of contract and engaged in the same or broadly similar work. This is not as clear-cut as it seems, as shown by the case of *Matthews v Kent and Medway Towns Fire Authority* (2006), in which there was an issue of whether part-time firefighters could compare themselves to full-time firefighters, given that while part-timers merely fought fires, full-timers had much broader duties, such as promotion of health and safety, and education. After losing up to the House of Lords, their Lordships decided by a 3:2 majority in the part-timers' favour, but the case shows that a comparison with a full-timer is not as clear-cut as it seems.

While it can be argued that part-time workers have always had protection under the Sex Discrimination Act 1975 (now Equality Act 2010), because often it is women who work part-time and any less favourable treatment could be seen as sex discrimination, this was not the case in relation to fixed-term working. As such the Fixed-Term Workers Directive was transposed into English law by the Fixed-Term Employees (Prevention of Less Favourable Treatment) Regulations 2002. Like the Part-Time Workers Regulations, they protect against less favourable treatment than a comparable permanent worker, unless the treatment can be objectively justified, and they also give protection in preventing the employer from employing a person on a series of fixed-term contracts, in that, after four such contracts, the fixed-term employee is regarded as permanent (reg 8(2)).

While the Regulations give some protection, certain factors should be noted. First, the protection is only for employees, whereas the protection for part-time working covers the wider category of workers. Second, the comparator is the same as the 2000 Regulations, which may cause problems. Third, in determining whether there has been less favourable treatment, the tribunal can look at the whole package rather than each term individually (reg 4). Such an approach is prohibited under the Equal Pay Act 1970 since the House of Lords' decision in *Hayward v Cammell Laird Shipbuilders* (1988). Thus while on the face of it there appears to be a great deal of protection, the reality may be different, particularly as the Court of Appeal in *Webley v DWP* (2005) held that non-renewal of a fixed-term contract is not less favourable treatment, pointing out that it 'was the essence of a fixed-term contract that it came to an end at the expiry of the fixed-term'.

While there is specific legislation protecting part-time and fixed-term workers/ employees, this is not the case with other atypical workers – namely, homeworkers, casual workers and agency workers. Any protection that such classes of worker may receive depends on whether they are classified as employees, and the tests used by the courts are more suited to those working in normal employment relationships rather than atypical ones. Over the years, the courts have used the multiple test originated in *Ready Mixed Concrete (South East) Ltd v MPNI* (1968) to establish that an employment relationship exists and have looked for control, personal service and mutuality of obligations between the parties. It is this final factor that works against many atypical workers.

Homeworkers are a group that, on the face of it, appears vulnerable. However, in *Airfix Footwear Ltd v Cope* (1978) and *Nethermere (St Neots) Ltd v Taverna* (1984), it was held that there was mutuality of obligations where the homeworker worked on a regular basis for the employer. Casual workers are also a group that, on the face of it, appears to fall foul of the requirement of mutuality and the case law bears this out. Cases such as *O'Kelly v Trust House Forte, Clark v Oxfordshire Health Authority* (1998) and *Carmichael and Leese v National Power plc* (1999) all state that casual workers are not employees as the nature of casual work is that there is no obligation on the employer to provide work, nor on the worker to accept work if it is offered despite the reality that work was offered and accepted on a regular basis. However, a recent EAT decision may offer a glimmer of hope. In *St Ives Plymouth Ltd v Haggerty* (2008), the EAT stated that the expectation of being given work, resulting from a practice over a period of time, can constitute a legal obligation to provide work and to perform the work provided. In that case, the worker regularly worked and had she refused to do so would have been taken off the list of regular casuals whom the employer employed. Elias P stated that the practical commercial consequences of not providing work, on the one hand, or of not performing it, on the other, could crystallise over time into legal obligations. Whether this becomes the general view of the courts has yet to be seen.

Lack of control is the factor that has led to decisions that agency workers are not employees of the agency (*Wickens v Champion Employment* (1984); *Bunce v Postworth Ltd t/a Skyblue* (2005)). However, this then leads to the possibility that the worker may be an employee of the client that does control the day-to-day work of the worker. While this was held to be the case in *Motorola Ltd v Davidson* (2001) and suggested obiter in *Dacas v Brook Street Bureau* (2004), this line of argument was not followed in later cases such as *Craigie v London Borough of Haringey* (2007). As a result of conflicting decisions in relation to agency workers, the President of the EAT stated that all such cases should be suspended pending the Court of Appeal ruling on the matter in *James v London Borough of Greenwich* (2008). The Court of Appeal upheld the decision of the EAT that Ms James was not an employee of the client. Given that the minimum requirement for a contract of employment is mutuality of obligations, and given that, when Ms James was absent, the agency provided another worker, the question of control was irrelevant. Further, in an agency relationship, the client is not paying directly for the work done by the worker as it is also paying for the services of the agency. If the contractual position is clear, there is no need to imply a contract of employment between the worker and the client, and this would only be necessary if there were some words or conduct that would entitle a tribunal to conclude that the documents no longer reflect the true situation. Passage of time on its own does not justify such an implication. Given *James*, it seems clear that, in the majority of cases, agency workers will be seen as self-employed and therefore unprotected to a large extent by the law, although as workers they will still have some limited employment rights and will be protected under anti-discrimination legislation, which protects those who personally provide services.

So there is some, but not complete, protection for certain classes of atypical worker, but from the case law it appears that casual workers and agency workers are likely to be classed as self-employed and thus have no protection. Things may be about to change in relation to agency workers, however. The Temporary and Agency Workers (Protection of Less Favourable Treatment) Bill, which failed to become law in the last Parliament, has been reintroduced. Meanwhile, in May 2008, the Department for Business, Enterprise and Regulatory Reform announced that the Government had reached an agreement with unions and employers that will see agency workers receiving equal treatment after 12 weeks' employment. However, equal treatment does not mean equal employment protection rights. It merely means that the same basic working and employment conditions will apply to such workers as if they had been recruited directly by the employer and it does not cover occupational social security schemes. The Department of Business and Regulatory Reform estimates that there are a million temporary workers in Britain at the moment. These workers have some limited protection under the National Minimum Wage Act 1998, the Working Time Regulations 1998 and under anti-discriminatory legislation, but they do not have protection against unfair dismissal and redundancy despite, in some cases, working for the same client for many years. It is true to say that the same is true of casual workers, but it is submitted that it is more likely that casual workers are just that: casual and not wishing to be in a permanent full-time relationship. Agency workers, on the other hand, often work for the same client for long periods of time and in reality are subject to the control of that client. While the agreement in May 2008 gives added protection, it still leaves over a million workers with no job security at a time when the government is promoting flexible working. As such, the law has still got some way to go to provide adequate employment protection for atypical workers.

Aim Higher ★

❖ There were a number of articles written when *Dacas* was decided. Incorporating this reading into your answer will gain you extra marks.

❖ Reading Reynolds (2006) 35 ILJ 320 and Wynn and Leighton (2006) 35 ILJ 301 will give you a critical analysis of the area.

Sources of Contractual Terms

INTRODUCTION

Many employment law exam papers will contain a question on the sources of the terms in an employment contract. This chapter and Chapter 4 will deal with all the terms, although this chapter will be dedicated to those terms that come from sources within the workplace and Chapter 4 will deal with the implied duties.

The issues to be considered are:

❖ express terms;
❖ collective agreements as a source of contractual terms;
❖ the contractual status of works rules – incorporation of disciplinary and grievance procedures;
❖ the status of the statutory statement;
❖ custom as a source of contractual terms; and
❖ implied terms.

Although general questions on the different sources of terms do come up, more often, a question will be set on one or two of the sources and will require an answer as to whether a term from a particular source has become part of the individual's contract of employment. This means that a detailed discussion of all the sources is unnecessary. To answer a specific question on this area, students need to be familiar with:

❖ interpretation of express terms and the process of variation;
❖ express and implied incorporation of collective agreements;
❖ the process of incorporation of other documents;
❖ the relationship between the statutory statement and contractual terms;
❖ the effect of a custom on the contract; and
❖ the judicial process of implication of terms.

Finally, it is important to note that while sources of terms may be a question in itself, a repudiatory breach of contract on the part of the employer can be a constructive dismissal. Knowledge of this area of the syllabus might, therefore, be required for other questions.

Checklist ✔

Students should be familiar with the following areas:

■ judicial interpretation of express terms — in particular, *Johnstone v Bloomsbury Area Health Authority* (1991);

■ judicial interpretation of flexibility and mobility clauses;

■ what constitutes a variation of terms;

■ enforceability of collective agreements between the collective and individual parties — in particular, cases such as *British Leyland (UK) Ltd v McQuilken* (1978), *Joel v Cammell Laird* (1969), *Duke v Reliance Systems Ltd* (1982), *Miller v Hamworthy Engineering Ltd* (1986), *Scally v Southern Health and Social Services Board* (1991), *Henry v London General Transport Services* (2001);

■ enforceability of works rules and disciplinary procedures — in particular, *Secretary of State for Employment v ASLEF (No 2)* (1972);

■ the status of the statutory statement — particularly the judgment of Browne-Wilkinson J in *System Floors (UK) Ltd v Daniel* (1981);

■ the implication of terms by the tests in *The Moorcock* (1889) and *Shirlaw v Southern Foundries Ltd* (1939);

■ the effect of restraint of trade covenants.

QUESTION 8

Production workers working for Webb Ltd have received a Christmas bonus every year for the last 15 years. During that time, the company has always traded at a profit but, last year, the company traded at a loss and no bonus was paid.

Last week, the company issued a new rule, which was posted on the noticeboard. The rule states that management reserves the right to require any employee to submit to a body search upon leaving the company premises, in order to check that property of the company is not being removed.

All the terms and conditions of employment of production workers working for the company are the product of a collective agreement negotiated between their union and the company, although the agreement has now terminated. One of the clauses in the agreement stated that redundancy selection would be on the basis of LIFO (last in, first out). The company now wishes to make five production workers redundant on the basis of 'lack of management potential'.

▶ Advise the company of the contractual implications of these changes.

Common Pitfalls

❖ The question is asking you to advise the company. If you were advising someone, you wouldn't give them a history of the present law, so don't do so in an answer such as this.

❖ Judicial implication of terms is a two-part test. The contractual tests indicate whether there should be a term or not and, if one should be implied, what the content should be. Don't go straight to the content and miss out the first stage.

Answer Plan

This question is looking at the implication of terms into an employment contract from three different sources: judicial implication; works rules; and collective agreements. The question asks the student to advise the company as to the contractual implications of its actions and thus is asking whether the company can enforce the changes it has introduced against the employees.

Therefore, the issues to be considered are:

❖ the contractual tests for implication of a term and the test for deciding the content of that term;

❖ whether works rules are contractual or merely orders from an employer and the consequences of any analysis;

❖ how far clauses in a collective agreement are appropriate for incorporation into an individual contract of employment;

❖ the process of incorporation of terms from a collective agreement into an employee's contract; and

❖ the effect on the employment contract of the termination of the agreement at the collective level.

ANSWER

The company is seeking advice as to the contractual implications of its actions. If, in each case, the company has lawfully amended the contracts of employment of the production workers, then it can compel the employees to comply with the amended terms. If, however, the company has unilaterally varied the contractual terms, the employees can refuse to comply with the changes and sue for damages should they suffer loss.

In the first situation, the company has paid a bonus for 15 years and now appears to have withdrawn it. If such payment has now become a term of the contract, this unilateral action on the part of the company may be a breach. The question to be asked is: given that it would appear that the contract is silent as to the issue of a Christmas bonus, would the courts imply such a term into the contract and, if so, what would the content of the term be? Implication of terms into a contract allows the court to fill in the gaps where the parties have failed to provide for a situation. In traditional contracts, there has been a presumption against adding in terms the parties have not expressed, but this presumption has not applied in employment contracts. There are two contractual tests that the courts use to imply terms into a contract. The first of these comes from the case of *The Moorcock* (1889) and implies a term because it is necessary to give the contract 'business efficacy'. The second test comes from *Shirlaw v Southern Foundries Ltd* (1939) and is known as the obvious consensus, or the 'oh, of course', test on the basis that, if a person were to ask the officious bystander if such a term should be in the contract, he would reply, 'oh, of course'.

Smith and Baker (*Smith and Wood's Employment Law*, 10th edn, 2010, Oxford University Press) argue that the old contractual tests have been modified in relation to employment contracts in three ways: first, there are inferred terms, which the courts are prepared to imply because they appear reasonable in all the circumstances rather than based on any supposed intention of the parties; second, implied duties that apply to all employment relationships; and third, what the authors describe as 'overriding terms' – that is, terms that are regarded as so important that they will be implied regardless of the parties' intentions. An example of such an overriding term is the duty to ensure the employee's safety, which, according to Stuart-Smith LJ in *Johnstone v Bloomsbury Area Health Authority* (1991), is so important that any express contractual term must be read subject to it.

In the case of the Christmas bonus, the first point to consider is whether the courts would hold that this has now become a term of the contract because it appears reasonable in the circumstances. An objective approach to this was seen in the case of *Mears v Safecar Security Ltd* (1982), in which the Court of Appeal gave guidance on the implication of terms into the contract. The Court said that a broad approach should be taken, and a term may be inserted based on all the evidence as to how the parties have worked the contract in the past. Thus, in that case, there was no implied term relating to sick pay, because the employees had never claimed it in the past. This approach can also be seen in *Courtaulds Northern Spinning Ltd v Sibson* (1988), in which Slade LJ said that the term the court should imply was one the parties would probably have agreed to if they were being reasonable. As such, a mobility clause was implied into the contract because the employee had always worked on different sites, even though there was no express term requiring him to do so.

For the past 15 years, the employer has paid a Christmas bonus. Given that this has happened for so long, it could be argued that it is reasonable that such payment has become contractual. In fact, it may also be argued that, under *Shirlaw*, the officious bystander would say 'oh, of course,' when asked if this has become a contractual term. This ignores, however, the situation in which the bonus has been paid. Over the last 15 years, the company has always made a profit; this year, it has made a loss. If, therefore, the old contractual tests are used to see if there should be a term relating to bonuses, and the concept of reasonableness is used to define the content of the term, then it could be said that there will be a term that the employees will receive a bonus when the company makes a profit. Thus, if this year the company was in profit, failure to pay the bonus will be a breach of contract and the employees can sue. If, as is the case, the company has made a loss, there will be no breach on the part of the company.

Another possibility is that the bonus has become a contractual term due to custom and practice. Smith and Baker state that for a custom to become legally binding it must be notorious, well established so that the employee must have taken employment subject to it, or have grown up while the employee was employed and thus the employee impliedly accepted it. In *Quinn v Calder Industrial Materials Ltd* (1996), the employers had paid enhanced redundancy benefits on four occasions between 1987 and 1994. When redundancies were declared in 1994 there were no enhanced benefits and the employees claimed that they were contractual due to custom. This was rejected by the EAT, which said that, on each of the four occasions, the decisions had been made by individual managers based on specific circumstances and there was no evidence that the employer intended the extra benefits to be contractual. This was followed in other cases until *Albion Automotive Ltd v Walker* (2002). In this case, the employer's predecessor had paid enhanced redundancy benefits on six occasions between 1990 and 1994. Enhanced benefits had been agreed with the union for the first lot of redundancies only, but had been paid for all of the others. When the complainant was made redundant, he claimed the enhanced benefits as a contractual right, a claim upheld by the Court of Appeal. The Court stated that the policy was known to the employees, it had originally come into operation by an agreement and reduced to writing, it had been applied frequently and automatically, the employees had a reasonable expectation of benefiting from it and the manner in which it was communicated implied contractual intent. While the policy regarding the bonus in the problem has not come into existence through an agreement, it is arguable that all the other points raised in *Albion* apply and the bonus may have become contractual through custom.

In respect of the new rule that the company has recently introduced, the issue to be decided is whether the rules have become contractual. If this is the case, then one party cannot unilaterally alter the terms of the contract and the employees must consent to the change before becoming legally bound. Lord Denning in *Secretary of State for Employment v ASLEF (No 2) (1972)* stated that works rules are 'in no way terms of the contract of employment. They are only instructions to a man as to how he is to do his work'. He reiterated this interpretation in the later case of *Peake v Automotive Products (1978)*, in which it was held that the rule book was non-contractual and only set out the administrative arrangements. On the other hand, given that some employers issue company handbooks with the employee's contracts, and employees often, in these situations, sign acknowledging receipt of the rules, in these circumstances it is likely that the parts of the rules that can be terms become part of the contract between the parties.

In the situation in the problem, there is no evidence of how the rules were originally communicated to the employees. It is safe to presume, however, that it was not done through a company handbook at the time contracts were issued, as this new rule has been placed on a noticeboard, suggesting that this is the method of communication. It is therefore more likely that the court will decide that the rules in this situation are orders from the employer (*ASLEF*) rather than contractual terms. Such an interpretation would, on the face of it, appear to give Webb Ltd carte blanche; however, the employer's right to issue and enforce rules is circumscribed by the concept of reasonableness. While the employee is under a duty to obey orders from the employer, this duty extends only to lawful, reasonable orders. In *Talbot v Hugh Fulton Ltd (1975)*, the dismissal of an employee for having long hair in breach of the works rules was held to be unfair because the rule did not say what constituted 'long' and, as there was no safety or hygiene risk, the rule was unreasonable. In the case of Webb Ltd, therefore, even though on interpretation of these particular rules it would appear that the company may act unilaterally and change the rules without consultation or agreement, the employees will not be bound to obey the order to submit to a body search if such an order is deemed to be unreasonable. Without evidence of how much the company is losing from thefts, what consultation took place before the introduction of the rule or what alternatives were considered, this rule would not appear to be reasonable and therefore the company cannot compel the employees to comply with it.

Collective agreements can be a source of terms of the employment contract. While such agreements are presumed not to be legally binding between the collective parties (s 179 of the Trade Union and Labour Relations (Consolidation) Act (TULR(C)A) 1992), if some of the clauses from the agreement become part of the individual contracts, those clauses are enforceable as contractual terms. Once the clauses are in the individual contracts, their enforceability stems from the contract and not the collective agreement, and the fact that the collective agreement between Webb Ltd and the union has now terminated will not affect those terms (Burroughs Machines Ltd v Timmoney (1977) and Whent v T Cartledge Ltd (1997)). Collective agreements may become part of an employee's contract by express or implied incorporation. On the wording of the question, it appears that there has been express incorporation, as all the terms and conditions are stated to be the product of a collective agreement between the union and the employer.

Not all terms of a collective agreement are suitable for incorporation into the individual contract, however. In British Leyland (UK) Ltd v McQuilken (1978), it was held that a clause of a collective agreement that stated a policy of offering redundant employees the choice between redundancy and retraining was not intended to create individual rights and, therefore, had not become part of the individual's contract. A similar conclusion was reached in Young v Canadian Northern Rly Co (1931) in relation to a redundancy selection policy. On the basis of these authorities, it would appear that the selection policy is not a clause that is appropriate for incorporation at the individual level. It may be, however, that the authorities can be distinguished.

While the policy in McQuilken would appear to be inappropriate for incorporation, a distinction between the case at Webb Ltd and Young is that the employee in Young was not a union member and was relying on the practice that collective agreements applied to all employees. In the case in question, it would appear that all the terms of the production workers have been collectively bargained and that the negotiations at the collective level were obviously intended to bind the individual parties. As such, it may be possible to argue that, based on the intention of the parties and the fact that the provision is specific and relevant to an individual employee, the selection procedure has become contractual, and the five production workers selected contrary to LIFO can sue for a breach of contract. The cases, however, would seem to go against this. Although the Court of Session in Anderson v Pringle of Scotland (1998) held that a LIFO was contractual, the Court of Appeal in Rover Group plc v Kaur (2005) has yet again decided that a redundancy selection policy is inappropriate for incorporation. The High Court, however, in Harlow v Artemis International Corporation (2008) held that an enhanced redundancy payment scheme was apt for incorporation. In other words, a redundancy selection scheme is a policy issue and cannot be incorporated, but payments under such a scheme can be.

QUESTION 9

While the law will protect an employer against an employee who divulges secret information during the currency of the employment relationship, it is less likely to protect an employer who inserts an express covenant into the contract, preventing an employee from working in a competing business, or divulging secret information, once that relationship has come to an end.

▶ With reference to case law, critically evaluate this statement.

Common Pitfalls ✗

◆ The question asks you to critically evaluate the statement and thus you must come to a conclusion as to whether the statement is accurate or not.

◆ The question states that you must reference case law, so ensure that you know the relevant cases before you start the question.

Answer Plan

This question is specifically about covenants in restraint of trade and how far the courts will uphold them against an ex-employee.

Particular issues to be considered are:

❖ **the doctrine of restraint of trade** – *Nordenfelt v Maxim Nordenfelt Guns and Ammunition Co* (1894); *Herbert Morris Ltd v Saxelby* (1916); *Mason Provident Clothing and Supply Co Ltd* (1913); *Faccenda Chicken Ltd v Fowler* (1986);

❖ **how a covenant may become contractual** – *Briggs v Oates* (1990); *Rex Stewart Jeffries Parker Ginsberg Ltd v Parker* (1988); *Marley Tile Co Ltd v Johnson* (1982); *Esso Petroleum Ltd v Harper's Garage (Stourport) Ltd* (1968);

❖ **what the employer can protect** – *Commercial Plastics Ltd v Vincent* (1965); *Forster & Sons Ltd v Suggett* (1918); *Turner v Commonwealth and British Minerals Ltd* (2000); *Littlewoods Organisation Ltd v Harris* (1978); *Strange v Mann* (1965); *Bowler v Lovegrove* (1921); *Office Angels Ltd v Rainer-Thomas and O'Connor* (1991);

❖ **what is reasonable in the public interest** – *Fellowes & Son v Fisher* (1976); *Spencer v Marchinton* (1988); *Greer v Sketchley Ltd* (1979); *Fitch v Dewes* (1921);

❖ **enforceability** – *Kores Manufacturing Co v Kolok Manufacturing Co* (1959); *Home Counties Dairies Ltd v Skilton* (1970); *White (Marion) Ltd v Francis*

ANSWER

The law does protect an employer against an employee divulging confidential information to unauthorised persons during the currency of the employment relationship. It does so by the implied duty of fidelity, and should an employee breach the duty, the employer will be able to sue for a breach of contract. However, this duty is very limited once the relationship comes to an end, and *Faccenda Chicken Ltd v Fowler* (1986) shows that setting up in competing business and approaching existing employees and customers is not a breach of contract once the relationship ends. As such, employers often insert into the contracts of employees who may be damaging to the employer once they leave a clause restricting their employment for a period of time. Such clauses are known as restraint-of-trade covenants. While such covenants would appear to offer the employer total protection from an ex-employee, historically, courts do not like them, as the court is balancing two conflicting interests. On the one hand, the employer wishes to protect its property; on the other, the employee should be free to work wherever and with whom he or she wishes. An enforceable restraint covenant will prevent this for a period of time.

In order to see if the covenant is enforceable, the court will go through a number of steps, the first of which will be to see if the covenant is contractually enforceable before looking at its validity. If the covenant has been imposed when the relationship has ended, it is unlikely to be enforceable unless the employer has given some consideration for the employee's promise. Likewise, if the employer commits a repudiatory breach, it is repudiating the whole contract, including the covenant, and as such it will be unenforceable (*Briggs v Oates* (1990)). There must be a repudiatory breach, however. In *Rex Stewart Jeffries Parker Ginsberg Ltd v Parker* (1988), a managing director of an advertising agency had a covenant in his contract that prevented him soliciting clients of the agency for 18 months after his employment had ended. After he was dismissed and given wages in lieu of notice, he set up in competition. He argued that the employer could not rely on the covenant because the employer had been in breach of contract by paying him wages in lieu and thus could not rely on the covenant. The Court of Appeal held that paying wages in lieu was not a breach of contract and the covenant was enforceable. Likewise the covenant does not have to be reiterated every time the contract is changed. In *Marley Tile Co Ltd v Johnson* (1982), the employee's original contract contained a number of covenants that were included in his second contract when he was promoted. When he was promoted again, the contract did not contain the covenants, nor did it reiterate details such as the company car or his expense account. The Court of Appeal held that the covenants were part of his final contract, as were provisions about a company car and the expense account. It held that the parties would assume the same provisions applied in all three contracts unless anything was said to the contrary.

The modern law on restraint-of-trade covenants is found in *Nordenfelt v Maxim Nordenfelt Guns and Ammunition Co* (1894), which, although not an employment law case, is pertinent to the area. The case involved the sale of a business and the contract contained a clause preventing the vendor from setting up in competition. The House of Lords held that a restraint of trade covenant will be void unless it can be shown that it is reasonable between the parties and reasonable in the public interest. *Esso Petroleum Ltd v Harper's Garage (Stourport) Ltd* (1968) states that both must be satisfied for a covenant to be enforceable. 'Reasonable between the parties' means that the employer must have a recognisable interest to protect; 'reasonable in the public interest' means that the employer can only give itself the protection it needs and no more. Thus if a covenant is too wide in area or is imposed for too long a period, the covenant will be void. If the covenant is not drafted as separate provisions, any part that is void will render the whole covenant void.

To establish that the covenant is reasonable between the parties, the employer must show that it has some proprietary interest to protect – in other words a trade secret, a secret process or customer connections, disclosure of which would damage the business. This means that the employer must establish that the employee has the knowledge of the trade secret or process, or is in a position in which customers could follow him if he left. Further, the employer can only restrain an employee in respect of the parts of the business in which the employee was employed and not the whole of the employer's business (*Tanner v Commonwealth and British Minerals Ltd* (2000)). In *Herbert Morris Ltd v Saxelby* (1916), there was a provision restraining an employee from working for a competitor for seven years. The employee had no knowledge of any trade secrets or secret processes and no contact with customers. It was held that the restraint was void.

A trade secret or secret process does not have to be patented but it must be confidential and not in the public knowledge. Valid restraints have covered a number of areas such as secret formulas (*Forster & Sons v Suggett* (1918)) and a detailed knowledge of the workings of a specialised business (*Littlewoods Organisation Ltd v Harris* (1978)). In respect of customers, the law only protects an employer in relation to employees who have established a relationship with customers, so there is a danger they will follow when the employee leaves. In *Strange v Mann* (1965), the manager of a firm of bookmakers had a clause stating that he couldn't engage in a similar business within a 12-mile radius when his employment terminated. It was held that, given that the manager had not built up a relationship with customers as most placed bets by phone, the employer had no interest to protect. The same conclusion was reached in *Bowler v Lovegrove* (1921) in respect of an estate agent whose major contact with customers was by phone. In addition, estate agents don't tend to have regular customers.

Where an employee does have contact with customers, the employer can only protect itself against those with whom the employee has had direct contact. In *Mason Provident Clothing and Supply Co* (1913), a covenant prevented the ex-employee from working for a competing business within a 25-mile radius of London. She had only had contact with customers within a particular area of London and the House of Lords ruled that, as the covenant covered customers she had not had contact with, it was too wide and void. A similar conclusion was reached in *Office Angels v Rainer-Thomas and O'Connor* (1991).

Even if the employer has a legitimate interest to protect, the covenant will still be void if it is not reasonable in the public interest. There are three ways in which this may happen. First, the covenant may be drafted in such a way that it is too broad and gives the employer more protection than it needs. In *Fellowes & Son v Fisher* (1976), a conveyancing clerk in Walthamstow agreed that, for five years after leaving employment, he would not be employed in or concerned with the legal profession anywhere within the postal district of Walthamstow and Chingford. The House of Lords held that it was too wide as it prevented from working in any part of the legal profession, even local government. In *Commercial Plastics Ltd v Vincent* (1965), an employee's contract prevented him working in the PVC calendaring field for one year after leaving his employment. As the employee had only been involved in the adhesive tape side of the business, again the covenant was too wide and void.

Second, the covenant may cover too wide an area either because it has no area in it and is therefore deemed to be worldwide, or because it prevents the employee from working in an area in which the employer has no interest. In *Spencer v Marchinton* (1988), the restraint covered a 25-mile radius but the employer had not expanded that far by the time the employee left. It was held to be too wide and void. Again a similar conclusion was reached in *Greer v Sketchley Ltd* (1979). Density of population may also affect the court. In *Fellowes*, the area was not wide but was densely populated. On the other hand, in *Fitch v Dewes* (1921), a lifelong restraint on a solicitor's clerk working within a seven-mile radius of Tamworth Town Hall was upheld by the House of Lords, as it was a modest area that was not densely populated.

The final way in which the covenant could be against the public interest is if it is too long in time. Often time and area are looked at together and the wider the area, the shorter the restraint should be. In *Commercial Plastics*, one year was too long given that the restriction was worldwide.

It can be seen that it takes a great deal of skill and knowledge to draft an enforceable covenant, but even if on the face of it the covenant appears unenforceable, there are two ways the court may save it. First, the courts will look at the reality and effect of the provision although they will not allow an employer to get a covenant through the back door by, for example, entering a contract with another employer that the employer will not employ ex-employees (*Kores Manufacturing Co v Kolok Manufacturing Co* (1959)). However, given that the courts look at the effect of the provision, they have been prepared in some cases to interpret clause in the way that the parties intended and not on their strict wording. In *Home Counties Dairies Ltd v Skilton* (1970) there was a clause in the contract of a milkman that said he should not serve or sell milk or dairy products after leaving employment. It was obviously too wide as it would, for example, prevent him working on a dairy counter in a supermarket. It was obvious, however, that the employer merely wanted to restrain his employment as a milkman, and thus the clause was interpreted in that way and upheld. Similarly, in *White (Marion) Ltd v Francis* (1972), a clause in a hairdresser's contract prevented her working in the hairdressing, business in any way. As it was obvious the restriction was only intended to cover hairdressing, it was interpreted in this way. A surprising case is *Littlewoods Organisation Ltd v Harris* (1978), in which a director of a mail order company was restrained from working for its main competitor General Universal Stores for 12 months after leaving employment. As GUS operated all over the world and in businesses other than mail order, the ex-employee argued that the clause was too wide and void. The Court of Appeal, however, said that, looking at the ex-employee's job and the intention of the employer, the clause would be interpreted to restraining him in relation to GUS's mail order business and was therefore valid.

Another way in which the court can rescue a covenant is by the 'blue pencil' rule. This can only happen when the covenant consists of separate provisions. If the court can sever the offending provision and still leave an enforceable covenant, it will do so (*Lucas (T) Co Ltd v Mitchell* (1974)). The court, however, will not rewrite a covenant. In *TSF Derivatives Ltd v Morgan* (2005), the High Court deleted a part of a covenant it felt was void but enforced the remainder. It also stated that if a clause is capable of two interpretations, one wide and the other narrow, a court should always adopt the latter.

If the covenant is upheld, then the employer can seek a remedy for breach. The two major remedies are damages or an injunction. Should the employer seek injunctive relief, it is likely that he will seek an interlocutory injunction to prevent continued breach, which could cause a great deal of damage to his business by the time of a full hearing. The rules governing the granting of an interlocutory injunction were discussed in *Lansing Linde Ltd v Kerr* (1991). Kerr had been employed by Lansing and had transferred when it was taken over by Linde. His new contract contained a number of restraint clauses and in contravention he left and went to work for a competitor. The employer sought an interlocutory injunction. The Court of Appeal looked at the guidelines laid down in *American Cynamid Co v Ethicon Ltd* (1975). That case stated that an interlocutory injunction can be granted if there is an arguable case and damages is an inappropriate remedy. If both parties are inconvenienced by the injunction, and damages are inappropriate for both parties, then an injunction should be given to the party who would suffer the most inconvenience if it were not granted. Taking this into account, the Court in *Lansing Linde* stated that in relation to the balance of convenience test there were three possible situations: first, there would be a situation in which only one party would suffer loss that damages could not compensate and in that situation an injunction would be granted; second, there would be the situation in which there would be a rapid full trial and the injunction would be given to the party who would suffer the most loss before the full hearing; third, there was the situation in which a full trial was unlikely, either because the interlocutory injunction decided the issue or because the time limit on the restraint meant that it would be inoperable by the time of the full hearing. In the case, the Court felt it unlikely there would be a full hearing given the restraint was only for 12 months. Also, the restraint was worldwide, whereas the employee only had knowledge of the UK marketing operation, and thus if it did go to a full hearing the Court felt that the employer would lose. As such, an injunction was refused. Given this ruling and the fact that most covenants are for short periods of time, it seems that injunctive relief may be difficult for an employer to obtain.

If the employer seeks damages instead, it may be difficult to quantify the loss it has sustained. However, in *AG v Blake* (2001), it was established that a defendant can be ordered to pay back the profit he has received as a result of the breach, even if the employer has suffered no financial loss. It was, however, envisaged by the court that this remedy would be exceptional where the remedy of an injunction would not compensate for the breach of contract.

The cases show a number of things. First, it is imperative that the employer has a legitimate interest to protect and only protects that interest and nothing more. While in some cases the law has looked to the intention rather than the words of the employer, these cases appear to be rare, although this may be more likely since *TSF Derivatives*. Writing a covenant as separate provisions may also allow the court to use the blue pencil rule, but this will not work if the area or time is too wide. Even if the covenant is valid, enforcement may prove difficult. The most effective remedy for an employer is an interlocutory injunction but *Lansing Linde* has shown that it may be difficult to obtain. It does appear from the cases that it is very difficult for an employer to protect itself and its business from an ex-employee and the law does very little to help. The conflict of interest that exists between the employer and ex-employee seems, more often than not, to benefit the ex-employee.

Aim Higher ★

◆   Very little has been written on restraint-of-trade covenants therefore reading those articles that have been written will give your answer more depth; for example, Cabrelli (2004) 33 ILJ 167.

◆   Denning MR, in his judgment in *Littlewoods Organisation Ltd v Harris* (1978) discusses some of the previous cases in some depth and is useful to discuss as background and context.

QUESTION 10

Despite the fact that collective agreements have a major impact on employees' terms and conditions, often regulating their changing content, their precise relationship with the contract of employment is often unclear and can lead to legal uncertainty as to their precise effect.

▶   With reference to case law, critically evaluate this statement.

Answer Plan

This question requires a detailed knowledge of the law relating to collective agreements and their impact on the contract of employment. It also requires the student to evaluate the law and to come to a conclusion as to whether the statement is accurate.

Particular issues to be considered are:

❖   the definition of collective agreement in s 178 of the Trade Union and Labour Relations (Consolidation) Act (TULR(C)A) 1992;

❖   the presumption in s 179 of the TULR(C)A 1992;

❖   terms that are appropriate for incorporation – in particular, cases such as *NCB v National Union of Mineworkers* (1986); *Young v Canadian Northern Rly Co* (1931); *Alexander v Standard Telephones and Cables Ltd* (1990); *Anderson v Pringle of Scotland Ltd* (1998); *Marley v Forward Trust Group* (1986);

* methods of incorporation into individual contracts – in particular, cases such as *NCB v Galley* (1958); *Robertson and Jackson v British Gas Corp* (1983); *Gibbons v Associated British Ports* (1985); *Whent v T Cartledge Ltd* (1997); *Cadoux v Central Regional Council* (1986); *Duke v Reliance Systems Ltd* (1982); *Ali v Christian Salvesen Food Services Ltd* (1997); *Singh v British Steel Corp* (1974); *Henry v London General Transport Services* (2001);
* conflicting collective agreements – in particular, cases such as *Clift v West Riding County Council* (1964) **and** *Gascol Conversions Ltd v Mercer* (1974).

ANSWER

Under s 178(1) of the TULR(C)A 1992, a collective agreement is 'any agreement or arrangement made by or on behalf of one or more trade unions or one or more employers or employers' associations and relating to one or more of the matters specified in s 178(2)'. Collective agreements have two functions: the procedural function – that is, the regulation of the relationship between the employer or employer's association and the trade union; and the normative function – that is, the regulation of provisions for individual employees who are members of the union. Collective agreements govern a large number of employees' terms and conditions of employment, yet there is a statutory presumption that they are not intended to be legally binding (s 179 of the 1992 Act). This, however, is misleading. Section 179 provides that they are not legally binding between the employer and trade union. Should terms of the agreement become terms of the individual employee's contract, then these terms will be legally enforceable by the employee against the employer. There is, however, legal uncertainty as to which terms within a collective agreement are appropriate for incorporation into an individual contract of employment.

In *NCB v National Union of Mineworkers* (1986), Scott J stated that terms that were appropriate for incorporation should be terms such as pay rates, hours of work, etc (the normative terms), whereas terms covering conciliation and other proceedings (that is, procedural terms) were not appropriate for incorporation because they are not intended to be contractually enforceable by employees. Even where an agreement has been expressly incorporated into an individual's contract, this will not incorporate procedural terms. Thus, what is a procedural or normative term is central to the decision of inferring contractual intent. The definition of procedural and normative terms, however, is an area in which there is legal uncertainty. This is particularly so in the case of redundancy procedures.

In *Young v Canadian Northern Rly Co* (1931), the Privy Council held that a redundancy selection policy of 'last in, first out' was inappropriate for incorporation into individual contracts, yet in *Marley v Forward Trust Group* (1986), a redundancy selection procedure that was in a personnel manual and which had been expressly incorporated into the individual's contract was held to be legally enforceable by the employee. The later case of *Alexander v Standard Telephones and Cables Ltd* (1990) again held that a redundancy selection procedure was inappropriate for incorporation, but in *Anderson v Pringle of Scotland Ltd* (1998), the Court of Session held that there was an arguable case that a redundancy selection procedure contained in a collective agreement could become part of the individual's employment contract. However, the later case of *Rover Group plc v Kaur* (2005) yet again refused to incorporate a redundancy selection procedure into the contract, and in *Harlow v Artemis International Corporation* (2008), the court said that an enhanced redundancy payment was appropriate for incorporation into the employee's contract. This would suggest that a redundancy selection procedure is deemed to be policy and therefore cannot be incorporated, but payments under a policy can be.

Where the term is normative, then it is appropriate for incorporation, but such a term may be incorporated either expressly or impliedly. Express incorporation is the most straightforward, as the contract of employment will expressly refer to the terms of the agreement. Such reference may include the whole of the agreement, as in *NCB v Galley* (1958), or may refer only to particular terms such as pay or hours, and they will be the only terms to be incorporated. Implied incorporation is more difficult. In this case, the courts look for evidence that both the employer and employee intended the agreement to become part of the contract. In *Joel v Cammell Laird* (1969), the court stated that, in order to be bound by a collective agreement, an employee must have specific knowledge of the agreement, and there must be conduct showing that the employee accepted the agreement and evidence that the agreement has been incorporated into the contract. In *Duke v Reliance Systems Ltd* (1982), the court further held that the employee needed to know of the existence, if not the content, of the term to be incorporated. The case of *Henry v London General Transport Services* (2001) has, however, thrown doubt on some of these decisions. In that case, the court held that an employee was bound by a collective agreement that by custom had become part of his contract. The Employment Appeal Tribunal (EAT) held that, for a term to be incorporated by custom, the custom must be reasonable, certain and notorious and it must be presumed that the term supports the intention of the parties. Until *Henry*, notoriety was the reason why custom as a source of contractual terms had fallen into disuse, because movement of workers in a modern society means that fewer workers will be aware of the customs. However, the EAT held that notoriety is not undermined if some employees do not know of it.

While the above appear to give guidance, the law may still be unclear. *Singh v British Steel Corp* (1974) stated that implied incorporation can apply only to union members and, in the case of non-union members, an agreement must be expressly incorporated for the employee to be bound. Furthermore, if an agreement is silent regarding a particular topic, the courts will not imply a term into the agreement (and hence the individual contract) on the basis that the omission must be deliberate (*Ali v Christian Salvesen Food Services Ltd* (1997)). Furthermore, in *Cadoux v Central Regional Council* (1986), a provision of an agreement that had been expressly incorporated was held not to be legally enforceable because the rules could be amended from time to time by the authority. This led the Court of Session to conclude that that part of the agreement was not incorporated because, given that the rules could be unilaterally altered by the council, the parties could not have intended them to be contractually binding. Thus, even where there is express incorporation, legal uncertainty may exist.

Once a term forms part of the contract, it is enforceable between the individual parties and it is irrelevant if one of the parties withdraws from the agreement. This can only affect the relationship between the collective and not the individual parties. In *Robertson and Jackson v British Gas Corp* (1983), the employer sought unilaterally to withdraw a bonus scheme that had been negotiated by collective agreement. The agreement was no longer in force, but the Court of Appeal held that the bonus scheme was contractual and the employer was in breach of contract. Also, in *Whent v T Cartledge Ltd* (1997), the employer withdrew from a national joint council agreement that regulated the employee's pay and conditions. It was held that the provision that the national joint council rates applied was contractual and the withdrawal of the employer from the agreement had no effect.

The precise relationship between collective agreements and contracts of employment is therefore unclear and thus there is legal uncertainty as to their precise effect. Whereas express incorporation seems simple, the legal uncertainty as to whether a term is appropriate for incorporation means that an employee will not know the precise content of his or her contract. The uncertainty that exists around implied incorporation, including the uncertainty created by *Henry*, means that often it is only when a case gets to court that both parties will know their responsibilities and rights.

QUESTION 11

Ian, Max and Roxy work for Walford Engineering, a firm manufacturing rides for fairs.

During the last two years, there have been periods of short-time working. Two years ago, there was an industrial dispute and all of the workforce were put onto a four-day week for the period of the dispute, which lasted from February to March. Six months later, another dispute occurred, which lasted for four months (from September to January) and again the workforce were put onto a four-day week. In both cases the two unions at the company, the CMU and the SWU, agreed to the cuts. In September last year, the CMU agreed that, in the event of future disputes, it would agree to a three-day week if it were to become 'economically necessary'. This agreement was stated to be binding in honour only.

Last month, there was another dispute and the company put the workforce on a three-day week for a month. Both Ian, a member of the CMU, and Max, a member of the SWU, are claiming four days' pay.

Roxy is a typist in the typing pool in the factory. She started work four weeks ago. Last week, she fell ill and has been told by her doctor that she will be unable to work for three weeks. Her statutory statement says she will be entitled to sick pay after two weeks of illness, but her contract, which was sent to her home this week, states that she is entitled to sick pay after three weeks of illness. In addition, the advertisement for Roxy's job stated that the company wished to recruit a 'personal assistant/typist', however, her job description on her contract is 'typist'. Roxy feels that she would not have applied for the job if it only involved typing.

▶ Advise Ian, Max and Roxy.

Common Pitfalls ✗

◆ In a question like this it is important to read the question properly. Although it says that there has been a dispute, it doesn't say that any of the parties were involved in that dispute.

◆ **Section 13** of the **ERA 1996** may be relevant as the exception in **s 14(5)** will not apply.

Answer Plan

This question raises the issue of collective agreements and their enforceability at the individual level. It raises a number of issues, in particular whether there is an implied term irrespective of the collective bargain. To some extent in relation to the first two parties, there needs to be some discussion in relation to implied duties, which are discussed in the next chapter. In addition, it addresses the problem of a conflict between the statutory statement and the contract and whether terms implied from sources outside the contract can modify express terms within it.

Issues to be considered are:

- the implied term in relation to payment during lay-off;
- how far conduct on the part of the employee can vary contractual terms;
- the implication of collective agreements into individual contracts;
- the effect at the individual level of a collective agreement stated to be binding in honour only;
- the relevance of s 13 of the ERA 1996;
- which prevails when there is a conflict between the statutory statement and the contract; and
- how far terms from documents such as advertisements can be implied into the contract.

ANSWER

Ian and Max have, in the past, accepted a four-day working week when there has been an industrial dispute. This is evidenced by the fact that they are only claiming four days' pay in relation to the last four-week lay-off. Generally, at common law, there is no right to work only a right to receive wages (*Collier v Sunday Referee Publishing Co Ltd* (1940)). This is only a general proposition, however.

In some cases, there is a duty to provide work where, for example, the employee needs to develop his skill or where the work must be done to earn the wages, as in the case of pieceworkers (*Devonald v Rosser & Sons* (1906)). The implied duty to pay may be ousted by an express term (*Hulme v Ferranti Ltd* (1914)) or the practice of the industry may imply a term that there is no pay during lay-off and this will oust the implied term (*Puttick v John Wright & Sons (Blackwall) Ltd* (1972)).

The first question to ask in relation to Ian and Max is whether there is a duty to pay during lay-off. In the past, both have accepted a four-day week when there has been an industrial dispute. Whereas there is a general duty to pay wages, this does not apply when the reason for the lack of work is totally outside the control of the employer. In *Browning v Crumlin Valley Collieries* (1926), Greer J held that the duty to pay wages did not apply when a land fault rendered the mine dangerous and therefore the men were unable to work. Walford Engineering may claim that the industrial dispute has rendered it impossible to provide five days' work, and on the basis of *Browning*, this is outside its control and therefore there is no breach of duty. As such, Ian and Max will have no claim.

On the other hand, if a tribunal feels that there is no impossibility, or that the industrial dispute is not outside the control of the employer, the question to be asked is whether there is a term in their contracts that allows for lay-offs without pay. In the past, both men have accepted a four-day working week. In addition, the unions have also agreed the four-day working week, although from the facts this does not seem to have been done by collective agreement, merely acquiescence. Could it be argued that Ian and Max's past conduct has now implied a term into their individual contracts that there will be a shorter working week when there is an industrial dispute? It appears that, until the recent lay-off, there were only two occasions in the past on which there was a four-day working week, although it happened for five months in total. In implying terms into the contract, the courts use the old contractual tests of business efficacy or obvious consensus to see if a term should be implied and then deduce the content of the term by what the parties would have agreed if they were being reasonable (*Courtaulds Northern Spinning Ltd v Sibson* (1988)). Thus it may be argued that, given that they have accepted a four-day working week in the past, this is now a term of their contracts.

A further argument that the employer may put forward is that a term of no pay during lay-off has become part of their contracts due to custom. To show that a custom has become part of the contract, it has to be certain, notorious and reasonable. To be notorious it must be well known in the industry so that the employee knew about it prior to taking the job (*Sagar v Ridehalgh & Sons Ltd* (1931)) or it began during the employees' employment, and by continuing to work the employee has accepted it, although du Parcq LJ said in *Marshall v English Electric Co Ltd* (1945) that mere continuance of working did not, of itself, imply acceptance as there may be other factors involved, such as a fear of dismissal as seen in *Samways v Swanhunter Shipbuilders Ltd* (1975).

The only way it could be argued that the custom is notorious is that it grew up while Ian and Max were employed, and by continuing to work they have accepted it. However, it could also be argued under *Samways* that they accepted the four-day week because of a fear of losing their jobs and thus by continuing to work this does not imply a new term into their contract. Even if there is a contractual term, it is in relation to a four-day working week not a three-day one. Ian's union, the CMU, has agreed a three-day week if this is 'economically necessary'. Although the agreement is stated to be binding in honour only, this is mere belt and braces because a collective agreement is not legally enforceable between the collective parties unless it is stated to be so by s 179 of TULR(C)A 1992. This, however, does not affect the enforceability between the individual parties and if the term has become part of the individual's contract, it is legally enforceable.

Even if the term from the collective agreement has not been expressly incorporated (and the facts do not say that there is an express term incorporating such agreements into the contracts), it may be impliedly incorporated. From *Joel v Cammell Laird* (1969) it appears that, for a term to be impliedly incorporated into a union member's contract, there must be knowledge of the agreement, conduct on the part of the employee to show he accepts the agreement, and evidence of incorporation. *Duke v Reliance Systems Ltd* (1982) says that in addition the employee must know of the existence of the term, if not its content, and in *Jones v Associated Tunnelling Ltd* (1981) the EAT held that continuing to work does not necessarily indicate that the employee has assented to the change.

Looking at the problem: if Ian knows of the agreement and the existence of the term, his lack of protest could indicate that he has accepted it, unless it is possible to argue, as in *Joel*, that given that it would take effect some time in the future, he can only accept it once it happens – which he clearly does not. Even if it is part of his contract, he could challenge the three-day week on the basis that it was not economically necessary. Max, on the other hand, is not a member of the union that negotiated the three-day week. As such, the term from the collective agreement can only become part of his contract if he expressly incorporates it into his contract (*Miller v Hamworthy Engineering Ltd* (1986)) and we have already noted that this does not appear to be the case from the facts. As such, the extra day's loss of pay during the four weeks is an unlawful deduction from wages under s 13 of the ERA 1996, as the employer has no contractual or statutory right to deduct and Max does not appear to have agreed to the deduction in writing prior to the event that led to it (*Tobacco and Confectionery Ltd v Williamson* (1993)). Thus Max is entitled to four days' pay.

In Roxy's case, there is a discrepancy between her contract and her statutory statement. Browne-Wilkinson J, in *System Floors (UK) Ltd v Daniel 1981*, said of the statement: 'It provides very strong prima facie evidence of what were the terms of the contract between the parties, but does not constitute a written contract between the parties.' Such an interpretation does not help Roxy. While in some cases the courts have accepted the statement as contractual, this is usually where there is no other written document, and where there is a conflict between the statement and the written contract, the contract will prevail (*Robertson and Jackson v British Gas Corpn* (1983)). As such, given the terms of her contract, she will not receive sick pay.

Roxy is also concerned that the job she has was advertised as personal assistant/typist but her contract states that her job is that of a typist and does not include personal assistant. The normal contractual rule is that an implied term cannot override an express term (*Deeley v British Rail Engineering Ltd* (1980)). In *Johnstone v Bloomsbury Area Health Authority* (1991), Stuart Smith LJ held that the implied duty to ensure the employees' safety overrode the express term in the contract allowing the employer to require junior doctors to work in excess of 88 hours a week. While this may appear to be an attack on the normal contractual principle, it is submitted that it is confined to the facts of the case. As such, on the basis of *Deeley*, Roxy is employed as a typist only.

Implied Duties

4

INTRODUCTION

In this text, implied duties are those terms implied into every contract of employment. The word 'duties' is used to distinguish the questions in this chapter from implied terms discussed in Chapter 3. By 'implied term', this text means terms implied into a specific individual contract because that is what the parties would have expressed if they had thought about it. On the other hand, 'implied duties' are in every contract of employment, irrespective of the parties' intentions, and can normally only be ousted by an express term. The majority of student texts split the duties into those of the employer and those of the employee. Examination questions may, however, mix the two areas and therefore it would be unwise to know one group of duties but not the other. In addition, this area impacts on others. Breach of these duties may constitute a repudiatory breach and thus a constructive dismissal, and so may be relevant to questions on unfair dismissal. Sexual harassment may be a breach of the duty of mutual respect as well as an infringement of the Equality Act 2010. As such, knowledge of this area will form a good foundation for a variety of questions that may come up on an examination paper.

General issues that the student needs to understand are therefore:

* the personal nature of the employment contract;
* the duties of the employer;
* the duties of the employee; and
* remedies for a breach of an employment contract.

Although breach of one of the implied duties may form the basis of other claims, it is important to see exactly what the question is asking for. If it is only on the area of such duties, a discussion of unfair constructive dismissal is not going to gain any marks. Detailed knowledge of the duties is therefore needed for specific questions on this area.

In particular, students need to be familiar with:

* whether there is a duty to provide work;
* the duty to pay wages;
* whether there is a duty to indemnify;

❖ the duty of mutual respect/trust and confidence;
❖ the duty to ensure the employee's safety;
❖ the duty of co-operation;
❖ the duty to obey lawful, reasonable orders;
❖ the duty to exercise reasonable care and skill;
❖ the duty not to accept bribes or secret commission;
❖ the duty not to disclose confidential information;
❖ the duty not to work for a competitor; and
❖ the ownership of inventions.

It can be seen from the list above that this is a vast area, which is expanding. Recent decisions have suggested that some of these duties are overriding ones and students should be aware of these developments.

Checklist ✔

Students should be familiar with the following areas:

■ the discussions in relation to the duty to provide work and the expansion of the exceptions in *Turner v Sawdon* (1901);

■ issues relating to the payment of wages: itemised pay statements, the concept of normal working hours, deductions from pay under the **Employment Rights Act (ERA) 1996**; payment during sickness and payment during lay-off;

■ whether a duty to indemnify exists;

■ the expansion of the duty of mutual respect/trust and confidence;

■ the specific aspects of the safety duty – in particular, safe place of work, safe system of work, safe plant and materials, and competent employees;

■ how far the duty of safety is an overriding one since *Johnstone v Bloomsbury Area Health Authority* (1991);

■ the employee duty of co-operation and the effect of a breach since *Ticehurst v British Telecommunications plc* (1992);

■ what constitutes reasonable orders;

■ the duty of confidentiality – that is, not to work for a competitor or disclose confidential information;

■ aspects of trust and confidence, such as working with reasonable care and the duty not to accept secret payments; and

■ judicial expansion of the employer's responsibility since *Johnstone v Bloomsbury Area Health Authority* (1991), *Scally v Southern Health and Social Services Board* (1991) and *Spring v Guardian Assurance* (1994).

QUESTION 12

Whilst the judges have, over the years, developed the implied duties of both the employer and employee, the duty of mutual trust and confidence is the one duty that has been greatly expanded since its inception in the 1970s and now encompasses a wide range of behaviour on both sides.

▶ Critically evaluate this statement.

Answer Plan

This question deals exclusively with the duty of mutual trust and confidence. It is important to note the word 'mutual' and to read the question properly. To look only at cases in which the employer has been held to be in breach of the duty is not fully answering the question.

Particular points to note are:

❖ the origins of the duty;
❖ the recognition of the duty in *Woods v W M Car Services (Peterborough) Ltd (1981)*;
❖ how the duty is reflected in the specific duties of the employee;
❖ the development of the term and its impact on employer behaviour; and
❖ the importance of the term in relation to unfair dismissal.

ANSWER

Prior to the introduction of the right not to be unfairly dismissed by the Industrial Relations Act 1971, there was no concept that the employment relationship was one that required mutual trust and confidence in order for the relationship to work. Prior to 1971, the only right an employee had was the right to notice, prior to dismissal, unless that dismissal was for gross misconduct, and certain rights in relation to the content of the contract of employment. However, the introduction of the right not to be unfairly dismissed established, arguably, the concept that an employer should treat its employees reasonably. This led Edmund-Davies LJ in *Wilson v Racher* (1974) to comment that older cases treated the relationship of employer and employee 'as almost an attitude of Czar–serf' and would be decided differently now: 'We have by now come to realise that a contract of service imposes upon the parties a duty of mutual respect.'

While a duty of respect has always been owed by the employee, the idea that such a duty was mutual was unknown until 1974. As such, the development of the duty has had more of an impact on employer behaviour. The duty became known as the 'duty of mutual trust and confidence' when Browne-Wilkinson J said in *Woods v WM Car Services (Peterborough) Ltd* (1981) it is clearly established that there is implied in a contract of employment a term that the employers will not, without reasonable and proper cause, conduct themselves in a manner calculated or likely to destroy or seriously damage the relationship of confidence and trust between an employer and employee.

Once the duty had been expanded to one of trust and confidence, it could be seen that some of the specific duties owed by employees are arguably a reflection of the duty. It has long been recognised that an employee owes a duty of fidelity towards his employer. This general duty can be subdivided into more specific duties, breach of which would destroy the trust and confidence an employer needs to have in its employee. These specific duties are the duty not to make a secret profit, disclosure of misconduct, the duty not to work in competition, the duty not to divulge confidential information, and the duty to serve the employer faithfully and not to wilfully disrupt its business.

As early as the 19th century, the courts recognised that employees were under a duty not to accept bribes or make a secret profit from their employment and to do so would be a fundamental breach of contract. In *Boston Deep Sea Fishing and Ice Co v Ansell* (1888), an employee was lawfully dismissed when it was discovered that he was accepting bribes from a supplier to ensure that orders were placed with that supplier. This was the case even though the employee had been summarily dismissed without grounds before the discovery of the bribe.

In respect of disclosure of misconduct, in the early case of *Bell v Lever Bros* (1932), the House of Lords held that an employee was not under an obligation to disclose his own misconduct to the employer. However, the duty was refined in *Sybron Corpn v Rochem Ltd* (1983). In that case, it was discovered after the retirement of the manager of the employer's European operations that he and a number of other employees had been passing business opportunities to a rival company that they had set up. The Court of Appeal held that he was in breach of a duty to disclose the wrongdoings of his subordinates, even if by doing so he would have revealed his own wrongdoing. This duty applied because he was a senior manager within the company and thus is not in all employment contracts. However, in *Neary v Dean of Westminster* (1999), it was held that the choirmaster, by not disclosing fees he had been paid for choir performances outside the Abbey, was in breach of the implied term of trust and confidence in addition to a breach of the term not to make a secret profit. Conversely, in *Nottingham University v Fishel* (2000), a researcher at the university, who used his staff to help with his private work, was held not to be under a duty to disclose the wrongdoings of his staff because he did not realise that they were acting in breach of contract. He was, however, in breach of the duty not to make a secret profit.

Part of the duty of fidelity is the duty not to set up in competition with your employer. In *Hivac Ltd v Park Royal Scientific Instruments Ltd* (1946), a group of highly skilled employees manufactured exactly the same products as their employer in their spare time. Lord Greene MR said: 'It would be deplorable if it were laid down that a workman could, consistently with his duty to his employer, knowingly, deliberately and secretly set himself up to do in his spare time something which would inflict great harm on his employer's business.' As such, an injunction was granted against the employees. It is, however, not a breach of the duty to intend to leave and compete with the employer (*Laughton and Hawley v BAPP Industrial Supplies* (1986)).

If in *Laughton* the employees were to have used confidential information while they were still employed, then there would be a breach of the final aspect of the duty of fidelity – that is, not to use the employer's confidential information. Protection in respect of ex-employees is very limited unless there is a restraint of trade covenant, but during employment the employee is under a duty not to disclose anything that the employer regards as confidential or to misuse that information in any way. In *Robb v Green* (1895), the employee had obtained his employer's customer list and approached customers when he set up in competition. It was held that the obtaining of the list while an employee was a breach of the duty of fidelity.

While it can be seen from above that the duty of fidelity has existed for many years and requires the employee not to act in a way that would destroy the trust an employer must have in the relationship, in *Secretary of State for Employment v ASLEF (No 2)* (1972), Lord Denning appeared to expand the duty to include an aspect that the employee should not act in a way that wilfully disrupts the employer's business. In the case, a work-to-rule, which was conducted to disrupt rail services, was held to be a breach of contract. A similar conclusion was reached in *British Telecommunications plc v Ticehurst* (1992), in which the Court of Appeal held that an employee, who, as part of industrial action, refused to sign an undertaking that she would work normally, was in breach of an implied term to serve her employer faithfully. Given that all industrial action is conducted with the aim of disrupting the employer, it would appear that the use of the implied term is far-reaching.

Thus it can be seen that the employee has always been under a duty not to undermine the trust the employer has in him. But as has already been noted, the idea that the duty was reciprocal is very recent. The duty on the employer is important since the case of *Western Excavating (ECC) Ltd v Sharp* (1978) when the Court of Appeal stated that a constructive dismissal can only take place where there is a repudiatory breach of contract on the part of the employer. Given that destroying trust and confidence is repudiatory, it follows that breach of the duty, should the employee resign as a result, can lead to an unfair dismissal claim. This begs the question, however, as to what conduct on the part of the employer is seen as a breach of the duty. The formulation of the duty by Browne-Wilkinson J in *Woods* above was approved in *Imperial Group Pension Trust Ltd v Imperial Tobacco Ltd* (1991) and by Lord Steyn in the House of Lords in *Malik v BCCI* (1997).

It is also clear from Browne-Wilkinson's exposition of the duty that the emphasis is placed on the impact of the employer's behaviour on the employee and not what the employer intended the impact to be. Behaviour that has been held to be a breach of the duty is wide-ranging. In *Bliss v South East Thames Regional Health Authority* (1985), it was held that insisting an employee underwent a psychiatric examination before he could return to work, where there was no evidence of psychiatric illness, was a breach of the duty. Other examples include: making unsubstantiated allegations of theft (*Robertson v Crompton Parkinson Ltd* (1978)); providing a reference alleging complaints from the public had been made against an employee of which she was unaware (*TSB Bank plc v Harris* (2000)); describing an employee as wholly unsuitable for promotion where there were no grounds for such an assertion (*Post Office v Roberts* (1980)); enforcing a mobility clause in a way that made it impossible for the employee to perform his job (*United Bank v Abktar* (1989)); and refusing to provide a grievance procedure (*WA Goold (Pearmak) Ltd v McConnell* (1995)).

The duty was recognised by the House of Lords in *Malik* (above), in which their Lordships held that whether there was a breach of the term had to be judged objectively in that it was not necessary that the employee had lost trust in his employer but whether the conduct was likely to bring about such a result. Nor was it necessary that the employee knew of the breach before his contract had terminated. This was important in the context of the case itself, which was a claim for damages based on the employee's loss of reputation in unwittingly being associated with a series of frauds committed by the employer.

In *Malik*, the argument was put forward that the employer was in breach by failing to provide the employee with information about the fraudulent dealings. The earlier case of *Scally v Southern Health and Social Services Board* (1991) held that the employer should have informed doctors of the opportunity to purchase extra benefits under their pension scheme within the time frame imposed by the scheme. Cases such as *Malik* and *Scally* are different from the others above in that they appear to be imposing positive duties to disclose on employers, whereas earlier cases prevent certain actions taken by employers. However, after *Malik*, case law has restricted the obligation on employers. In *BCCI SA v Ali* (1999) and *University of Nottingham v Eyett* (1999), the courts restricted the idea that the employer is under a positive duty to provide information to its employers to maintain trust and confidence. In *Ali*, it was held that the employer was not under an obligation to reveal information to the employees about the fraudulent dealings, and in *Eyett*, the employer was not under an obligation to inform employees of the most advantageous way to exercise pension rights, although in *Ibekwe v London General Transport Services* (2003) the Court of Appeal followed *Scally* in deciding that an employer had done enough to inform its employees of changes to the pension scheme by attaching a letter to their payslips detailing the changes. It should be noted that a wide-ranging duty to give relevant information to employees would place a corresponding duty on employees to do the same and we have already seen that there is no duty on an employee to inform his employer of his own wrongdoing.

So it is true to say that the duty of trust and confidence has been greatly expanded since its initial inception. While in the vast majority of cases it has restricted employers' behaviour, cases like *Ticehurst* have also placed further restrictions on the behaviour of employees, particularly in the area of industrial action. What the courts do not seem to be prepared to do, however, is expand the duty to include a positive requirement on employers to provide information to employees and have imposed such a duty in limited circumstances. As Deakin and Morris (*Labour Law*, 5th edn, Hart) note, 'at one level these decisions seem incompatible with the idea of mutual trust and confidence as the core obligation at the heart of the employment relationship'.

Aim Higher ★

❖ A great deal has been written on the duty of trust and confidence.
❖ Reading and citing articles in your answer will gain you extra marks – for example, Brodie (2008) 37 ILJ 329 and Cabrelli (2005) 34 ILJ 284.

QUESTION 13

Riskit, Duck and Dodge have worked at Lax Ltd for ten years. Riskit and Duck work in the machining room at one of the two sites operated by the company. Riskit has to cut two inches off a metal bolt. The correct method, as he knows, is to use a milling machine to file it off. Since this process is rather lengthy, Riskit decides to use a circular saw. During this process, the blade of the saw disintegrates along with part of the bolt. Metal fragments shower from the machine and bolt and, while taking evasive action, Riskit injures his head on the corner of the saw table. One of the fragments flies into the eye of Duck, who had left his machine at the other end of the factory in order to fill in his pools coupon jointly with Riskit.

Dodge works at the other site of Lax Ltd, which is five minutes away from the main site. The finishing machine on which Dodge works has broken down and will take two months to mend. As a result, Lax Ltd has closed down the factory and has laid off

Dodge for two months without pay. Lax Ltd argues that, without the machine, there will be a build-up of unfinished products that it cannot sell or store.

▶ Advise Riskit and Duck whether they may claim compensation from Lax Ltd, and Dodge whether he is entitled to payment of wages during the two-month lay-off.

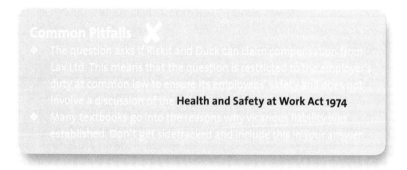

Common Pitfalls ✗

❖ The question asks if Riskit and Duck can claim compensation from Lax Ltd. This means that the question is restricted to the employer's duty at common law to ensure its employees' safety and does not involve a discussion of the **Health and Safety at Work Act 1974**

❖ Many textbooks go into the reasons why vicarious liability was established. Don't get sidetracked and include this in your answer.

Answer Plan

This question deals with two separate implied duties: the duty to ensure the employee's safety; and the duty to pay wages. The question in relation to one party is whether there is a complete defence to the employee's claim and, in relation to the second, whether any duty is owed at all.

Particular points to raise are therefore:

❖ the general duty to ensure the employee's safety;
❖ the duty to provide a safe system of work;
❖ the duty to provide safe plant and materials;
❖ defences to a claim;
❖ the duty to provide reasonably competent fellow employees;
❖ vicarious liability; and
❖ the duty to pay during lay-off.

ANSWER

The employer is under an implied duty to ensure its employees' safety. The duty arises under *Donoghue v Stevenson* (1932), in that, because of the proximity of the relationship between employer and employee, the employer must take reasonable care to ensure that its acts or omissions do not cause the employee foreseeable injury. The standard is that of a reasonable employer and should the employer do all that is reasonable, it will not be liable for any injury sustained by the employee (*Latimer v AEC Ltd* (1953)).

In *Wilsons and Clyde Coal Co v English* (1938), the House of Lords identified specific aspects of the duty. One of these aspects is the duty to provide a safe system of work; another is the provision of safe plant and materials. In relation to Riskit, it is necessary to see if one or both of these aspects of the duty have been broken.

Riskit injures his head when the blade of a saw disintegrates while sawing a bolt. Riskit, however, knows that he should use a milling machine to cut the two inches off the bolt. It would appear therefore that Riskit has been told the correct and safe way of performing the job and chooses an unsafe way. While one of the aspects of the duty to provide a safe system of work is training and supervision, Riskit has worked for the company for ten years and appears to be experienced. Even if the employer supervised his work at the beginning, he should know and observe the correct method of cutting the bolt after ten years. In addition, the employer is entitled to assume that the employee will take some responsibility for his own safety (*Smith v Scott Bowyers Ltd* (1986)) and is entitled to assume that the employee has a modicum of common sense (*Lazarus v Firestone Tyres and Rubber Co Ltd* (1963)). As such, it is unlikely that the court will find that Lax Ltd is in breach of its duty to provide a safe system of work.

While Riskit is using the saw, the blade disintegrates and causes injury to both Riskit and Duck. While the employer is under a duty to provide safe plant and materials, breach of this duty depends on the employer's knowledge (*Davie v New Merton Board Mills* (1959)). Once the employer knows of a defect, if it does nothing to protect its employees, it will be in breach. In *Taylor v Rover Car Co* (1966), the employee was using a chisel that was badly hardened and which shattered, causing him injury. A chisel from the same batch had shattered previously without causing injury. It was held that the employer was in breach of duty because, given the previous incident, it should have known that the batch was faulty and withdrawn it from use. Here, the cause of the injuries was the saw blade. If Lax Ltd knew that the blade was dangerous (for example, because another one from the same supplier had disintegrated), then, by analogy with *Taylor*, it could be argued that Lax Ltd is liable to Riskit. A similar conclusion would be reached if the reason the saw blade shattered was because of lack of maintenance by the employer (*Bradford v Robinson Rentals Ltd* (1967)). If, however, Lax Ltd can show that it was the misuse of the blade that caused it to disintegrate, then there will be no breach on the part of the employer. In this case, however, if there is a hidden defect, by the **Employers' Liability (Defective Equipment) Act 1969** any defect attributable to the negligence of a third party will be deemed to be attributable to the negligence of the employer. Thus, by statute, Lax Ltd will be liable and will be able to recover any compensation paid to Riskit from the manufacturer.

Even if it is held that Lax Ltd is in breach of the common law duty in relation to Riskit, there are two defences that Lax Ltd could raise. The first is lack of causation – that is, that the employer's breach of duty did not cause the employee's injury. Riskit was wrongly using a circular saw. If he had used the correct method to cut the bolt, no injury would have been sustained. It could also be argued that the action he took to avoid the fragments and the injury to his head was not foreseeable. If this is successful, then the injury was caused by Riskit and not the breach of duty and, as such, Lax Ltd can negate its liability (*Horne v LEC Refrigeration Ltd* (1965)).

Alternatively, Lax Ltd may raise the defence of contributory negligence under the Law Reform (Contributory Negligence) Act 1945. Such a defence will reduce the employer's liability, as damages will be reduced to reflect the proportion of the blame that can be attached to the employee's own negligence. In *Bux v Slough Metals* (1973), the employer was held to be in breach of its common law duty when it provided goggles for the employees but did not ensure that they were worn. Damages were reduced by 40 per cent, however, because of the employee's own negligence in failing to wear the goggles. Thus, even if the employer is in breach, it can be argued that Riskit's negligence in using the saw in the first place contributed to his injury and damages should be reduced accordingly.

Fragments from the saw hit Duck in the eye. Duck may be able to claim compensation from Lax Ltd in one of two ways. First, he could argue along similar lines to Riskit – that is, that Lax Ltd is in breach of the duty to provide a safe plant and materials. The success or otherwise of this line of argument is demonstrated above. Conversely, Duck could argue that Lax Ltd had not provided him with a reasonably competent fellow employee in that it was due to Riskit's negligence that Duck was injured in the first place. The basis of the liability under this head is again knowledge. If Lax Ltd had no idea that Riskit was using unsafe methods, there will be no breach of duty (*Coddington v International Harvester Co of Great Britain* (1969)). On the other hand, if Lax Ltd did have this knowledge, then a breach will have occurred (*Hudson v Ridge Manufacturing Co Ltd* (1957)).

Should Duck not succeed in establishing a breach of the primary duty, he may be able to establish that Lax Ltd is vicariously liable for Riskit. Vicarious liability arises when the employee injures someone by his or her negligence while within the course of employment. 'Course of employment' appears to mean while the employee is doing an authorised act in an authorised manner or an authorised act in an unauthorised manner (*Limpus v London General Omnibus Co* (1862)). It does not cover acts specifically forbidden by the employer (*Conway v George Wimpey* (1951)) but may do if such an act benefits the employer (*Rose v Plenty* (1976)). The House of Lords, however, has recently redefined the common law definition of 'course of employment'. In *Lister v Helsey Hall Ltd* (2001), their Lordships held that the correct approach to determine whether an employee's act is committed during the course of his or her employment is to concentrate on the relative proximity between the nature of the employment and the act committed. As such, a boarding school was vicariously liable for the sexual abuse of boys by a school warden because the nature of his employment meant that he had close contact with the boys and this created a sufficiently close connection between the acts of abuse and the work he was employed to do to make it fair to hold the employer liable. On this wider definition of course of employment, it can be argued that as Riskit is employed to cut bolts and he injures someone while doing that incorrectly, there is a sufficiently close connection between his employment and the wrongful act to establish vicarious liability. Even under the narrower definition of course of employment prior to *Lister*, Riskit is authorised to cut the bolt. The employer cannot argue that he is only authorised to cut the bolt with the milling machine. Once the authorisation has been given, the employer cannot then limit the way in which the employee performs that authorised act (*Limpus*). As such, Lax Ltd is vicariously liable for Riskit.

Again, the employer may have a defence. Duck is injured when coming over to Riskit to complete his pools coupon. As such, is the injury to Duck a foreseeable consequence of the negligence of either Lax Ltd or Riskit? It is reasonably foreseeable that, if the saw blade disintegrates, an employee will be injured because the saw is in the workplace. It could be argued, therefore, that, given that some injury is foreseeable, the injury to Duck is a natural consequence and thus liability is established. It may be possible, however, for Lax to argue contributory negligence on the part of Duck.

Dodge has just been informed that he will be laid off for two months without pay. While generally there is no duty on the employer to provide work, there is a duty to pay wages (*Collier v Sunday Referee Publishing Co Ltd* (1940)). This is the consideration the employer provides under the contract and breach of the term is repudiatory. There are two situations in which the duty will not apply. First, as the duty is implied, it can be overridden by an express term (*Hulme v Ferranti Ltd* (1918)) or a term implied by custom (*Puttick v John Wright and Sons (Blackwall) Ltd* (1972)), although the right to lay off without pay may only be exercised for a reasonable length of time (*Dakri (A) and Co Ltd v Tiffen* (1981)). Second, the duty will not be implied when the failure to provide work is outside the control of the employer. In *Browning v Crumlin Valley Collieries* (1926), a colliery had to close down when a land fault necessitated repairs. Greer J held that the employer was not under a duty to pay the laid-off employees because the reason for the lay-off was totally outside its control.

In the case of Dodge, there appears to be no term in the contract allowing a lay-off without pay and thus the general implied duty will apply unless Lax Ltd can show that the lay-off is totally outside its control. In this case, it appears that the reason Lax Ltd has closed down the factory is because it does not want to stockpile unfinished articles. In other words, work is possible but inconvenient to the employer. In *Devonald v Rosser and Sons* (1906), an economic recession was held not to be sufficient reason to lay off piece workers without pay. This would suggest that the situation facing Lax Ltd does not fall within the exception in *Browning* and therefore the employer is under a duty to pay Dodge. Should it be held that the duty is not applicable, Dodge will be entitled to a guaranteed payment under ss 28–32 of the Employment Rights Act (ERA) 1996.

QUESTION 14

Vanessa worked for Dodgey Investment Consultants for four years. She was entitled to a bonus calculated according to the annual profits of the company. By virtue of this arrangement, Vanessa should have received £1,000 for the year ending 31 December. However, mistakenly, she was paid £2,000. Vanessa, being unaware of the mistake, paid for a £2,000 holiday for herself and her room-mate with the money.

Under a 'garden leave' clause in her contract, Vanessa was entitled to be paid wages during her one-month notice period, although she was under no obligation to work. Vanessa was given one month's notice to terminate her contract, but at the end of the month she received no pay (when she should have received £1,500) because the company had discovered its mistake in overpaying the bonus and wished to recoup the bonus and a sum of £500 that it had paid out in damages to a client of Vanessa to whom Vanessa had given bad investment advice. Just before she was given her notice, Vanessa signed a document saying that she would repay any monies owed to the company on the termination of her employment.

▶ Advise Vanessa as to her legal position in contract and under the ERA 1996.

Answer Plan

This question deals essentially with the employer's duty to pay wages, but is also looking at the remedies an employee may have when payment is not forthcoming. As such, it brings in actions under the ERA 1996. Many employment law courses cover the ERA 1996 under the duty to pay wages and that is why it is part of a question under implied duties. Vanessa's 'garden leave' clause is important because it means that her employer will pay her at the end of the leave rather than pay her wages in lieu of notice.

Particular issues to be considered are therefore:

❖   whether the employee owes a duty to indemnify the employer;
❖   when the employer is entitled to recover an overpayment of wages;

❖   what constitutes a legal deduction under s 13(1) of the Employment Rights
     Act (ERA) 1996;
❖   which deductions are excluded by s 14;
❖   what is a deduction; and
❖   what constitutes wages.

ANSWER

The question asks for advice to be given to Vanessa on both her contractual rights and
her rights under the ERA 1996. As such, the question will be dealt with in two parts.

In relation to her contractual claim, the employer is arguing that Vanessa owes £1,000
in respect of the overpaid bonus and a further £500 to repay damages the employer
has incurred due to Vanessa's negligence. In relation to the overpayment of the bonus,
Vanessa was unaware that she had been overpaid and, in fact, spent the money as
soon as she received it. In *Avon County Council v Howlett* (1983), an employee who was
off sick was inadvertently overpaid. When the employer attempted to recover the
overpayment, the employee argued on the basis of estoppel by representation. In
other words, the employee had relied on the representation by the employer that he
was entitled to the money and had altered his legal position as a result (that is, he had
spent the money). The defence succeeded, but the later House of Lords' case of *Lipkin
Gorman v Karpnale Ltd* (1992) said that future cases based on *Howlett* should be dealt
with not on the basis of estoppel, but on the general defence of change of position in
the law of restitution. These decisions, however, are on the basis that the employee
does not realise that an overpayment has occurred.

If the employee, on realising that there has been an overpayment, then spends the
money, this will constitute theft under s 5(4) of the Theft Act 1968. In Vanessa's case,
she was unaware that she had been overpaid by £1,000 in relation to the bonus. On
the basis of *Howlett* and *Lipkin*, she altered her legal position by buying a holiday. As
such, Dodgey Investment Consultants is not entitled to recover the £1,000 and
Vanessa can sue for recovery as she does not legally owe it the money. The agreement
she signed prior to leaving will not cover this overpayment.

In relation to the £500 that the company has paid out in damages to Vanessa's client,
this may be recoverable if there is an implied duty in the contract that the employee
will indemnify the employer against loss incurred due to the employee's negligence.
Harmer v Cornelius (1858) is said to be the authority for the proposition that the
employee owes the employer a duty of care. As such, should the employee be in

breach of the duty, this would give the employer the right to sue for damages. In the case of *Janata Bank v Ahmed* (1981), an employee was successfully sued by his employer for the recovery of £34,640, which the employer had lost due to the employee's failure to exercise proper care and skill as implied by his contract. In the case of Vanessa, it would appear that the employer is arguing breach of contract. In some circumstances, an employer will join the employee as joint tortfeasor under the Civil Liability (Contribution) Act 1978. In the problem, this has not occurred and Dodgey Investments is now trying to recover damages it has already paid. In other words, it is claiming an indemnity from Vanessa.

The leading case in this area is *Lister v Romford Ice and Cold Storage Co Ltd* (1957), in which the House of Lords clearly held that the implied duty to indemnify the employer against damage caused by the employee's negligence exists. The case, however, has been severely criticised. The main basis of the criticism is that, given that the employer has to pay damages because it is vicariously liable for its employee (and given that although liability arises through notional control of the employee by the employer, the principal rationalisation of vicarious liability is that the employer – or its insurers – has the financial ability to pay damages), creating a right of indemnity is inconsistent. In *Lister* (1957), the employee tried to argue that there was a further implied term in the contract that the employer will ensure that the employee is insured against such liability before the right of indemnity can arise, but this was rejected by the House of Lords.

There have been attempts to avoid the decision in *Lister*. In *Harvey v RG O'Dell Ltd* (1958), it was held that the indemnity did not arise when the employee was doing work he was not normally employed to do but when he was helping his employer. This decision has been criticised by Jolowicz ('The Master's Indemnity: Variations on a Theme' (1959) 22 MLR 71 and 189), however, in that it gives a very narrow view of what the employee is employed to do. Another way of avoiding *Lister* can be seen in *Jones v Manchester Corp* (1952), in which the Court of Appeal held that a hospital board was not entitled to an indemnity from a young inexperienced doctor who had caused injury to a patient through his negligence because the board was at fault in failing to adequately supervise him. This stems from the common law rule that a contribution can be claimed from a joint tortfeasor if that tortfeasor is not wholly innocent, as opposed to being liable through principle rather than action (as in most cases of vicarious liability). While this does not prevent the court from apportioning damages under the Civil Liability (Contribution) Act 1978, it prevents the contractual claim arising.

In the problem, Vanessa has worked for the company for four years. There is no evidence that she is inexperienced, as in *Jones*, and it is unlikely that a court would feel that she needed supervision unless there were evidence of problems in the past. As such, it would appear that the only reason that the employer has had to pay the £500 is because of the imposition of vicarious liability rather than any negligence on the company's part and thus *Jones* will not apply. This means that, given that the right of indemnity does apply although it is rarely enforced, Dodgey Investments will have a contractual claim to recover the £500 if the loss was caused by Vanessa's negligence.

It would appear, therefore, that the company has no contractual right to the £1,000 overpayment but does have a contractual right to the £500. The question that must now be asked, however, is whether the money was deducted correctly.

The Wages Act 1986 (now the ERA 1996) was brought in to deal with deductions from wages made incorrectly by employers. It gives employment tribunals jurisdiction over deductions that contravene the Act. The issue of legal entitlement to the money deducted is irrelevant. The Act merely lays down an administrative structure of how and when the employer can deduct. Section 13(1) of the ERA 1996 states that the employer cannot make a deduction from the wages of an employee unless the deduction is required or authorised by stature, required or authorised by a provision in the employee's contract, or agreed to previously by the employee in writing before the deduction was made. Section 14, however, contains a list of exceptions to s 13(1), and s 14(1)(a) and (b) covers deductions in respect of an overpayment of wages or expenses.

'Wages' is defined by s 27 of the ERA 1996 and includes 'any fee, bonus, commission, holiday pay or other emolument referable to his employment' (s 27(1)(a)). As such, it would appear from the problem that the overpayment of the £1,000 was an overpayment of wages for the purpose of s 14 of the Act. At one time, it was thought that if the employer had no contractual right to recover the overpayment, s 14 did not apply (*Home Office v Ayres* (1992)). This has now been overruled, however, and even though Dodgey Investments does not have a contractual right to recover, Vanessa cannot use the tribunal jurisdiction under the Act but must use the contractual jurisdiction (*Sunderland Polytechnic v Evans* (1993)). In relation to the deduction of the £500, however, the situation is different. Vanessa was under a 'garden leave' clause. While the decision in *Delaney v Staples t/a De Montfort Recruitment* (1992) states that wages in lieu of notice are damages for a breach of contract and therefore not wages for the purposes of the Act, Vanessa will be paid at the end of the period although there is no requirement to work. As such, her final payment will be wages under s 27(1)(a). A further point is that, in reality, Vanessa received no money whatsoever rather than a reduction in money. Can a total failure to pay constitute a deduction for the purposes of the Act? The Court of Appeal in *Delaney* stated that a non-payment was a 100 per cent deduction and therefore fell within the tribunal jurisdiction. The House of Lords did not hear this point on appeal and it therefore appears that this is still the law. Vanessa has thus suffered a deduction from her wages. The question must therefore be asked: did the deduction comply with s 13(1)?

There is no requirement to deduct the sum by statute, nor is there evidence that Vanessa's contract allowed such a deduction. Vanessa did, however, sign a document allowing the deduction to be made just before she was given notice. Until the early 1990s, such an agreement would have meant that the Act had been complied with, but, in *Discount Tobacco and Confectionery Ltd v Williamson* (1993), the Employment Appeal Tribunal (EAT) held that such an agreement had to be signed before the event causing the deduction and an agreement signed after the event but before the deduction was made did not comply with s 13(1). Here, Vanessa signed the agreement after she gave the bad advice and caused the company loss. Therefore, the deduction is in breach of s 13(1) and can be recovered.

QUESTION 15

In addition to the long-standing applications of the general implied duty on the employer to exercise care, another area of considerable modern concern has taken this duty much further than its origins in physical injury to the employee in a workplace accident. This is the expanding law relating to workplace stress-induced injuries.

▶ With reference to case law, critically evaluate the extent of an employer's liability for workplace stress-induced injuries.

Answer Plan

This question asks the student to look at how far the employer's health and safety duties have been expanded over recent times to include workplace stress-induced injuries. Given that the first case in this area was 1995, the student needs to track the development of the duty since that time, and evaluate whether in reality the duty of the employer has actually been increased or whether the cases demonstrate a reluctance on the part of the courts to do this. It is also necessary to consider the impact on this area of the Protection from Harassment Act 1997 and the Equality Act 2010.

Particular issues to be considered are:

❖ the origins of the duty in *Walker v Northumberland County Council* (1995);
❖ the application of the duty in *Waters v Commissioner of Police of Metropolis* (2000);
❖ the principles laid down in the Court of Appeal decision in *Sutherland v Hatton* (2002);

❖   application of the principles in recent cases such as *Barber v Somerset County Council* (2004); *Simmons v British Steel* (2004); *Hartman v South Essex Mental Health and Community Care NHS Trust* (2005); *Melville v Home Office* (2005); *Intel Corporation (UK) Ltd v Daw* (2007); *Deadman v Bristol City Council* (2007);

❖   the impact of the **Protection from Harassment Act 1997** and *Majrowski v Guy's and St Thomas's NHS Trust* (2006); and

❖   the impact of the **Equality Act 2010**.

ANSWER

While an employer has always owed a duty to take reasonable care to protect its employees against foreseeable injury, until the case of *Walker v Northumberland County Council* (1995) this duty had only be applied in respect of physical injury. In *Walker*, however, an employee successfully sued his employers in respect of a second nervous breakdown, having already suffered one in the past and having returned to work with the offer of extra support, which never materialised. It was held that, given the first nervous breakdown, it was reasonably foreseeable that without extra staff the complainant's health would suffer and there was no reason why the employer should not be liable for psychiatric damage to an employee as well as physical damage. This was extended by the House of Lords in *Waters v Commissioner of Police for the Metropolis* (2000), in which the House of Lords held that an employer could be liable for psychological harm, caused by failing to take a complaint of sexual assault by a fellow officer seriously and by allowing the employee to be subjected to victimisation and harassment by fellow officers after she had made the complaint. The expansion of the common law duty was eventually reviewed by what is now the leading case of *Sutherland v Hatton* (2002) in the Court of Appeal.

The judgment of the court was given by Hale LJ in which she gave a series of 16 practical propositions of which Smith and Baker (*Smith and Wood's Employment Law*, 10th edn, 2010, Oxford University Press) identify the key points: (1) the ordinary principles of employer's liability apply to the area of work-induced stress, which focuses on the foreseeability of the injury; (2) mental disorder will be inherently more difficult to foresee than physical injury and the employer is entitled to assume the employee can withstand the normal pressures of work; (3) there are no inherently dangerous jobs in relation to stress and much will depend on whether the demands made of that employee are excessive, perhaps evidenced by a history of illness (including that of other employees) and complaints; (4) the employer is normally entitled to take what the employee says at face value; (5) the employer is only in breach if it has failed to take steps that it could have reasonably been expected to take, which may involve considering the size of the undertaking and its resources and the need to treat other employees fairly; (6) an employer who offers a confidential counselling service is unlikely to be found in breach of duty; (7) if the only way to protect the employee was to dismiss or demote him, an employer will not be in breach of duty by allowing a willing employee to continue working; (8) causation must be proved – that is, that the injury has been caused by the breach of duty not simply by the stress; (9) where the stress was caused only partly by work, the employer need only pay that part of the damages for which its actions are responsible.

The application of these principles were seen in *Barber v Somerset County Council* (2004), in which the House of Lords said that the employer had to take the initiative, rather than wait and see as suggested by the Court of Appeal. In *Simmons v British Steel* (2004), their Lordships confirmed this, saying that while physical injury had to be reasonably foreseeable for an employer to be liable, this was not essential in cases of psychiatric injury. Employers become liable to take action once they are aware of the employee's condition.

While the principles laid down in *Sutherland* have given some guidance, later cases have shown that the courts still find the principles difficult to apply in stress cases, a point made by the Court of Appeal in *Hartman v South Essex Mental and Community Care NHS Trust* (2005). In that case, the Court reiterated that the duty on employers is to prevent foreseeable injury and employers are only liable if a failure to take action results in an employee suffering foreseeable loss. An employer may be aware of this through the way the work is organized or because the employee has a health problem. It is the responsibility of the employee to make the employer aware of the health problem and complaining about overwork or a possible risk to health is not enough. In *Hartman*, the employee had a breakdown. She had told the occupational health department about problems and a previous breakdown, but did not want the information disclosed to her managers and because she was passed as fit to work, the Trust did not receive the information. When she started suffering problems again, the Trust offered counselling and leave, both of which she refused. She suffered no real difficulties at work and could not identify an event at work that had led to her second breakdown. As such, the Trust was not liable. It did not have the knowledge of the earlier problems and thus her breakdown was not foreseeable. Even if there had been a breach of duty, it would be unlikely that there was causation under the *Sutherland* principles. However, further clarification of the employer's duty was given by the Court of Appeal in *Melville v Home Office* (2005). In this case, a healthcare worker, responsible for removing the bodies of suicide victims in a prison, suffered a breakdown. The employer was aware of the stressful nature of the job. The Court of Appeal, holding the employer liable, stated that if the employer could foresee the risk of harm, because of the nature of the job, the employer did not have to foresee harm to a particular employee.

While this may or may not challenge certain of the guidelines in *Sutherland*, *Intel (UK) Ltd v Daw* (2007) shows that they are still being refined. In that case, the employee had a nervous breakdown caused by an excessive workload. The employer knew that she had a history of depression and the High Court found the employer in breach of duty. Intel appealed, arguing that it had a confidential counselling service. The Court of Appeal dismissed the appeal saying that the mere provision of a counselling service was insufficient to discharge the employer's duty. However, in *Deadman v Bristol City Council* (2007), the employee suffered from depression after an allegation of sexual harassment was made against him. He argued a breach of duty, stating that the way in which the employer handled the case against him, in breach of contract, led to him suffering stress. The Court of Appeal held that a policy to handle such complaints 'sensitively' was aspirational and not part of the contract. Although having a panel of two rather than three members was a breach of contract, it was not reasonably foreseeable that the employee would suffer stress as a result. Further, the employer was not in breach by leaving a letter stating the decision on his desk. It was the content of the letter and not the way in which it was disclosed that was important.

In *Melville v Home Office* (2005), the Court of Appeal stated that if the employer could foresee the risk of harm because of the nature of the job, it didn't have to foresee harm to a particular employee, and thus the Home Office was liable for the breakdown of a healthcare worker in a prison who had the job of removing the bodies of suicide victims. The Court of Appeal in *Dickens v O2 plc* (2009) seem to suggest that the *Hatton* requirements of reasonable foreseeability, breach and causation may not be as strict as first thought. In finding the employer liable for stress-induced injury, the Court stated that, in relation to foreseeability, it was sufficient that the employee had previously complained about the stress of the job, had regularly been late for work and had told her manager she didn't know how long she could keep going before she became ill. Further, in *Corr v IBC Vehicles Ltd* (2008), the House of Lords held the employer liable for the suicide of an employee after an accident at work had left him severely disfigured, and after which he suffered severe headaches and had problems sleeping. After the accident, he was hospitalised; he took his own life some six years after the accident. The House of Lords held that the employee would not have committed suicide if it had not been for the accident caused by the employer's negligence. An employer is liable when it can reasonably foresee damage caused by the commission of a tort but there is no necessity to foresee the precise form of that damage. Suicide is a reasonably foreseeable consequence of severe depression and the depression was caused by the employer's negligence. These cases show that the law in this area is still developing.

There are two other possibilities, outside of the common law duty, in which an employer may be liable for workplace stress-induced injury. First, if the injury lasts for more than 12 months and has a substantial adverse effect on the employee's ability to carry out normal day-to-day activities, it may constitute a disability under s 6 of the Equality Act 2010, since the removal of the requirement that a mental impairment has to be a clinically well-recognised illness. In this situation, liability will turn on what reasonable adjustments the employer has put in place to counter any disadvantages in the workplace that the disabled employee encounters.

A more recent development in this area comes from the case of *Majrowski v Guy's and St Thomas's NHS Trust (2006)*, which potentially leaves the employer with no defence and in which foreseeability does not play a part. In that case, an employee claimed that his manager had subjected him to harassment under the Protection from Harassment Act 1997, for which his employer was vicariously liable. The House of Lords held that this was the case. The importance of this decision cannot be underestimated. First, the Protection from Harassment Act was brought in to protect people from stalkers and was never intended to apply in employment situations but their Lordships held that it was so broadly drafted that it could so apply. Second, since *Lister v Helsey Hall Ltd (2001)*, the concept of vicarious liability has been widened so that an employee's conduct must only have a reasonable connection to his work. Third, harassment does not have to cause mental injury and finally, if harassment and vicarious liability are established, there is no defence.

The question asks about employer's liability in relation to workplace stress-induced injury. While guidelines were laid down in *Sutherland* in respect of the employer's common law duty, later cases appear to still be refining and clarifying the law, so it cannot be said with any certainty whether the employer's duty has expanded or whether the established duty is merely being applied to modern injuries. Perhaps what is more worrying for employers, however, is *Majrowski*. The application of the Protection of Harassment Act to employment claims leaves an employer particularly vulnerable, given that there is no breach of duty on its part and it is liable for the acts of its employees even if it took reasonable steps to prevent such conduct. It is clear that the duties of an employer in this area are still expanding.

Aim Higher ★

◆ It has been noted above this is an area that is in flux. The law is developing quickly in this area, so you need to keep abreast of it and include very recent cases to get good marks.
◆ A number of writers have published in this area and referring to them in your answer will increase your marks – for example, Barrett (2002) 31 ILJ 285, Barrett (2005) 34 ILJ 182 and Brodie (2004) 33 ILJ 261.

5 Discrimination

INTRODUCTION

Discrimination is an area that has rapidly expanded recently. It has been affected greatly by European Court decisions, and is an area in which a complainant not only has rights under national law, but may also have rights under European law in the form of the Equal Treatment Directive (76/207/EEC). Both discrimination and equal pay, discussed in Chapter 6, are areas in which European law has probably had the greatest impact and, to answer questions on these topics, it is necessary to understand the relationship between national law and European law and how far an individual in a Member State can enforce European law in the national courts.

Until the passing of the Equality Act 2010, there were a myriad of Acts and regulations affording protection from discrimination. All of these have now been repealed and placed under one Act. The Act, in s 4, lists the protected characteristics. These are:

- age;
- disability;
- marriage and civil partnership;
- pregnancy and maternity;
- race;
- religion or belief;
- sex;
- sexual orientation.

All of these were previously protected by various pieces of legislation. Sections 5–12 then define the protected characteristics in more detail. Most importantly race includes colour, nationality, and ethnic or national origin (s 9), so removing problems introduced by the Race Relations Act 1976 (Amendment) Regulations 2003. The majority of the Act will be in force in October 2010. Importantly, the Act for the first time allows a claim for direct discrimination on a combination of two of the protected characteristics – for example, sex and race (s 14) – although this provision will not come into force until April 2011. Given the time of writing, case law under the old legislation has been used in the problem questions as the majority of the Act is a consolidation of the previous law.

In addition, questions in this area may also include the Part-Time Workers (Prevention of Less Favourable Treatment) Regulations 2000 (as amended) and the Fixed-Term Employees (Prevention of Less Favourable Treatment) Regulations 2002.

In any problem question on discrimination, the starting point should always be to identify the type of discrimination that has occurred, because this will then lead on to whether a potential defence exists. The next stage is to identify the specific act of discrimination committed and finally any defence, if one is available. Furthermore, if the employer is an organ of the state, be aware of the possibility of a claim under a directive, in addition to any claim under national law.

For questions on the area of discrimination, general issues that the student needs to understand include:

❖ the relationship between national and European law in this area;
❖ the concept of discrimination;
❖ direct discrimination;
❖ indirect discrimination;
❖ victimisation;
❖ harassment;
❖ post-termination discrimination;
❖ the acts of discrimination;
❖ the role of the Commission;
❖ occupational requirements;
❖ exceptions to the legislation; and
❖ enforcement and remedies.

Questions in this area may come in the form of either essays or problems, and problem-type questions will often include different types of discrimination. In particular, therefore, students should be familiar with:

❖ the definition of discrimination;
❖ the burden of proof;
❖ the concept of continuing acts;
❖ the comparator in a direct discrimination claim;
❖ the definition of indirect discrimination;
❖ the defence in an indirect discrimination claim;
❖ the limitations in a victimisation claim;
❖ the statutory definition of harassment;

* what constitutes post-termination discrimination;
* the specific acts of discrimination;
* dual-characteristics claims; and
* remedies and how compensation is assessed.

Finally, given the impact of European law, no student should attempt a question in this area without a knowledge of the major cases in the European Court of Justice (ECJ) and their impact on national law.

Checklist ✔

Students should be familiar with the following areas:

■ the concept of discrimination – in particular, cases such as *James v Eastleigh Borough Council* (1990) and *Showboat Entertainment Centre v Owens* (1984);

■ the burden of proof ;

■ the necessary comparison in direct discrimination ;

■ the enforceability of the **Equal Treatment Directive** – in particular, in cases such as *Marshall v Southampton and South West Hampshire Area Health Authority (No 2)* (1993); *Foster v British Gas plc* (1991); *Doughty v Rolls Royce plc* (1992); *Francovich v State of Italy* (1992); *Marleasing SA v La Comercial Internacional de Alimentacion SA* (1992);

■ the elements of indirect discrimination and, in particular, cases such as *Enderby v Frenchay Health Authority* (1994); *Jones v University of Manchester* (1993); *Bilka-Kaufhaus GmbH v Weber von Hartz* (1987); *Hampson v DES* (1989); *Cobb v Secretary of State for Employment and Manpower Services Commission* (1989); *Falkirk Council v Whyte* (1997); *London Underground v Edwards (No 2)* (1998); *R v Secretary of State for Employment ex p Seymour-Smith and Perez* (1999) ECJ, (2000) HL; *Allen v GMB* (2008);

■ problems of interpretation of the specific acts of discrimination;

■ the statutory definition of harassment;

■ occupational requirements;

■ potential conflicts between the characteristics of sexual orientation and religion or belief;

■ principles in the award of compensation in particular cases, such as *City of Bradford Metropolitan County v Arora* (1989); *AB v South Western Water Services Ltd* (1993); *Deane v Ealing London Borough Council* (1993);

- The impact of European law on legislation – in particular, the effect of *Marshall (No 2)* above and the earlier *Marshall* (1986) decision *R v Secretary of State for Employment ex p EOC* (1994) *R v Secretary of State for Employment ex p Seymour-Smith and Perez* (1999) ECJ, (2000) HL
- the impact of the **Human Rights Act (HRA) 1998**;
- the **Part-Time Workers (Prevention of Less Favourable Treatment) Regulations 2000 (as amended)** and **Fixed-Term Employees (Prevention of Less Favourable Treatment) Regulations 2002**

QUESTION 16

Alexis, Crystal and Blake work for Dynasty Products Ltd. Alexis has just discovered that she is pregnant. She was due to go on a two-month training course in two weeks' time, but Dynasty has now refused to send her, saying that it will be wasted because, shortly after she returns, she will be on maternity leave. Another employee is now being sent in her place. The company has said that it would treat a man on long-term sick leave in the same way.

Crystal applied for a promotion recently. During her interview, she was asked about her childcare arrangements and about her husband's new job 100 miles away. In the end, no one interviewed was offered the promotion because the post was frozen as a result of cutbacks. Crystal has now learned that the interview panel had decided before the post was frozen that she would not be offered it, because Dynasty assumed that the family would be moving shortly because of her husband's job.

Blake works on the shop floor. He has objected because women on his shift can leave half an hour earlier on a Friday than the men in order to do their shopping. The women are not paid for this half an hour but Blake feels that he should be given the opportunity to leave early.

▶ Advise Alexis, Crystal and Blake whether they may pursue claims under the **Equality Act 2010** against Dynasty Products Ltd.

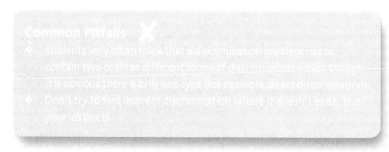

Common Pitfalls

- Students very often think that a discrimination problem has to contain two or three different forms of discrimination – even though it is obvious there is only one type (for example, direct discrimination).
- Don't try to find indirect discrimination where it doesn't exist. Trust your instincts.

Answer Plan

This question deals with allegations of direct sexual discrimination and, as seen in previous questions, the easiest way to approach it is to deal with each party individually. In the case of all the parties, it looks unlikely that a genuine occupational qualification exists, so it is a waste of valuable time to discuss this issue.

Particular issues to be considered are:

* the burden of proof;
* the definition of direct discrimination;
* the problems in s 23(1)) of the Equality Act 2010 (EqA);
* denying access to promotion, training or transfer, or any other benefits, facilities or services in s 39(2)(b);
* the problems caused by *Thorn v Meggit Engineering* (1976) and whether *Brennan v Dewhurst Ltd* (1984) can apply;
* whether assumptions can be discriminatory; and
* the problems caused by *Peake v Automotive Products* (1978) and the effect on the problem of *MOD v Jeremiah* (1980).

ANSWER

In the case of Crystal and Blake, any potential claim against Dynasty Products Ltd will be of direct sexual discrimination. The definition of direct discrimination is found in s 13 of the EqA 2010 and occurs when a woman, on the grounds of her sex, is treated less favourably than a man. This is perhaps misleading, however, because the Act further protects against discrimination on the grounds of marital status (s 13(4)) and applies equally to men (s 11(a)).

The burden of proof is found in s 136, which provides that where a complainant proves facts from which the tribunal could conclude, in the absence of an adequate explanation from the respondent, that the respondent has committed an act of discrimination, the tribunal shall uphold the complaint unless the respondent proves that he did not commit the act. Thus, the Act imposes a statutory duty on the tribunal to shift the burden of proof where the complainant establishes a prima facie case of discrimination.

While s 13(1) talks of less favourable treatment, the question to be asked is: less favourable than what? This is answered by s 23(1), which requires a tribunal to consider the treatment of the complainant and compare it to that of a person of the opposite sex where 'there is no material difference in the circumstances relating to each case'. This means that, in the case of Crystal and Blake, it must be shown that their treatment was different from that of a person of the opposite sex whose circumstances were not materially different, and that the reason for the different treatment was the complainant's sex. Should this be proved to the satisfaction of the tribunal, the employer's motive for its actions is irrelevant (*Grieg v Community Industries* (1979)). In *James v Eastleigh Borough Council* (1990), the House of Lords said that the question to ask was: 'Would the complainant have received the same treatment but for his or her sex?' If the treatment would have been different if the complainant's sex were different, discrimination has occurred and the reason for that discrimination is irrelevant. On the other hand, if the employer shows that it would have treated both sexes in the same way, there is no discrimination. In *Home Office v Coyne* (2000), Coyne complained of sexual harassment, but her complaint was not dealt with for two years and she was eventually dismissed. The Court of Appeal held that for a complaint to lie, she had to show that, but for her sex, the complaint would have been dealt with. In that case, however, there was no evidence that the Home Office would have dealt with a complaint by a man in a more favourable way and thus her complaint failed. It is submitted that this is a narrow interpretation of the law and allows a bad employer to escape liability on the basis that it treats all employees equally badly.

In the case of Alexis, she has been turned down for training because she is pregnant. Alexis may be discriminated against because of the protected characteristic of pregnancy. Section 18(2)(a) provides that a person discriminates against a woman if, in the protected period in relation to her pregnancy, he treats her less favourably because of her pregnancy. The protected period is the period of the pregnancy and any statutory maternity leave to which she is entitled (s 18(6)). The potentially discriminatory act is refusing her access to training in s 39(2)(b) and this is because of the protected characteristic of pregnancy. Unlike other areas of discrimination, Alexis does not need a comparator; she merely needs to establish that the reason for the less favourable treatment was her pregnancy as such.

Dynasty's argument that it would treat a man on long-term sick leave in the same way is irrelevant.

Therefore, in relation to pregnancy, the comparison required by s 23(1) is not required and the only reason that Alexis has not been selected for her training course is her pregnancy and it is actionable. Given that it is an action under s 18, Dynasty will have no defence.

Crystal was interviewed for a promotion but was not offered the post because the interview panel assumed she would be moving because of her husband's new job.

Crystal's case raises a variety of issues. First, it must be decided what is the less favourable treatment. If Crystal argues that it is not getting the promotion, she may have problems because no one was promoted because the post was frozen. In *Thorn v Meggit Engineering Ltd* (1976), a woman was rejected for a job because of her sex but in the end no one was appointed. The tribunal held that there had been no sex discrimination, as she had not been treated less favourably than a man because a man did not get the job. This can be contrasted with the case of *Roadburg v Lothian Regional Council* (1976), in which in similar circumstances, a woman was refused a job that was offered to a man, but then the post was frozen and so no one actually took up the job. In that case, it was held that there was discrimination in that the less favourable treatment was not being offered the job in the first place. Thus, to choose the lack of an offer may not lead to a finding of discrimination despite the fact that the reason for the refusal to make an offer was because of a sex-based assumption – that is, that her husband is the breadwinner and therefore she will move with his job (*Horsey v Dyfed County Council* (1982)). As no man was offered the promotion, Crystal will not satisfy s 23(1).

Crystal may, however, be able to argue that the interview itself was where the less favourable treatment occurred. In *Gates v Wirral Borough Council* (1982), it was held that asking questions about childcare arrangements of women, when the same questions were not asked of men, was discriminatory. In *Saunders v Richmond-upon-Thames Borough Council* (1978), it was held that questions in an interview for a golf professional, such as 'are you blazing a trail for women', were not discriminatory when not asked of men. In *Brennan v Dewhurst Ltd* (1984), a girl applied for a job as a butcher's assistant but was turned down for the job because of her sex. The post was then frozen and no one was appointed. She was successful in her claim for direct discrimination on the basis that the interview was the incident of discrimination in that the questions made it clear that the employer did not want to appoint a woman and, therefore, her action lay under s 39(1)(a) (arrangements for determining who shall be employed) rather than s 39(1)(b). Crystal was asked questions about her husband and her childcare arrangements. If men were also interviewed and were not asked similar questions, she can argue less favourable treatment on the grounds of her sex, given that it appears that they had no intention of appointing her in the first place. The predecessor of the Equality and Human Rights Commission, the Equal Opportunities Commission (EOC), argued that such questions should not be asked until the job is offered. This makes sense, in that, if the men were asked the same questions, it would be difficult to show less favourable treatment. The point, of course, is that it is the answers to the questions that will influence the employer because, even in today's society, the majority of childcare responsibilities will still fall to women.

Blake feels that he is receiving less favourable treatment in that he has to work an extra half an hour on Fridays. **Section 39(2)(b)** covers discrimination in access to benefits, facilities or services. In *Peake v Automotive Products* (1978), Mr Peake claimed discrimination on the basis that women were allowed to leave five minutes early every day to avoid the rush to leave when the factory closed. In the EAT, Peake won his case, and Phillips J said that 'benefit' in s 6(2)(a) (now s 39(2)(b)) 'meant no more than advantage'. The Court of Appeal, however, overruled the EAT, Lord Denning MR stating that rules for safety and good administration could not be discriminatory and that Peake's claim was *de minimis*. The case caused some criticism as it suggested that motive was relevant in direct discrimination and a later Court of Appeal, in *MOD v Jeremiah* (1980), overruled the first part of the decision but upheld it on *de minimis*. In Blake's case, the difference between his situation and *Peake* is five minutes a week, albeit that, in Blake's case, it all happens in the one day. How far the courts will invoke the *de minimis* principle is unclear. In *Birmingham City Council v EOC* (1989), the House of Lords held that deprivation of choice is sufficient to constitute less favourable treatment and, in *Gill v El Vino Co Ltd* (1983), Eveleigh LJ said:

> I find it very difficult to invoke the maxim *de minimis* non curat lex in a situation where that which has been denied to the [claimant] is the very thing that Parliament seeks to provide, namely, facilities and services on an equal basis.

On the basis of these cases, it would appear that *de minimis* is unlikely to succeed. There is one important difference between Blake's case and *Peake*, however. In *Peake*, the women were paid for the five minutes; in Blake's case, they are not paid for the time off. In *Jeremiah*, men were required to work in dirty conditions, for which they were paid extra, but the women were not so required. It was held that forcing men to work in such conditions was discriminatory and it was irrelevant that they received extra pay; an employer cannot buy the right to discriminate. On this authority, the fact that the women do not receive pay is irrelevant. The lack of choice is because of Blake's sex (*James v Eastleigh Borough Council*) and should the courts reject *de minimis*, which seems likely, Blake will be successful in his claim for direct discrimination.

QUESTION 17

Northbury Health Authority has recently advertised internally for a supervisor to take charge of domestic staff. Deirdre, who is 36, worked for the health authority full-time as a supervisor until five years ago when she left to have children. Until that time, she had worked for the health authority for ten years. She now works part-time as a domestic auxiliary to fit in with her children, and is prepared to work to job share. She is not interviewed for the job because the authority tells her that post is not open to part-time staff, nor can the job be shared.

The health authority has recently dismissed Harvinder, a Sikh, from his job as mortuary attendant. The reason for his dismissal, according to personnel, is that he cannot wear a protective surgical cap when attending post-mortems because of his turban and his long hair. He has been frequently warned about this and had taped some of the conversations with personnel secretly, in case of such an eventuality. The discovery of the tapes coincided with his dismissal, although the authority claims that the tapes had no bearing on its decision to dismiss.

▶ Advise Northbury Health Authority.

Common Pitfalls

❖ Students very often get confused by the concept of direct or indirect discrimination. For indirect discrimination, there must be a provision, criterion or practice that puts one group at a disadvantage when compared to another.

❖ If there is no such provision, etc, it cannot be an indirect discrimination claim.

Answer Plan

This question covers both sex and race discrimination. Again, it is easier to deal with each party separately and identify the type of discrimination first and then the act of discrimination that may have been committed.

Particular issues to be considered are:

❖ the requirements for an actionable indirect discrimination claim;
❖ what constitutes a provision, criterion or practice – comparing cases such as *Holmes v Home Office* (1984); *Clymo v Wandsworth London Borough Council* (1989); *Falkirk Council v Whyte* (1997);
❖ the defence and, in particular, cases such as *Bilka-Kaufhaus GmbH v Weber von Hartz* (1987); *Hampson v DES* (1989); *Cobb v Secretary of State for Employment and Manpower Services Commission* (1989); *Allen v GMB* (2008);
❖ the acts of discrimination in s 39 of the EqA 2010;
❖ the concept of racial discrimination;
❖ the concept of victimisation – in particular, *Aziz v Trinity Street Taxis* (1988);
❖ the possibility of a claim under the religion or belief characteristic.

ANSWER

This question deals with a variety of issues in relation to discrimination claims. By s 136 of the EqA 2010, where a complainant proves facts from which the tribunal can conclude, in the absence of an adequate explanation from the employer, that an act of discrimination has occurred, the tribunal must uphold the complaint unless the respondent proves that it did not commit the act. Thus, the Act imposes a statutory duty on the tribunal to shift the burden of proof where the facts establish a prima facie case of discrimination.

Deirdre is at present employed part-time, but worked full-time for the authority before she had her family and is prepared to job share. The authority has told her that the job is not open to part-time staff, nor can it be job shared. To establish a prima facie case, Deirdre must convince the tribunal that the facts give rise to a prima facie case of discrimination. The type of discrimination that Deirdre must try to establish is indirect discrimination ((s 19) of the Act) in relation to access to opportunities for promotion (s 39(2)(b)).

By s 19, indirect discrimination occurs where the employer applies a provision, criterion or practice: that it applies, or would apply, equally to a man; that puts, or would put, women at a particular disadvantage when compared with men; that puts women at that disadvantage; and that the employer cannot show to be proportionate means of achieving a legitimate aim.

There are considerable differences between this definition and the original definition in the previous legislation. The previous definition required the complainant to show that: the employer was imposing a condition or requirement that applied equally to both sexes; the proportion of women who could comply with the condition or requirement was considerably smaller than the proportion of men who could comply; the employer could not justify the imposition of the condition or requirement irrespective of sex; and it was to the complainant's detriment that she could not comply.

The differences are immediately apparent. The phrase 'provision, criterion or practice' is wider than the more restrictive 'condition or requirement'. The woman no longer has to show a difference in the proportions of men and women affected. The defence now means that the employer must show that the discrimination is a proportionate means of achieving a legitimate aim.

The old 'condition or requirement' was interpreted as meaning something that was necessary for the job (*Perera v CSC (No 2)* (1983)). This interpretation meant that if an employer merely expressed a preference, then it was not imposing a condition or requirement – a view expressed as unfortunate by the Court of Appeal in *Meer v Tower*

Hamlets (1988). In *Falkirk Council v Whyte* (1997), however, the EAT held that if a factor described as a preference was in reality the deciding criterion in who was offered a job or promotion, it was a condition or requirement. Under the previous definition, therefore, it is clear that working full-time is a necessary requirement for the supervisor's job because she is told that she cannot apply because she is part-time and that the job cannot be job shared. Thus, full-time working would be classed as a condition or requirement pre-2001 and most certainly would be a provision, criterion or practice under the amended section.

Second, Deirdre must show that working full-time puts women at a particular disadvantage. This will involve some consideration of a comparative group. While *Holmes v Home Office* (1984) decided that the imposition of full-time working was indirectly discriminatory to women, *Kidd v DRG (UK)* (1985) demonstrated that it is necessary for Deirdre to choose the correct comparative group. In *Pearse v Bradford Metropolitan District Council* (1988), one of the requirements of eligibility to apply for the post of senior lecturer in a college was that the applicants had to work full-time. Pearse argued that the requirement was discriminatory and produced statistics that, out of all the academic staff, 21.8 per cent of women worked full-time compared with 46.7 per cent of men. The EAT held that the wrong comparative group was used. The group should have been those academic staff eligible to apply for a senior lectureship due to qualifications and experience. On this comparison, there was little difference in the proportions and therefore no discrimination. A similar wrong choice of comparative group was seen in *Jones v University of Manchester* (1993). In establishing the comparative group, therefore, Deirdre must choose those at the workplace who are qualified to apply for the post of supervisor. If, when looking at this group, the proportion of women working part-time is considerably smaller than the proportion of men working part-time, she will have established the second requirement for an indirect discrimination claim – that is, that the provision of full-time working puts women at a particular disadvantage. This is supported by *London Underground v Edwards (No 2)* (1998), in which the Court of Appeal upheld the EAT in finding that a difference of just under 5 per cent constituted indirect discrimination; this must now be subject to the ECJ decision in *R v Secretary of State for Employment ex p Seymour-Smith and Perez* (1999), in which, although the Court held that it was up to member States to determine the relevant difference, the Court did not feel that a difference of less than 10 per cent indicated indirect discrimination. The ECJ added, however, that a smaller, persistent and constant disparity over a long period of time could indicate discrimination. This interpretation was adopted by the House of Lords when it decided *ex p Seymour-Smith* in February 2000.

The third requirement that Deirdre must establish is that the imposition of the provision is not a proportionate means of achieving a legitimate aim. It should be noted that the decision of the Court of Appeal in *Allen v GMB* (2008) has now given detailed guidance on the differences between legitimate aims and proportionate means. The GMB recommended to female equal pay claimants that they accept a single status deal that grossly underestimated the compensation that was due. The Court of Appeal held that while the objective of achieving a single status deal was legitimate, the means used to obtain it – that is, misleading the claimants as to the amount of back pay they would get – was not proportionate and, as such, the union had indirectly discriminated against the female claimants.

The defence available to the employer is very similar to that under the old law and has had a chequered history. In *Steel v UPOW (1978)*, Phillips J stated that the employer had to establish that the condition was necessary and not merely convenient to establish the defence. This stringent test was watered down by the Court of Appeal in *Ojutiku v Manpower Services Commission (1982)*, in which it was said that whether the employer was justified in imposing the requirement depended on whether its decision 'would be acceptable to right thinking people as (having) sound and tolerable reasons for doing so'. The ECJ in *Bilka-Kaufhaus GmbH v Weber von Hartz (1987)* stated that the employer had to show 'objectively justified' grounds, and that the factors that have a disparate effect 'correspond to a real need on the part of the undertaking, are appropriate with a view to achieving the objectives pursued and are necessary to that end'. *Hampson v DES (1989)* stated that to show that a condition is justifiable 'requires an objective balance to be struck between the discriminatory effect of the condition and the reasonable needs of the party who applies that condition'. Wood J in *Cobb v Secretary of State for Employment and Manpower Services Commission (1989)* said:

> It was for the tribunal . . . to carry out the balancing exercise involved, taking into account all the surrounding circumstances and giving due emphasis to the degree of discrimination caused against the object or aim to be achieved – the principle of proportionality.

In Deirdre's case, therefore, the employer must establish an objectively justified reason for the imposition of the provision that only full-time staff can apply for the job. From the facts, it would appear that the authority feels that the job can only be adequately performed full-time. This is indicated by the refusal to consider job sharing.

Despite *Holmes*, above, this may be justifiable in relation to certain types of job. In *Clymo v Wandsworth London Borough Council (1989)*, the EAT held that the refusal of an employer to allow a woman to job share a managerial post was not discriminatory, in that full-time working was an inherent characteristic of the job rather than a condition or requirement. If such an argument can be validly raised in respect of a supervisor's job, then the requirement that the job be performed full-time will not be discriminatory. This, however, is not the only argument put forward by Northbury. The authority is refusing part-timers the opportunity to apply for the post, whether such workers are prepared to work full-time or not. What the authority appears to have done is to make an assumption that because Deirdre works part-time at present, due to her childcare responsibilities, she cannot work full-time. Northbury is therefore making assumptions based on Deirdre's sex. Such assumptions are discriminatory (*Horsey v Dyfed County Council* (1982)) and therefore the provision that the applicants must work full-time at the time of their application is not justifiable.

The final hurdle for Deirdre is to show that she has been put at a disadvantage. Under the old law, a woman had to show that she had suffered a detriment. Detriment is not defined by the EqA, other than by saying it does not include conduct that amounts to harassment (s 212) but Lord Brandon, in *MOD v Jeremiah* (1980), said that it meant no more than 'putting under a disadvantage'. In this case, Deirdre has suffered a disadvantage when compared to men because she cannot apply for a promotion due to the provision or criterion imposed by the authority. She is unable to apply for the supervisor's job because of the provision that the job must be worked full-time and not job shared. Although there is no longer the additional hurdle that she has suffered a detriment because she cannot comply with the provision of full-time working, in this particular case, that is the reason why she has been put at a disadvantage. As such, under the old law, Deirdre would be likely to succeed in an indirect discrimination claim. As such, Deirdre will have made out her prima facie case and the tribunal must uphold the complaint unless the employer can show that sex is not the reason for the provision.

Harvinder has been dismissed ostensibly because his turban and long hair mean that he cannot wear the surgical cap when attending post-mortems. Harvinder, however, may be able to argue that the real reason for his dismissal is that he taped the warnings he received and therefore he has been the subject of victimisation. If we look at the reason given by Northbury first, it would appear that the authority is imposing a provision that surgical caps should be worn during post-mortems.

The requirements of s 136 mean that should Harvinder establish a prima facie case of race discrimination, the burden will shift to Northbury to put forward another reason for his treatment. Again, by s 19 of the Act, indirect discrimination occurs when: the employer applies a provision, criterion or practice that it applies or would apply equally to a person not of the same race or national or ethnic origins as Harvinder; the provision, criterion or practice puts, or would put, persons of the same race or national or ethnic origins as Harvinder at a particular disadvantage when compared with other persons; the employer cannot show the provision, criterion or practice to be a proportionate means of achieving a legitimate aim; and the provision, criterion or practice puts Harvinder at a disadvantage.

Harvinder can argue that a provision, criterion or practice is being applied, in that it is necessary for his job as a mortuary attendant that he wears a protective surgical cap when attending post-mortems. The House of Lords in *Mandla v Dowell Lee* (1983) decided that Sikhs were a race within the meaning of the Act. The provision that those attending post-mortems must wear surgical caps is likely to put Sikhs at a particular disadvantage when compared to other races who do not wear turbans. It may also be possible for Harvinder to argue that he is also suffering indirect discrimination under the religion or belief characteristic. Jurisprudence under the European Covention on Human Rights, however, interpreting Art 9 of the Convention and to which employment tribunals must have regard under the HRA 1998 suggests that if an employee knows of employer requirements before taking a post, the Article will not uphold their rights (for example, to dress in a particular way due to religious beliefs) as the employee knew the requirements and still took the job (*Kontinnen v Finland* (1996)). In *Kontinnen*, the Commission held that, given the conflict, the employee was free to leave his job and held that he was not dismissed because of his religious beliefs but because he refused to work the hours required by his employer. On the same basis, it is argued that Harvinder will have no claim for discrimination on the grounds of religion as he freely took the job knowing the dress requirements.

If Harvinder is successful in showing indirect race discrimination, the authority may have a defence if it can show that such a provision is a proportionate means of achieving legitimate hygiene aims and that alternatives will not work (*Singh v Rowntree Mackintosh Ltd* (1979)). This will require the tribunal to balance the aims of the employer with the rights of Harvinder. In *Saint Matthias Church of England School v Crizzle* (1993), a tribunal held that the needs of the Church of England School to have a headmaster who was a communicant outweighed the discriminatory impact on the complainant, who was Asian and a Christian but a non-communicant.

Harvinder may have an alternative claim of victimisation under s 27 of the EqA. This occurs when a person has been treated less favourably because he or she has brought proceedings under the Act, has given evidence in such proceedings, done anything under or by reference to the Act or has alleged that the discriminator has contravened the Act, unless that allegation is false and made in bad faith. The Court of Appeal, in *Cornelius v University College, Swansea* (1987), has said that it is the conduct listed above that is the basis of a victimisation claim and not the complainant's race. Harvinder taped his interviews with personnel and once this was discovered he was dismissed. To show that he was the subject of victimisation, he must show that the reason for his dismissal was that he taped the interviews to use in evidence in a race discrimination claim and that it was because of the potential use of the tapes that his dismissal occurred – in other words, that a person who taped such interviews for another purpose would not have been dismissed.

In the leading case of *Aziz v Trinity Street Taxis* (1988), a person was dismissed for secretly recording conversations he intended to use in discrimination proceedings. The employer argued that the reason for his dismissal was the fact that he had taped the conversations and not because of their eventual use. Given that the employer argued that it did not know the eventual use of the tapes, the Court of Appeal held that there was no victimisation. Given *Aziz*, Harvinder would have to prove that the reason for his dismissal was, by s 27(2)(c), the fact that he was going to use the tapes in discrimination proceedings. This means that he must show that it was the discovery of the tapes that led to his dismissal, not the problem with the surgical cap, and that it was because of the eventual use of the tapes and not the fact that the tapes were made. On the facts, this may be difficult, given the number of warnings he has received in relation to his headwear during post-mortems. It appears, therefore, that this is the true reason for his dismissal and that the authority may have the defence of justification to defeat an indirect discrimination claim.

QUESTION 18

The Equality Act 2010, as with previous pieces of anti-discrimination legislation, has the concept of victimisation. The concept, however, is not based on unfavourable treatment because of a protected characteristic but on the basis that the complainant has undertaken a protected act. As such, victimisation involves looking at different questions when compared to the other forms of discrimination and, as such, is very difficult to establish.

▶ Critically evaluate this question.

Answer Plan

This is quite a detailed question and requires a detailed knowledge of the definition of victimisation and how case law has interpreted it. It also requires the student to evaluate whether a claim of victimisation is difficult to establish.

Issues that need to be considered are:

❖ the definition of victimisation;
❖ what constitutes a protected act, looking at cases such as *Waters v Commissioner of Police of the Metropolis* (1997) and (2000);
❖ the comparator – in particular, looking at *Kirby v Manpower Services Commission* (1980); *Aziz v Trinity Taxis* (1988); *Cornelius v University College of Swansea* (1987); *Chief Constable of West Yorkshire v Khan* (2001);
❖ the causal link between the protected act and the less favourable treatment, looking at *Nagarajan v London Regional Transport* (1999); *Khan* (2001); *Cornelius* (1987); *Derbyshire v St Helens Metropolitan BC* (2006); and
❖ the relevance of motive.

ANSWER

In the Equality Act 2010 there is a concept of victimisation. The Act defines victimisation in s 27 as subjecting a person to a detriment by reason that the person victimised has done a protected act or the employer believes that the person has done a protected act. A protected act is:

(a) bringing proceedings against the discriminator or any other person under the Act; or

(b) giving evidence or information in connection with proceedings under the Act; or

(c) doing any other thing for the purposes of or in connection with the Act; or

(d) making an allegation (whether or not express) that the employer or another person has contravened the Act.

> A complainant is not protected if the less favourable treatment was because he/she made a false allegation in bad faith.

Thus, for a victimisation claim to be successful, the complainant must show that: he or she committed one of the protected acts above; he or she was treated less favourably; and the less favourable treatment was by reason that he or she did the protected act. It is the final causal link that has proved difficult for complainants to establish.

While the first two protected acts seem self-explanatory, the second two are more complex. Paragraph (c) is quite wide and has covered, for example, secret taping of conversations to provide evidence of race discrimination in Aziz v Trinity Taxis (1988). Paragraph (d), on the other hand, is very narrow because it states that the act alleged must be a contravention of the legislation. The importance of this is seen in Waters v Commissioner of Police of the Metropolis (1997) (CA). Waters, a police officer, made an allegation of rape against a fellow officer while they were both off-duty. No action was taken against the officer, and after Waters' complaint, she was subjected to verbal abuse, amongst other things, from fellow officers, taken off special duties and required to be psychologically analysed to ensure she was fit for duty. She complained of victimisation, alleging that her employer had treated her in that way because she had alleged a contravention of the then Sex Discrimination Act (SDA) 1975. The Court of Appeal, however, said that given the sexual assault took place outside work, the employer could not be liable under the then s 41 (now s 109) as the assault did not take place in the course of the officer's employment. Thus the employer had not contravened the Act, and thus could not be said to be victimising Waters because of her allegation. While the House of Lords in 2000 upheld the Court of Appeal's interpretation, it did allow Waters' appeal that her employers had been negligent. However, it shows how narrow the scope of para (d) is compared to the much wider para (c). Some writers have suggested that if Waters had used para (c) she would have won, as the only issue would have been whether her allegations were false and not made in good faith.

Previous definitions of victimisation required the complainant to have a comparator. The revised definition in the EqA has removed this restriction and thus the basis of the claim is the detriment because the employer knows or believes that the employee did the protected act, and not as previously that the employer treats the employee less favourably than a person who had not committed the protected act. This removes the problems created by cases like *Kirby v Manpower Services Commission* (1980), in which the complainant alleged victimisation when he was transferred after his employers discovered that he had disclosed confidential information alleging suspected discrimination by some employers. The EAT rejected his claim on the basis that anyone disclosing confidential information would have been transferred. However, the Act does require that the employee has suffered a detriment. This raised an interesting issue in *Chief Constable of West Yorkshire v Khan* (2001). In this case, Khan was pursuing a race discrimination claim against the Chief Constable and as such the Chief Constable refused to provide a reference in support of a job application that Khan was making. Khan was shortlisted but not appointed. However, it was acknowledged that, had the Chief Constable provided the reference, Khan would not have been shortlisted. The Chief Constable argued that in fact Khan had received more rather than less favourable treatment (that is, he had not suffered a detriment). However, the House of Lords stated that the perception of the victim was important and if the victim reasonably believes the treatment to be less favourable and thus a detriment, that is sufficient.

The final part of a victimisation claim is the causal link between the protected act and the detriment. The language of the definition is that the employer subjected the employee to a detriment because he or she did the protected act. In other words, that the protected act was the reason behind the detriment. As such, in *Aziz*, the employer argued that it was the breach of trust in secretly taping conversations that had led to Aziz's dismissal and not the fact that he intended to use them in a race discrimination claim. However, this interpretation introduced an element of motive, which was unnecessary in direct discrimination claims (which was the basis of a victimisation claim pre-EqA) in which it is only necessary to show the less favourable treatment and not the reason behind it. In *Nagarajan v London Regional Transport* (1999), a claimant was interviewed for a job with London Regional Transport against which he had brought several race discrimination claims. The House of Lords held that if the protected act was an important factor leading to the less favourable treatment, then a victimisation claim existed, even if the protected act was only one reason for the treatment and not even the main reason. This seemed to remove the requirement of motive and to adopt the test seen in the direct discrimination case of

James v Eastleigh BC of 'but for' – that is, but for the protected act would the complainant have been subjected to the detriment.

However, two years later, the House of Lords took a different approach in *Khan*. The Court of Appeal, using the 'but for' test, stated that Khan had been victimised, but the House of Lords reversed the decision. Their Lordships accepted the argument of the employer that it would have refused a reference to anyone with an existing claim against it whether it was for discrimination or not and thus the treatment was not because the claim happened to be under the anti-discrimination legislation. In other words, if the employer has a general policy, such as in *Khan*, then the less favourable treatment is not racially (or for any of the other discriminatory grounds) motivated and will not constitute discrimination. So if an employer treats everyone badly, it will not be liable – a proposition described as 'an absurd result' by the Court of Appeal in *Aziz*. Furthermore, in *Khan*, the House of Lords stated that the employer had acted reasonably and honestly in accordance with advice, appearing to add another dimension.

This was adopted by the Court of Appeal in *Derbyshire v St Helens Metropolitan BC* (2006), in which 510 staff brought an equal pay claim. Most compromised but 39 continued and the council wrote to them saying that if they were successful, mass redundancies would be the result. As such, they compromised the claim but then sued for victimisation. The Court of Appeal held that the council had acted reasonably and honestly in trying to settle the claim and thus although there was a detriment, there was no victimisation. The House of Lords (2007) reversed the Court of Appeal, so preventing a defence for the employer that its actions are honest and reasonable, something that was never part of the definition of victimisation.

Thus, from an examination of the case law, it does seem that victimisation is difficult to prove. Judges have struggled with the causal link between the detriment and the House of Lords itself has reversed its previous decision in *Nagarajan* and in *Khan*. It is hoped that the simplification of the definition in the 2010 Act and the removal of the need for a comparator will mean that more cases will succeed in future.

Aim Higher ★

◆ Reading relevant articles and incorporating the ideas into your answer (properly accredited) will gain you extra marks – for example, Connolly (2009) 38 ILJ 149.

◆ Analysing the old law carefully and comparing it to the new law will show that the definition has been widened considerably. Reflect this in your answer.

QUESTION 19

The Equality Act 2010 has eliminated the problems of having different pieces of anti-discriminatory legislation devised piecemeal and intended for particular target groups

▶ Critically evaluate this statement in relation to the protected characteristics.

Common Pitfalls

❖ The question is asking the student to critically evaluate the statement.

❖ A common pitfall in a question of this type is to not mention the problems before the Act and just to list the changes it has introduced without evaluating whether this will solve the problems.

❖ This is not a question asking what the **Equality Act** has changed but asking you to come to some sort of view as to whether the old problems have been resolved or will still exist.

Answer Plan

This question asks the student to look at the changes made by the Equality Act 2010. It also requires the student to evaluate whether the Act has eliminated the problems that existed where there were a number of pieces of legislation, each one aimed at one particular group.

The issues to be discussed here are:

❖ a brief discussion of the problems that existed pre-2010 in relation to the protected characteristics;

❖ whether the EqA 2010 has or has not eliminated these problems; and

❖ whether problems still exist.

ANSWER

The major pieces of legislation that gave protection from discrimination were the Sex Discrimination Act 1975 (SDA), the Race Relations Act 1976 (RRA), the Disability Discrimination Act 1995 (DDA), the Employment Equality (Sexual Orientation) Regulations 2003 (SO Regs), the Employment Equality (Religion or Belief) Regulations 2003 (RB Regs) and the Employment Equality (Age) Regulations 2006 (Age Regs). All of these pieces of legislation were amended during their currency. It can be seen therefore that each piece of legislation was targeted at a particular group and was often introduced or amended to comply with EU requirements. As such, the legislation often contained slightly different definitions that added to its complexity.

A few examples can be noted. All of the pieces of legislation had the concept of indirect discrimination, apart from the DDA, which had the concept of disability-related discrimination and the duty to make reasonable adjustments. However, the protection from disability-related discrimination was restricted by the House of Lords' decision in *London Borough of Lewisham v Malcolm* (2008), in which their Lordships decided that the comparator in such a claim was a person with the same material circumstances but without the disability, so overruling *Clarke v Novacold* (1998). This meant that for a disabled person who had been off for six months, five of which were for disability-related reasons, the comparator would be a non-disabled person who had been off for six months. This severely reduced the number of disabled persons who could pursue a disability-related claim, whereas had there been the concept of indirect discrimination within the Act, disabled claimants would still have had protection.

In addition, the legislation talked of discrimination on the grounds of race etc, apart from the SDA, which talked about the grounds of her sex. This meant that a woman had less protection that other protected groups as seen in *Showboat Entertainment Centre v Owens* (1984), in which an employee who was dismissed for refusing to obey a racist order was held to have been discriminated against on racial grounds. This would not have been the case if the employee had been dismissed for refusing to obey a sexist order as the dismissal would not have been on the grounds of his or her sex.

Other anomalies existed. The SDA and RRA had the concept of genuine occupational qualifications (GOQs), whereas the SO and RB Regs had the concept of genuine occupational requirements (GORs). The legislation did not protect against discrimination by association, which was in conflict with the EU Employment Directive (2007/78/EC) according to the ECJ in *Coleman v Attridge Law* (2008). A further anomaly, which arose as a result of the implementation of the Directive, was that the definition of indirect discrimination was harmonised across the majority of the legislation (excluding the DDA); however, as the Directive only applied to race or national or ethnic origins – a narrower interpretation than under the RRA – the old definition of indirect discrimination still applied when discrimination was on the grounds of colour or nationality. Furthermore, a more stringent burden of proof applied to these grounds. Another issue was if the person discriminated against had grounds under different pieces of legislation – for example, if the person was female and black. This meant that the person had to choose one piece of legislation only and could end up choosing the wrong one. Thus, by the time of the enactment of the EqA 2010, it was fair to say that the existing legislation was piecemeal and complex, often protection differing depending on which specific ground was being pleaded. The question is whether these problems have been eliminated.

The Equality Act 2010 repeals all the former anti-discriminatory legislation and covers all aspects of discrimination where discrimination has occurred on the basis of a protected characteristic. The protected characteristics are the old grounds for discrimination plus pregnancy and maternity. It also states that civil partnership is a protected characteristic. The Act defines such characteristics (ss 5–12), but importantly, in the definition of race in s 9 the definition includes colour and nationality, so removing the anomaly noted above. This ensures that the same definition of indirect discrimination and the same burden of proof applies whether discrimination is on the grounds of colour, race, nationality, or ethnic or national origins.

The definition of direct discrimination is simply treating a person less favourably because of a protected characteristic (s 13) and is wide enough to include persons discriminated against because of association with someone with the protected characteristic, so implementing the ECJ decision in *Coleman* above. However, this does not apply where the discrimination is because of marriage or civil partnership, in which case the victim of the less favourable treatment has to be the spouse or civil partner (s 13(4)). The definition also clarifies that where the protected characteristic is religion, it does not matter that the religion or belief is also the discriminator's religion or belief (s 13(6)).

Perhaps, most importantly, the Act introduces a new provision of discrimination arising from a disability. Section 15 (replacing disability-related discrimination) provides that a person discriminates against a disabled person if he treats the person in a particular way because of the person's disability, if the treatment amounts to a detriment and if the employer cannot show that it is a proportionate means of achieving a particular aim. A claim does not lie where the employer did not know, and could not be reasonably expected to know, that the employee was disabled and it is irrelevant that the employer has complied with the duty to make reasonable adjustments. On the face of it, this is intended to overrule *Malcolm* above on the basis that the limitations in *Malcolm* no longer provided enough protection from disability-related discrimination. This is an interesting section because it talks about the disabled person suffering a detriment rather than less favourable treatment. How this will be interpreted will be vital, particularly if the courts feel that a detriment is something that is more than just unfavourable treatment. The Explanatory Notes to the Act also state that it is also intended to protect a disabled person from unfavourable treatment arising out of the disability or in consequence of the disability, such as the need to take disability-related absence. Again, whether this is the interpretation the tribunals will adopt remains to be seen. One thing that is important to note is that s 15 does not require a comparator, hence the overruling of *Malcolm*, and thus is to be welcomed. In addition, there is further protection for disabled people in that, for the first time, the definition in s 19 of indirect discrimination also applies to the protected characteristic of disability. This means that if the employer has a policy, which would put disabled persons at a disadvantage when compared to non-disabled people, they have a potential claim if they are or would be put at a particular disadvantage. It is suggested that both s 15 and s 19 considerably increase protection for disabled people.

The Act repeals the concept of genuine occupational qualifications (GOQs) and replaces them with the concept of occupational requirements (ORs), which apply across all of the characteristics. While genuine occupational requirements had been introduced into later legislation, the SDA only had the concept of GOQs and the RRA had both GOQs and GORs. Both GOQs and GORs provided an exception to a direct discrimination claim in which having a particular characteristic was necessary for the job – for example, female toilet assistants in female toilets. GOQs were quite specific in their nature – for example, the holder of the job provided personal services that would lead to objections if the job was held by a member of the opposite sex – whereas GORs were much wider and less specific. The old definition of a GOR stated that to hold, for example, a particular belief was a genuine and determining occupational requirement and it was proportionate to apply it in the particular case. The definition of ORs in the Equality Act is different from that in earlier legislation. Schedule 9, para 1 states that a person does not contravene the provision relating to direct discrimination by applying in relation to work a requirement to have a particular characteristic if it can be shown, having regard to the nature or context of the work, that the characteristic is an occupational requirement and the application of the requirement is a proportionate means of achieving a legitimate aim.

This differs from the old legislation in three ways. First, it also applies to disability and further allows an employer to positively discriminate in favour of disabled persons. Second, the notion that the requirement must be genuine has been removed. While this may seem to increase the power of the employer, it is suggested that the removal of the word genuine is countered by the additional requirement that not only does the requirement have to be proportionate, but it must also be imposed to achieve a legitimate aim. Again, until there is case law, it remains to be seen whether the change in wording widens or narrows the exception.

Finally, the EqA deals with the issue of combined discrimination by introducing the concept of direct discrimination on the basis of dual characteristics in s 14. The characteristics that can be combined are age, gender reassignment, race, religion or belief, sex and sexual orientation. The comparator is a person who does not share either of the characteristics. The claimant does not have to show that a claim of direct discrimination in respect of each characteristic would be successful if pursued. ORs equally apply in respect of dual-characteristics claims. This is a totally new form of claim and while the majority of the Act was brought into force in October 2010, s 14 will not come into force until April 2011.

Has the EqA eliminated all of the problems that existed by having different pieces of legislation targeting different groups? On the face of it, yes. Certainly, protection for disabled persons has been brought into line with other protected areas and strengthened by the introduction of s 15. Employees will be protected from discrimination by association and employees who have been discriminated against on two grounds will now be able to take a dual-discrimination claim. The changes in the wording in respect of occupational requirements may mean employers have a greater ability to impose requirements on jobs but it is suggested that the need to show that the requirement is a proportionate means of achieving a legitimate aim should prevent this from happening. The fact that the law is contained in one Act and to a large extent has been harmonised across all of the characteristics has, it is suggested, eliminated the problems the previous law caused.

QUESTION 20

Lyndsay works for ACME Engineering. She began work as an accounts secretary four months ago. Since the beginning, she has been the subject of unwelcome advances from Tom, the company accountant. These have consisted of unwanted remarks concerning the way she dresses. Yesterday evening, after working late, Tom put his arm around Lyndsay's waist and said: 'Come on, love, it's obvious you're fair game.' Lyndsay was then subjected to a particularly humiliating assault.

On arriving at work the next morning, Lyndsay reported the assault to the works manager, who informed her that a one-off incident gave her no cause for complaint. He also said that, should she decide to take the matter further, he would have no choice but to mention Lyndsay's liberal attitude to matters of a sexual nature.

▶ Advise Lyndsay whether she may take any action against the company.

Answer Plan

This question looks short but it requires students to discuss a number of different issues. In Lyndsay's case, there is the question of sexual harassment under the EqA 2010, and whether the time of the assault means that she has no claim. Her treatment by the works manager could also potentially be direct discrimination or victimisation and both need to be discussed, as does vicarious liability on the part of the employer.

Particular issues to be considered are therefore:

- the definition of direct discrimination in s 13 of the EqA 2010 – in particular the 'but for' test in *James v Eastleigh Borough Council* (1990) and *Home Office v Coyne* (2000);
- the definition of 'subjecting to' in s 39(2)(d) of the EqA 2010;
- the statutory definition of harassment in s 26 of the EqA 2010 and, to aid interpretation, a discussion of the old law – in particular, *Porcelli v Strathclyde Regional Council* (1985); *Snowball v Gardner Merchant* (1987); *Bracebridge Engineering Ltd v Darby* (1990); *Insitu Cleaning Co Ltd v Heads* (1995); *Stewart v Cleveland Guest Engineering Ltd* (1994); *Wileman v Minilec Engineering Ltd* (1988); *Reed and Bull Information Systems Ltd v Stedman* (1999); *British Telecommunications plc v Williams* (1997); *Driskel v Peninsula Business Services Ltd* (2000); *Pearce v Governing Body of Mayfield Secondary School* (2003);
- whether the action by the works manager was a detriment or victimisation under s 27 – in particular, *Aziz v Trinity Street Taxis* (1988) and *Nagarajan v London Regional Transport* (1999);
- whether the time of the assault is relevant – in particular, *Waters v Commissioner of Police of the Metropolis* (2000) and *Chief Constable of Lincolnshire v Stubbs* (1999);
- vicarious liability of the employer under s 109 of the EqA 2010 – in particular, *Jones v Tower Boot Ltd* (1997); *Waters*; *Stubbs* (above); and
- the burden of proof in s 136.

ANSWER

Lyndsay may have a claim for direct sex discrimination. In order for her claim to be successful, she would have to show that she has been treated less favourably on the grounds of a protected characteristic – that is, her sex (s 13 (1) of the EqA 2010). In addition, she will have a claim under the harassment provisions in s 26(1) of the EqA.

Prior to changes introduced in 2005, in order to claim sexual harassment, a complainant argued direct discrimination and that she had suffered a detriment. This often proved difficult. In the early days of sexual harassment claims, it was thought that the detriment had to be a contractual detriment; however, *Porcelli v Strathclyde Regional Council* (1986) stated that sexual harassment per se constituted the detriment for the purposes of the Act. To aid interpretation, the Equal Opportunities Commission produced a code of practice that defined sexual harassment as 'unwanted conduct of a sexual nature, or other conduct based on sex affecting the dignity of women and men at work', and although not binding, the code was relied upon in cases such as *Wileman v Minilec Engineering Ltd* (1988) and *British Telecommunications plc v Williams* (1997). Williams also established that there was no need for a comparator in a sexual harassment claim, but the House of Lords in *Pearce v Governing Body of Mayfield Secondary School* (2003) stated that this was the wrong approach and that the fact that the conduct was gender-specific did not prove that the reason for the conduct was sex-based. This seemed to clarify a number of decisions, some of which stated that there was no need for a comparator (*Williams* above and *Insitu Cleaning Co Ltd v Heads* (1995)) and others of which said the normal test in *James v Eastleigh Borough Council* (1990) applied (*Stewart v Cleveland Guest Engineering Ltd* (1994) and *Driskel v Peninsula Business Services Ltd* (2000)). In other words, after *Pearce*, a complainant had to show that 'but for' her sex she would not have been subjected to the harassment, thus requiring the need for a male comparator. The reintroduction of a male comparator in this area was seen as unfortunate by many academic writers. A further problem with the use of detriment in the area of sexual harassment was that the complainant had to show that she had been 'subjected to' a detriment. While the phrase was given a broad interpretation in *Burton v De Vere Hotels* (1996), this was overturned in the House of Lords' decision in *Pearce*, thus causing more difficulties for complainants alleging sexual harassment.

In October 2005, a concept of sexual harassment was introduced into the legislation. These provisions are now replicated and expanded in s 26 (1) of the EqA 2010 and cover the protected characteristics of sex and gender reassignment. The section provides that a person subjects a woman to harassment when:

(a) A engages in unwanted conduct related to a protected characteristic that has the purpose or effect
    (i) of violating her dignity, or
    (ii) of creating an intimidating, hostile, degrading, humiliating or offensive environment for her,
(b) A engages in any form of unwanted verbal, non-verbal or physical conduct of a sexual nature that has the purpose or effect
    (i) of violating her dignity, or
    (ii) of creating an intimidating, hostile, degrading, humiliating or offensive environment for her, or
(c) on the ground of her rejection of or submission to unwanted conduct, he treats her less favourably than he would treat her had she not rejected, or submitted to, the conduct.

Section 26(3) states that the conduct shall be regarded as harassment, if having regard to all the circumstances, including in particular the perception of the victim, it should reasonably be considered as having that effect.

There are a number of things to note about the definition. First, it is clear that harassment does not have to be intentional as it is sufficient that the conduct has an effect on the complainant. Second, the definition talks about unwanted conduct related to a protected characteristic, which should widen the protection compared to the previous law, which talked about 'on the grounds of her sex'. Third, the conduct will only be regarded as harassment if in all the circumstances it should reasonably be regarded as having that effect – that is, there is an objective element. However, the tribunal is particularly directed to take into account the perception of the complainant. Fourth, if the complainant suffers an unpleasant atmosphere because she has rejected or accepted sexual overtures, this can also constitute harassment.

How will the new definition benefit Lyndsay's claim? The question states that Lyndsay has been the subject of unwelcome advances from Tom, therefore his conduct has been unwanted. He put his arm around Lyndsay's waist, which was unwanted physical conduct of a sexual nature. He then subjected her to 'a particularly humiliating assault'. Such action would have the effect of violating her dignity at least and creating an intimidating, degrading and humiliating environment for her; it appears to have done so in the problem as she has reported the incident to the work's manager. Although he told her he would have to mention her liberal attitude to matters of a sexual nature should she take the matter further, this is irrelevant if Lyndsay feels that her dignity was violated, etc, because of Tom's actions. As such, it is likely that a tribunal will hold that Lyndsay has suffered sexual harassment.

When Lyndsay complains to the works manager, she is told that she has no claim. However, Lyndsay may therefore have two further potential claims in respect of the action by the works manager. She may be able to argue that the failure to do anything constituted a detriment (s 39(2)(d)) or that she has suffered victimisation (s 27).

In *Home Office v Coyne (2000)*, a complaint of sexual harassment was not dealt with by a manager, and Coyne argued that the failure to deal with the complaint caused her to suffer a detriment and was thus sex discrimination. The Court of Appeal held that Coyne had to show that, but for her sex, the complaint would have been investigated. There was no evidence to suggest that the Home Office would have dealt with a complaint by a man more favourably and thus Coyne had not shown that the failure to deal with her complaint was on the grounds of her sex. On this basis, even under the new definition of related to sex, if the works manager argues that he would have treated any complaint by ignoring it, whether from a man or a woman, Lyndsay will not be able to prove the lack of investigation constituted a detriment she suffered because of her sex.

However, Lyndsay may be able to argue that she has suffered victimisation under s 27 of the EqA 2010. Victimisation occurs when a person is treated less favourably because he or she has done a protected act. A protected act is that she: has brought proceedings under the Act; has given evidence in such proceedings; has done anything by reference to the Act; or has alleged that the discriminator has contravened the Act. *Aziz v Trinity Street Taxis* (1988) makes it clear that it is the doing of one of the acts in the now s 27 that is the basis of the claim and not the sex of the person. *Nagarajan v London Regional Transport* (1999) further establishes that the motive of the discriminator is irrelevant if the action was significantly influenced by her sex. Thus, if Lyndsay can show that the reason the works manager failed to do anything was because she was alleging sexual harassment, and that if her complaint had been about, for example, her hours of work, it would have been investigated, she may be able to pursue a claim of victimisation.

Her claims are in relation to the actions of two employees. This raises the issue of the vicarious liability of the employer. Section 109 states that an employer shall be liable for the acts of its employees during the course of their employment unless the employer can show that it took all reasonable steps to prevent the unlawful acts being perpetrated. In the race discrimination case of *Jones v Tower Boot Ltd* (1997), a claim under the equivalent provision in the then RRA 1976, it was originally argued that the phrase 'in the course of employment' should be interpreted in the same way as at common law – that is, the employee is doing an authorised act in an authorised way or an authorised act in an unauthorised way. On this interpretation, it was held that an employer was not liable for the severe racial harassment of an employee because such harassment would not be an authorised act or an unauthorised way of conducting an authorised act. This initial decision was severely criticised on the basis that the more serious the harassment, the less likely that the employer would be held liable. The Court of Appeal in *Jones* reversed the decision, stating that the course of employment had to be given its ordinary meaning – that is, the act was committed by the employee whilst at work.

While this is a much more sensible interpretation, the question that must be asked is: where does this leave Lyndsay? While it appears that the sexual comments by Tom occur during working hours, the problem states that the assault took place after they had been working late and it is the assault that the works manager will not investigate. In *Waters v Commissioner of Police of the Metropolis* (1997), the Court of Appeal held that a female police officer who felt that she had been victimised because she had complained about a sexual assault committed by a fellow officer at a party outside of working hours had no claim for victimisation, because the original assault had not taken place during the course of employment. In other words, a victimisation claim could only be upheld if the employer was legally liable for the original act. While the employer was held to be liable in negligence by the House of Lords on appeal (2000), this restriction on 'course of employment' was seen as unfortunate. The decision was limited before the appeal by *Chief Constable of Lincolnshire v Stubbs* (1999), which held that an employer was liable for sexual harassment suffered by a female at a work-related party held outside working hours because the party was pre-arranged and linked to the employer. On the basis of this, it can be argued that, as the assault on Lyndsay took place while she and Tom were working late on the employer's premises, the assault was committed during the course of Tom's employment and thus ACME is liable under s 109.

QUESTION 21

To what extent do you consider that amendments made by the Equality Act 2010 ensure that those discriminated against on the grounds of disability have the same protection as those discriminated against on other grounds?

Answer Plan

The first thing to note about this question is that it involves a discussion of the amendments made by the 2010 Act to the previous provisions protecting against discrimination on the basis of disability and how this increases, or otherwise, the previous protection. It is also asking if protection for disabled people is the same as for those discriminated against on the grounds of other protected characteristics. As such, the student needs to know what changes the amendments have made to the previous law and then come to a conclusion as to whether the amendments give the same or different protection to those who are disabled.

Particular issues to consider are:

❖ the new definition of disability;
❖ pre-employment health enquiries;
❖ the definition of direct discrimination and the endorsement of *Coleman v Attridge Law* (2008);
❖ the definition of discrimination arising from disability and the overruling of *London Borough of Lewisham v Malcolm* (2008);
❖ the duty to make reasonable adjustments in s 20;
❖ whether the duty to make reasonable adjustments remains the same;
❖ the introduction of indirect discrimination into the area of disability;
❖ disability as an occupational requirement; and
❖ how protection against discrimination on the grounds of disability compares to protection against discrimination on other grounds.

ANSWER

Since the introduction of protection against discrimination for disability in 1995, it became apparent that in some areas the protection was wider than in other protected areas. For example, the fact that only a disabled person could sue under the legislation allowed for positive discrimination in respect of disabled persons. In addition, the duty to make reasonable adjustments only applied under disability discrimination and not to discrimination under any other ground. That said, over the years, deficiencies in the legislation became apparent – never more so than in the case of *London Borough of Lewisham v Malcolm* (2008) when the decision of the House of Lords virtually wiped out protection for those who had been discriminated against on the basis of a disability-related reason. As such, the government used the Equality Act 2010 to remedy some of the deficiencies that had become apparent.

To fall within the Act, a person must have a disability (s 6(1)) or have had a disability (s 6(2)). A disability is defined as a physical or mental impairment that has a substantial and long-term adverse effect on the person's ability to carry out normal day-to-day activities (s 6(1)(b)). In other words, the impairment must be the cause of substantial and long-term adverse effects. There is no definition of physical impairment or mental impairment. Until amendments in 2005, a mental impairment had to be clinically well recognised – so in *Goodwin v Patent Office* (1999), the EAT held that an employee dismissed because of paranoid schizophrenia had been dismissed on the grounds of disability. Critics felt that the original definition placed hurdles in front of a complainant who was obviously mentally ill but had not been diagnosed. As such, the amendments remove the requirement that a mental impairment must be clinically well recognised.

The impairment must have an adverse effect on the ability to carry out normal day-to-day activities; the previous list of normal day-to-day activities has been removed as the government felt that this placed additional burdens on disabled people. 'Substantial' is not defined, although Sched 1, para 4 gives the power to make regulations for the effect of a condition on the ability to carry out normal day-to-day activities to be treated as substantial or not. 'Long-term' means that the effect must have lasted 12 months, and be expected to last 12 months or for the rest of the person's life (Sched 1, para 2). As under the old law, for certain progressive conditions, a person is treated as disabled from the date of diagnosis and not from the time the condition starts to have an adverse effect (Sched 1, paras 6 and 8). In *Clark v Novacold* (1998), the EAT held that a manual worker who could not walk short distances or lift heavy loads after injuring his back, an effect likely to last for more that 12 months, was disabled. Conversely, in *Foord v J A Johnston & Sons* (1998), an applicant who had fallen arches and therefore could not stand for long periods of time was not disabled. She could cope within her normal working hours of 8 am to 2 pm and only experienced difficulty when, on one occasion, she had to work an extra two hours. In *Hewett v Motorola Ltd* (2004), the EAT said that normal day-to-day activities included someone who had difficulty understanding normal social interaction, such as someone with Asperger's syndrome, and in *Kapadia v London Borough of Lambeth* (2000), the EAT said that a tribunal had erred in ignoring medical evidence and basing an opinion on how the applicant had given evidence. Schedule 1, para 2(2) states that if the impairment ceases to have an adverse effect, it will still be treated as a disability if the effect is likely to recur – again, this is similar to the old law. In *Swift v Chief Constable of Wiltshire Constabulary* (2004), the EAT considered the position in relation to recurring conditions that are not defined in the Act. The EAT said that if an impairment had had a substantial adverse effect on day-to-day activities, the tribunal had to ask itself if the substantial effect was likely to recur. It was likely to recur if it was more probable than not that the effect would recur and it is irrelevant that the tribunal does not think the recurrence will last 12 months. The important thing is to look at whether the effect will recur, not the illness.

The government felt that asking pre-employment health-related questions was one of the main reasons why disabled persons failed to get interviews, therefore s 60 of the Act addresses this. This is a new provision and provides that an employer must not ask about a job applicant's health until that person has been offered a job or been included in a pool of suitable applicants to be offered a job where one arises. There are specified circumstances under which such questions may be asked: finding out whether an applicant would be able to participate in an assessment to test their suitability; making reasonable adjustments to enable a disabled person to participate in the recruitment process; finding out what reasonable adjustments could be made to allow an applicant to undertake an intrinsic function of the job; monitoring diversity in job applicants; supporting positive action; and enabling an employer to identify a suitable person where disability is an occupational requirement. Any question asked outside of the above is actionable by the EHRC (s 120(8)).

The definition of direct discrimination in s 13 of the Act talks about a person being treated less favourably because of a protected characteristic, not because of that person's protected characteristic. This reinforces the ECJ decision in *Coleman v Attridge Law* (2008) and protects persons who are discriminated against because of association with a disabled person. Section 13 furthers allows positive discrimination in favour of a disabled person by providing that a non-disabled person has no remedy if the disabled person receives more favourable treatment (s 13(3)).

Section 15 of the Act attempts to overrule the *Malcolm* decision. In *London Borough of Lewisham v Malcolm* (2008), the House of Lords, overruling *Clark v Novacold* above, held that the correct comparator in a disability-related claim was a non-disabled person. This effectively wiped out protection under this head. Section 15 introduces the concept of discrimination arising from disability. It arises where an employer treat a disabled person in a particular way and because of the disability the treatment amounts to a detriment. The employer has a defence if it can show that the treatment is a proportionate means of achieving a legitimate aim. Section 15 does not apply if the employer did not know, and could not reasonably have been expected to know, that the person had a disability (s 15(2)) and it is irrelevant that the employer has complied with the duty to make reasonable adjustments (s 15(3)). The important difference between this definition and the definition of disability-related discrimination is the fact that, under s 15, the complainant does not have to have a comparator, so overruling Malcolm.

In addition to a new type of discrimination under s 15, the Equality Act includes disability as a protected characteristic in the definition of indirect discrimination in s 19, so introducing the concept into disability discrimination for the first time. Section 6(3)(a) states that the protected characteristic is a particular disability and s 6(3)(b) states that references to persons who share the same protected characteristic are references to persons who have the same disability. This seems strange as, for example, one person's visual impairment may be totally different from another's. It is suggested, however, that the other provisions of the Act will mean that a claim for indirect discrimination will be rare as other provisions such as the duty to make reasonable adjustments will pick up on most acts of discrimination.

The previous duty to make reasonable adjustments is to a large extent replicated by the EqA 2010 in s 20. There is an additional duty, however, which previously only applied in respect of goods and services and premises. This is where, but for the provision of an auxiliary aid, a disabled person would be at a substantial disadvantage. There is a duty to take such steps as are reasonable to provide that aid (s 20(5)). As under previous law, the duty will not apply where an employer could not be reasonably expected to know that a disabled person would be placed at a disadvantage (Sched 8, para 20). As with the previous law, therefore, the duty on the employer is reactive not proactive and there will still be a requirement on the disabled person to show the employer the disability, unlike other protected characteristics such as sex, in which cases the claimant does not have to prove that they are one sex or another.

The old law always allowed an employer an exception to a direct discrimination claim where a particular characteristic was a requirement of the job. Previously a mixture of genuine occupational qualifications and genuine occupational requirements, the EqA has harmonised this across all protected characteristics as occupational requirements and for the first time these also apply to disability (Sched 9, para 1). In addition, in a change of wording from previous law, the employer is no longer required to show that the requirement is genuine and determining merely that it is a proportionate means of achieving a legitimate aim. This further endorses that an employer can positively discriminate in favour of a disabled person where having such is an occupational requirement.

On paper, therefore, it appears that the EqA has harmonised protection in relation to disability and the other protected characteristics, but in addition has preserved areas in which a disabled person has more protection. Thus only disabled persons can sue under the provisions; the discrimination arising out of disability does not require a comparator unlike indirect and direct discrimination. The duty to make reasonable adjustments applies only to the protected characteristic of disability and the prohibition on pre-employment health questions will in the main benefit only disabled persons. While, as under previous law, some of the protections will be dependent on an employer's actual or assumed knowledge, it can be said that to a large extent that the EqA has harmonised protection for those with the protected characteristic of disability with those with the other protected characteristics.

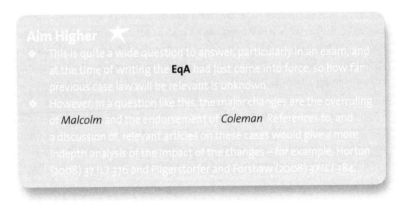

Aim Higher ⭐

◆ This is quite a wide question to answer, particularly in an exam, and at the time of writing the **EqA** had just come into force, so how far previous case law will be relevant is unknown.

◆ However, in a question like this, the major changes are the overruling of *Malcolm* and the endorsement of *Coleman*. References to, and a discussion of, relevant articles on these cases would give a more indepth analysis of the impact of the changes – for example, Horton (2008) 37 ILJ 376 and Pilgerstorfer and Forshaw (2008) 37 ILJ 384.

Equal Pay

INTRODUCTION

Equal pay is an area that often comes up on examination papers since, like discrimination in Chapter 5, it is an area on which European law has had a great impact. To answer questions in this area, students need to understand the relationship between European law and national law and, in particular, the enforceability of European law in the national courts. It is necessary, therefore, to understand fully the applicability of Art 141 of the EC Treaty and the Equal Pay Directive (75/117/EEC) and recent decisions of the European Court of Justice (ECJ) affecting the interpretation of national law. At the time of writing, the relevance of the old cases on the interpretation of the Equality Act 2010 (EqA) is unknown. Therefore the previous case law has been used in this chapter to show how the 2010 Act may be interpreted.

For questions in this area, general issues that the student needs to understand are:

- ❖ the different routes to equal pay under the EqA 2010;
- ❖ the two possible routes to equal pay under European law;
- ❖ who constitutes a valid male comparator;
- ❖ the different procedures to claim equal pay;
- ❖ how the tribunal decision is applied; and
- ❖ the defence available to the employer on a like work, or work rated equivalent, or equal value claim.

Although this area can lend itself to essay-type questions, it is more common to have problems and thus it is important that students understand the steps involved in an equal pay claim.

In particular, students should be familiar with:

- ❖ the implied sex equality clause in the contract;
- ❖ the concept of equal work in s 65 of the EqA 2010;
- ❖ the definition of a 'male comparator' in s 79;

❖ the definition of 'like work', 'work rated equivalent' and 'work of equal value' in s 65;
❖ the importance of cases such as *Hayward v Cammell Laird Shipbuilders (No 2) (1988)* and *Pickstone and others v Freemans plc (1988)*;
❖ the problems with the equal value route to equal pay;
❖ the defence of material factor in s 69;
❖ the difference between the EqA 2010 and a claim under Art 141 of the EC Treaty;
❖ ECJ decisions that have impacted on the interpretation of the EqA 2010.

Finally, given the impact of European law on this area, any answer will almost certainly discuss the Treaty Article, the Directive and ECJ decisions made thereunder. A detailed knowledge of this area is therefore essential to answer an examination question fully.

Checklist ✔

Students should be familiar with the following areas:

■ the operation of *Pickstone v Freemans plc (1988)* on the choice of the route to equal pay;

■ the choice of comparator – particularly *Ainsworth v Glass Tubes and Components (1977), McCarthys v Smith (1980), Scullard v Knowles (1996), Lawrence v Regent Office Care (2002), Allonby v Accrington and Rossendale College (2004)*;

■ the different components in a like work claim – particularly cases such as *Capper Pass Ltd v Lawton (1977)* and *Coomes (Holdings) Ltd v Shields (1978)*;

■ the operation of **s 65(4)** and **(8)** and the guidance given in *Eaton v Nuttall (1977)*;

■ the importance of *Hayward v Cammell Laird Shipbuilders (1988)* and *Murphy v Bord Telecom Eireann (1988)*;

■ the definition of a material factor – in particular, *Clay Cross (Quarry Services) v Fletcher (1979), Rainey v Greater Glasgow Health Board Eastern District (1987), Jenkins v Kingsgate Clothing Productions Ltd (1981), Strathclyde Regional Council v Wallace (1998), Enderby v Frenchay Health Authority and Secretary of State for Health (1994), Ratcliffe v North Yorkshire County Council (1995), British Road Services v Loughran (1997)*;

■ actions under **Art 141 (formerly 119)** – in particular, *Defrenne v SABENA (1976), Garland v British Rail Engineering Ltd (1982), Rinner-Kühn v FWW Spezial Gebäudereinigung GmbH (1989), Barber v Guardian Royal Exchange Assurance Group (1990), Barry v Midland Bank plc (1999)*.

- actions under the Directive – in particular, cases such as *Marshall v Southampton and South West Hampshire Area Health Authority* (1986); *Marshall (No 2)* (1991) and (1993); *Foster v British Gas plc* (1991);

- time limits – in particular, *Biggs v Somerset County Council* (1996); *Preston v Wolverhampton Health Care NHS Trust* (2001); *Margorrian v Eastern Health and Social Services Board* (1998)

QUESTION 22

Dot, Lou and Pauline work for Midshire University. Dot is a secretary. She feels that her work is of equal value to that of the computer technicians who work on a different site from her. She feels that her qualifications and experience are similar to those of the technicians. Dot works 9 am to 5 pm and has six weeks' holiday a year. The technicians work 12-hour shifts (because they need to be available when part-time classes run in the evenings) and get four weeks' holiday a year. Dot receives £5.50 per hour. The technicians receive £7 per hour.

Lou is a cleaner. She claims that her job is of equal value to that of the caretakers at the same site. There is no difference in the number of hours worked by the cleaners and the caretakers, but the caretakers receive £1 an hour more than the cleaners. All of the cleaners are women apart from one man. All of the caretakers are male.

Pauline is a cook. She feels that her job is of equal value to that of the university administrative assistants in terms of qualifications and experience. The administrative assistants earn £1,500 per annum more than Pauline, although Pauline gets free meals and free transport, provided by the university, to and from work. Midshire says that to increase Pauline's pay would involve restructuring the pay scales of all the catering staff both on the main campus and in the halls of residence and this would involve a great deal of extra administrative work.

▶ Advise Dot, Lou and Pauline.

Common Pitfalls

❖ Students often get work rated equivalent and work of equal value muddled.

❖ If the question does not mention that a job evaluation scheme has been conducted, it cannot be a work rated equivalent claim.

Answer Plan

This question raises a variety of preliminary issues in an equal pay claim and also involves a detailed discussion of possible defences. All the parties are claiming that their jobs are of equal value and, given the special procedure in such claims, it is worth briefly describing the procedure in relation to all the parties, before discussing each individual case.

Particular issues to be considered are therefore:

❖   the procedure in an equal value claim;
❖   the definition of a male comparator in s 79 of the EqA 2010;
❖   what are common terms and conditions within the section and, in particular, *Leverton v Clywd County Council* (1989) and *O'Sullivan v Sainsbury plc* (1990);
❖   the exclusivity of the routes in s 65(6) and the effect of *Pickstone v Freemans plc* (1988);
❖   the meaning of pay within Art 141;
❖   the term-by-term approach in s 66 and the effect of *Hayward v Cammell Laird Shipbuilders (No 2)* (1988);
❖   the defence in s 69 and, in particular, *Clay Cross (Quarry Services) v Fletcher* (1979); *Rainey v Greater Glasgow Health Board Eastern District* (1987); *Strathclyde Regional Council v Wallace* (1998).

ANSWER

All the parties in the problem wish to claim equal pay with their male colleagues. In all cases, the parties are arguing that their jobs are of equal value to those of the men. The equal value route was introduced by the Equal Pay (Amendment) Regulations 1983 after the case of *Commission of the European Communities v United Kingdom* (1982), when the ECJ held that the original Act did not satisfy the principle of equal pay for work of equal value contained in the Equal Pay Directive. Prior to the change in the legislation, the only two ways in which a woman could claim equal pay was by showing that she was on 'like work' – that is, work that was the same or broadly similar to that of her male comparator (s 65(2)) – or that she was on 'work rated equivalent' to that of her male comparator (s 65(4)). While the second route appeared to satisfy the purpose of the Directive, in reality, a woman can only use s 65(4) if her employer has conducted a job evaluation scheme (JES) and there is no statutory requirement that employers do so. This meant that until 1984, when the Regulations came into force, in the vast majority of cases, a woman could only claim equal pay if she was on the same or similar work. The 1983 Regulations sought to remedy this defect and created a third route to equal pay, that of equal value, now contained in s 65(6) of the 2010 Act.

The Regulations introduced a new procedure, contained in s 131 of the Act, and a new defence for equal value claims, and all three parties in the problem will have to use this procedure. Briefly, after conciliation, the tribunal will decide if there are grounds for an equal value claim. If there are not, it will dismiss the claim and must do so if a JES has given the complainant's job a different value, unless the JES is discriminatory (*Neil v Ford Motor Co* (1984)). If the tribunal thinks that there are grounds for the claim, the employer must raise its defence. If the defence is upheld, the claim will be dismissed. If the defence is rejected or not raised, the tribunal may commission an independent expert who will assess both the complainant's job and that of her male comparator and report back to the tribunal. The tribunal will then make a finding based on the report, although it is not conclusive or binding on the tribunal (*Tennants Textile Colours Ltd v Todd* (1989)). In the past, a major criticism of the procedure was the length of time the procedure entailed. Changes introduced in 2004 now reduce considerably the length of time a claim will take. If the tribunal does not appoint an expert, it will make a decision as to whether the work is of equal value. The changes envisage in this situation that a claim should take 25 weeks. Where an expert is appointed, the claim should take 37 weeks. Also, until recently, where the complainant was successful in an equal pay claim, the tribunal could only award back pay for two years. Decisions such as *Levez v TH Jennings (Harlow Pools) Ltd* (1999) (ECJ) and the ECJ and House of Lords' decisions in *Preston v Wolverhampton Health Care NHS Trust* (2000) (ECJ) and (2001) (HL) questioned the compatibility of this with European law. As such, the Regulations in 2003 amended the law, allowing back pay to be claimed for up to six years before the institution of proceedings (s 132(4)).

In each case, the woman must find a male comparator to start her equal pay claim. The definition of the male comparator is contained in s 79. Such a comparator is a man employed by her employer or an associated employer of her employer, and employed at the same establishment, or at a different establishment in Great Britain where common terms and conditions are observed for that class of employee. It is the responsibility of Dot, Lou and Pauline to find their own comparator and not the responsibility of the tribunal (*Ainsworth v Glass Tubes and Components* (1977)).

We will turn first to Dot's situation. She wishes to claim equal pay with the computer technicians and therefore it is necessary to see if one of the technicians will fall within the definition of male comparator in s 79. Without doubt, the technicians are employed by her employer, but they work at a different site from her and therefore at a different establishment. This means that she must show that common terms and conditions of employment are observed. In *Leverton v Clywd County Council* (1989), a nursery nurse employed by the county council compared herself to higher paid clerical workers at other establishments, also employed by the council. She worked 32.5 hours a week and had 70 days' holiday a year. Her comparator worked a 37-hour week and had about 20 days' holiday a year. All the council employees were employed on terms derived from a collective agreement known as the 'purple book'. Both the EAT and the Court of Appeal held that she had no valid comparator because two important terms, hours and holidays, were fundamentally different. The House of Lords, however, took a wider view of common terms and conditions. Lord Bridge held that the test in s 79 did not mean a comparison of the terms of the contract of the woman with those of the comparator, but to see if there are general terms that apply across the establishments operated by the employer, covering a wide range of employees, but where there will be variations among individuals. His Lordship felt that a collective agreement applying to all employees was the paradigm of common terms and conditions contemplated by the section.

We have no evidence in Dot's case that the terms and conditions of non-academic staff have been negotiated by a collective agreement. If there is such an agreement, and if it applies across all the establishments and is not only applicable to the site where Dot works, by *Leverton*, she has a valid comparator and, given that it does not appear that the university has a defence in her case, the tribunal could appoint an independent expert to assess the two jobs. On the other hand, if there is no such agreement, then it would appear that the tribunal will be required to analyse the individual terms to discover a broad similarity. In contrast to the earlier decisions in *Leverton*, in *O'Sullivan v Sainsbury plc* (1990), it was held that there were common terms when holiday, sick provisions and maternity provisions were common. Given the vast difference in hours and holidays in Dot's case, in the absence of a collective agreement covering herself and the technicians at the other site, it is unlikely that she has a valid comparator within s 79 and her claim will therefore fail.

Lou is a cleaner and claims that her work is of equal value to that of caretakers. There is no mention that there are no caretakers working at the same establishment as Lou; therefore, the question of common terms and conditions does not arise. The route of equal value is found in s 65(1)(c) of the Act. Section 65(6) states that A's work is of equal value to B's work if it is neither like B's work nor rated equivalent to B's work, but nevertheless equal to B's work in terms of the demands made on A by reference to factors such as effort, skill and decision-making. In other words, an equal value claim can be pursued if the work in question is not like work or work rated equivalent. The interpretation of s 65(1)(c) was the question for the courts in *Pickstone v Freemans plc* (1988). In this case, the applicant sought equal value with a comparator doing a different job, but there was a man doing the same job as her. Until the case reached the House of Lords, it was successfully argued that the interpretation of s 65(1)(c) meant that if a man was doing like work or work rated equivalent, the applicant could not bring an equal value claim using another male comparator and that the equal value route existed only if no like work or work rated equivalent route was available (although the Court of Appeal upheld the applicant's claim on the basis of Art 141). Thus, because Mrs Pickstone had a man doing like work, she was unable to compare herself to another man doing totally different work on an equal value claim. The House of Lords held that this was a misinterpretation of s 65(1)(c). On true construction of the Act, the starting point was for the applicant to choose her male comparator. It was after this that s 65 applied, and if her chosen comparator was doing like work, her route lay under s 65(1)(a), and if he was doing work rated equivalent, her route was under s 65(1)(b). If neither of those applied, she could claim equal value. In this case, Mrs Pickstone had chosen a comparator who was doing a totally different job from her and where no JES existed; thus, she could pursue an equal value claim. To construe the section any other way would mean that the employer could place a man doing the same work as women and defeat any possible equal pay claims. This would frustrate the purpose of the Act. Following this decision, it is irrelevant in Lou's case that one man is doing like work to her. If she chooses a caretaker as her male comparator, given that the work is different and there is no JES, she can claim that her work is of equal value and the procedure described above will start. It is her choice of comparator that determines her route to equal pay and not the route that determines the comparator.

Pauline is also arguing that her work is of equal value to a man doing another type of job. Again, if the comparator falls within the definition in s 79, Pauline is not prevented from pursuing her claim if there are male cooks (Pickstone). The university, however, may try to argue on two points. First, although the administrative assistants earn more money than Pauline, she gets non-cash benefits in terms of free meals and transport. How far can these non-cash benefits be taken into account when assessing the pay differential? Article 141 describes pay as 'the ordinary, basic or minimum wage or salary and any other consideration, whether in cash or in kind, which the worker receives, directly or indirectly, in respect of his employment from his employer'. In Hayward v Cammell Laird Shipbuilders (No 2) (1988), the applicant claimed that her work was of equal value to her male comparators. She, however, received non-cash benefits that they did not, and the employer argued that, by reference to the definition of pay in Art 141, the court was obliged to look at the pay package as a whole and put a cash value on the non-cash benefits. The House of Lords disagreed, saying that s 66 stated that if a woman showed that she was entitled to equal pay, the term in the woman's contract that was less favourable than that of the man should become as favourable, and any beneficial term in his contract not contained in the woman's should be included in her contract. In other words, the court should not do a whole-pay package approach, but a term-by-term comparison. Thus, the fact that Pauline receives extra non-cash benefits does not prevent her cash pay being equalised to that of the administrative assistants.

The university has attempted to raise a defence, however. In relation to an equal value claim, the employer has a defence if it can show that the difference in pay is due to a material factor that is not the difference of sex (s 69(1)(a)). In addition, if the factor puts a specific sex at a particular disadvantage, the defence holds if the employer can show it is a proportionate means of achieving a legitimate aim (s 69(2)). By s 69(3), a long-term objective of reducing inequality between men's and women's terms of work is always to be considered a legitimate aim.

Originally, market forces could not be raised as a material factor (*Clay Cross (Quarry Services) v Fletcher* (1979)). However, there was a major revision of the defence in *Rainey v Greater Glasgow Health Board Eastern District* (1987), in which the House of Lords held that the restriction of the defence in *Fletcher* was unfortunate and that the defence could include objectively justified grounds that were connected with economic factors affecting the efficient carrying on of the employer's business. In *Rainey*, therefore, there were objective reasons for putting new male entrants on a higher rate (because of the need to expand the service) and objectively justified administrative reasons for not increasing the pay of one group of NHS employees whose pay was determined by the Whitley Council. Thus, if the university can show an objectively justified reason for the difference in pay, the defence will be made out. In *Enderby v Frenchay Health Authority and Secretary of State for Health* (1993), the ECJ ruled that different bargaining structures per se were not objectively justified factors allowing a difference in pay where the disadvantaged group is almost exclusively women. Therefore, if there are different pay bargaining structures within the university, this in itself is not a defence if the different structures predominantly disadvantage women. Whether the court would accept the argument raised by the university about the extra administrative work is debatable. In *Rainey*, a shortage of prosthetists led to the health authority bringing in private practitioners to meet demand.

In addition, if the applicant had been successful, this would have created an anomaly for one group of NHS workers on the Whitley Council grades, an anomaly that would have been permanent. The university is not arguing about the need to attract persons into the administrative assistant jobs, but is merely arguing that to restructure the pay of the catering staff would involve a lot of work. As such, it is unlikely that there is an objectively justified reason for the difference in pay that affects the efficient carrying on of the university and the defence will fail.

QUESTION 23

The problems inherent in the Equal Pay Act 1970 will not be eradicated by the Equality Act 2010.

▶ Critically evaluate this statement.

Common Pitfalls

❖ The student needs to know both the new and the old law to answer this question and compare them.
❖ A list of the changes made by the **EqA** is not enough; you must argue whether they do or do not eradicate the problems.

Answer Plan

This question is asking the student to look at the problems within the original Equal Pay Act 1970 and whether the changes to equal pay, introduced by the Equality Act 2010, has eradicated them. Note that the question is asking for a critical evaluation and therefore just listing the problems with the EPA and the changes introduced by the EqA will not be enough. The question is asking for a judgement to be made.

Particular issues to be considered are:

❖ the problems with the definition of a male comparator under the EPA;
❖ the problems of the concept of same employment under the EPA;
❖ the procedure for an equal value claim under the EPA;
❖ the defences to an equal pay claim;
❖ the effect of *Enderby v Frenchay Health Authority and Secretary of State for Health* (1994);
❖ the impact of *Lawrence v Regent Office Care Ltd* (2002) and *Allonby v Accrington and Rossendale College* (2004);
❖ the consequences of *Evesham v North Hereford Health Authority* (2000); and
❖ whether the issues discussed are resolved or not by the EqA 2010.

ANSWER

While the intention of the EPA 1970 was to remove the differences between men's and women's pay by 2010, there is still a substantial difference of nearly 20 per cent between the pay of men in full-time work and women in full-time work. The difference between genders in part-time work is even greater. Many, such as Fredman, argue that the problem lay within the Act itself and therefore it is proposed to look at the problems with the 1970 Act and see if these are replicated in the EqA 2010.

In order to claim equal pay, a woman has to find a male comparator. If she can prove she is on equal work to that of her comparator (defined in s 65(1)), this will activate the sex equality clause in her contract (s 66) and then any term in her contract that is less favourable than his becomes as favourable and any favourable term in his contract that is not in hers becomes part of her contract (s 66(2)). The old definition of male comparator in the EPA has, to a large extent, been replicated by the EqA 2010. Thus s 79 states that a male comparator is a man employed by the woman's employer or associated employer and employed at the same establishment or different establishment where common terms apply at the establishments either generally or as between the man and the woman. The Act specifies in s 64(2) that the comparator does not have to be working at the same time as the woman. While this would seem to restate the law in *Macarthys Ltd v Smith* (1979), and cover predecessors, recent case law has stated that a comparator cannot be a successor (*Walton Centre for Neurology and Neurosurgery NHS Trust v Bewley* (2008)) although the EqA is silent on the matter and it may be that the definition has been widened. The issue of common terms has been migrated into the EqA. A common collective agreement was seen as the paradigm of common terms by Lord Bridge in *Leverton v Clwyd County Council* (1979). Even if there are different collective agreements, the terms only need to be broadly similar and not identical. If, however, there are two collective agreements and the terms are not broadly similar, the woman must show that her comparator, if he was employed at her establishment, would be employed on terms broadly similar to the ones he enjoys (s 76(4)(c)).

A further problem with the choice of male comparator is that he must be real. Unlike other strands of discrimination, where a woman is claiming equal pay, she cannot use a hypothetical comparator. However, the EqA 2010 appears to allow a woman to use a hypothetical comparator in a specific case. This is where the sex equality clause has no effect – for example, because there is no male comparator on equal work, because the employer only employs women. Section 71 allows a claim for direct sex discrimination under s 13 or direct dual-characteristic discrimination under s 14 so allowing the use of a hypothetical comparator. Section 71 is, however, limited to direct discrimination claims not indirect discrimination and only applies to terms related to pay, although the definition of such is wide under Art 141, and not to other contractual terms, which the rest of ch 3, which is entitled 'Equality of Terms', does. The limitations aside, this is a major difference from the old law and should provide a remedy for women employed by employers who only employ women to prevent equal pay claims. The effect of this may, however, be limited as the ECJ in cases such as *Lawrence v Regent Office Care Ltd* (2002) and *Allonby v Accrington and Rossendale College* (2004) has held that a woman can only pursue an equal pay claim if there is a single source that can remedy the discrimination. This means that a woman cannot choose a comparator employed by an employer with no relationship to her own and argue that if her employer were to employ a man to do her job, he would pay him more. This may be difficult to prove.

A final problem is that the woman must choose her comparator (*Ainsworth v Glass Tubes and Components* (1977)) and she is only entitled to equal pay with her comparator. The tribunal has no power to give her more pay because, for example, her work is of a higher value or she has more experience (*Evesham v North Hereford Health Authority* (2000)). This means she must be careful in her choice, particularly looking for a comparator who has the same experience as herself.

The EqA uses the concept of equal work in s 65 and although this was not a concept in the EPA, in essence it is the same as equal work and is defined as like work, work rated equivalent or work of equal value (s 65(1)). The definition of like work is the same as the old law and as such any differences do not render the claim unsupportable if they are infrequent or not of practical importance (s 65(2)). In respect of work rated equivalent, this is where a JES gives an equal value to the jobs in terms of the demands made on the worker, or would give an equal value in those terms if the evaluation was not made on a sex-specific system (s 65(4)). A sex-specific system is one that, for one or more of the demands, sets different values for men and women (s 65(5)). While this allows a tribunal to allow a woman to claim equal pay on the basis that her work would have been given an equal value in a non-discriminatory scheme, it does not allow a tribunal to correct a flawed scheme, which means that the woman would have to start again on an equal value claim. Such is allowed by s 131(6), which allows a woman to claim equal value, even if a JES has rated her job lower than that of her comparator, provided that she can establish that the JES or its application discriminated because of sex. There was a similar provision in the EPA and thus does not really address the problems of JESs.

The third route to equal pay, that of equal value in s 65(6), is virtually identical to the definition in the EPA and thus requires the tribunal, on its own or with the help of independent experts, to assess whether the claimant's work is of equal value to her male comparator. Under the old law this was perhaps the most complicated route to equal pay, often resulting in years of litigation. The Employment Tribunals (Constitution and Rules of Procedure) Regulations 2004, Sched 6 introduced a new procedure for equal value claims. This is now supplemented by s 131 of the EqA 2010. Essentially, there is a three-stage procedure. Stage 1 is the weeding-out stage. The tribunal decides whether or not to appoint an independent expert and whether the expert should assist on determining the facts on which the expert's report will be written. It will also decide whether to strike out the claim if the claimant's job has been given a lower value that that of her comparator under a JES (s 131(5)–(7)) as discussed above and consider the employer's defence. Stage 2 is the fact-finding stage and stage 3 is the hearing. The Rules of Procedure envisage that if no independent expert is appointed, the whole process should take 18 weeks. Where an independent expert is used, the envisaged timetable is 37 weeks. While the procedure introduced in

2004 does reduce the time for pursuing a claim from the average of 20 months prior to its introduction, the procedure is still long and complex and this has not been addressed by the new Act. The fact that the procedure remains the same fails to take into account other criticisms. First, there is the cost of taking an action. An unofficial comment from a member of the EOC in 1991 put the cost of an equal value claim then at £150,000. Given the lack of legal aid in tribunals, a claimant needs the support of a trade union or the Equality and Human Rights Commission to start a claim. Furthermore, unlike other areas of discrimination, a claimant is still limited to back pay for six years only (s 132(4)). As such, the cost of taking equal value claims and the relative small sums that can be awarded means that for many such claims are prohibitive. None of these issues have been addressed by the EqA.

Section 69 of the Act rewrites the defence available to an employer. Under the EPA, the employer has a defence if it could show that, in the case of like work or work rated equivalent, there was a genuine material factor that was not the difference of sex and which was a material difference between her case and his. In the case of equal value, the genuine material factor may be a difference between her case and his. The EqA removes the word 'genuine' from this definition, but in reality the word added nothing to the defence. The new wording, however, is derived from previous case law such as *Rainey v Greater Glasgow Health Board* (1987), in which in effect the judiciary created the concept of indirect discrimination even though this was not mentioned in the EPA. For example, in *British Coal Corporation v Smith* (1996), the House of Lords held that the employer had to objectively justify the differences in pay between the claimants and their comparators where statistics showed a difference in pay between a group that was predominantly female and a group doing equal work that was predominantly male. Section 69 provides that the sex equality clause will not operate where the difference is because of a material factor reliance on which does not involve treating A less favourably than B because of A's sex (direct discrimination) (s 69(1)(a)) or because of the factor A and persons of the same sex doing work equal to A are put at a particular disadvantage where compared to persons of the opposite sex doing work equal to A's, unless the employer can show that the factor is a proportionate means of achieving a legitimate aim (indirect discrimination) (s 69(1)(b) and (2)). By s 69(3), the long-term objective of reducing inequality between men's and women's terms of work is always to be regarded as a legitimate aim. While this is putting into statutory form what in reality already existed, it means that the problems with indirect discrimination are still here. There are issues around the correct pool for comparison. For example, in *Pearse v Bradford Metropolitan District Council* (1998), the eligibility to apply for the post of senior lecturer was confined to people who worked full-time. Pearse argued that this was discriminatory to women as only 21.8 per cent of female staff could apply compared to 46.7 per cent of male staff. The EAT held that the comparative group was too wide and should only include those with the qualifications to apply for a senior lecturer post. Within that group, there was no disparate impact on women and thus no indirect discrimination. What evidence is required to show a disparate impact and issues around proportionate means and legitimate aims. In addition, the section in reality gives the employer two chances and places more burdens on the claimant. If the employer proves that the factor was not one of sex thereby disproving direct discrimination, the claimant then has to show that the factor produces a disparate impact on women doing equal work to men. If she cannot do so, the employer will not have to justify his actions, as per the decision reached in *Strathclyde Regional Council v Wallace* (1998). The problem this creates is that it is introducing a new definition of indirect discrimination into the law. It uses the term 'factor' not 'provision, criterion or practice' as in s 19 and the comparison is only with someone on equal work, not the much broader comparison in s 19. Furthermore, as the claimant cannot use a hypothetical comparator, she will be unable to challenge this defence where only women are employed because, as has already been noted, s 71 only applies to direct discrimination.

Does the EqA eradicate the problems inherent in the EPA? Given the discussion above, the answer must be 'no'. Apart from the limited new right in s 71 and the possibility that the claimant may be able to compare herself to a successor, all the problems in the EPA have been replicated in the EqA. The procedure and costs in an equal value claim, the need for a real rather than hypothetical comparator and the limit on compensation to six years' back pay means that equality of terms is treated less favourably than the other strands of discrimination and the EqA is a missed opportunity.

Aim Higher ★

❖ Read up on the criticisms of the **EPA** – for example, Fredman (2008) 37 ILJ 193, Steele (2006) 35 ILJ 338 and Steele (2008) 37 ILJ 119.

❖ It is unclear how far old case law will be used to interpret the **EqA 2010** but an excellent introduction to the Act is B Doyle et al, *Equality and Discrimination: The New Law* (Jordans, 2010).

QUESTION 24

Vicky, Gail, Sally and Denise work for Coronation Products Ltd.

Vicky is a clerical assistant. Steve is also a clerical assistant, but is paid a higher hourly rate than Vicky. Coronation argues that this is because all the male clerical assistants have to work compulsory overtime and the collective agreement negotiated with the union in the workplace has negotiated higher hourly rates when some of the hours are overtime hours. The men do work the overtime. None of the women are members of the union because Coronation discourages female membership. Gail works in the printing shop. She feels that she is entitled to equal pay with the men who work in the paint shop. A recent JES gave Gail's job a lower rating than that of the paint shop workers. The reason for this is that although Gail's job has more responsibility, the paint shop is dirty and the work involves heavy lifting. As such, the job has been given a higher rating because of the working conditions and the amount of lifting that has to be done. None of the female staff has ever been allowed to work in the paint shop.

Sally and Denise job share. They both work a single machine, Sally working the machine from 8 am to midday and Denise taking over at 1 pm until 5 pm. Coronation pays them a lower hourly rate than the full-time machine operators. Coronation argues that this is because job sharing is less productive than full-time working.

▶ Advise Vicky, Gail, Sally and Denise whether they will be successful in their equal pay claims against the company.

Answer Plan

This question mixes preliminary issues in relation to eligibility to claim with possible defences, and emphasises again that if students have a logical structure, all the points raised in a question should be covered. Thus, if the student first determines eligibility, second determines the route, and lastly, looks at defences, that should leave no stone unturned.

Particular issues to be considered are therefore:

❖   the definition of the male comparator in s 79 of the EqA 2010;
❖   the definition of 'like work' in s 65(2);
❖   the defence of 'material difference' in s 69;
❖   how far different bargaining structures can be a defence – particularly *Enderby v Frenchay Health Authority* (1994) and *British Road Services v Loughran* (1997);
❖   the definition of a JES in s 65(4) and (5) and *Eaton v Nuttall* (1977);
❖   the effect of a JES on an equal value claim; and
❖   how far economic reasons can be a defence under *Jenkins v Kingsgate Clothing Productions* (1981).

ANSWER

All four parties wish to claim equal pay against Coronation Products Ltd. To do so, they must establish that they have a route to claim equal pay under the EqA 2010, or that they have an action under Art 141 of the EC Treaty. None of the parties has the additional route under the Equal Pay Directive as Coronation Products Ltd is not an emanation of the state.

Vicky wishes to claim equal pay with Steve. She must first establish that Steve is a valid male comparator under s 79 and, should he be so, her choice of comparator determines her route to equal pay (*Pickstone v Freemans plc* (1988)). To be a valid male comparator under s 79, Steve must be employed by his employer or an associated employer and work at the same establishment, or at a different establishment where common terms and conditions are observed for that class of employee. Steve works for the same employer, and Coronation Products Ltd does not appear to operate on more than one site. Therefore, Steve is a valid male comparator within the definition in s 79.

As Vicky has chosen Steve, and as he is doing a job with the same title, it would appear that Vicky's route to equal pay is the like work route in s 65(2). The section defines like work as work that is the same or broadly similar, and any differences between the things that the woman does and the things done by her comparator are not of practical importance. In *Capper Pass Ltd v Lawton* (1977), Phillips J said that the tribunal should take a broad view, looking to see if the work is generally similar, if there are differences and, if there are, if those differences are of practical importance. Thus, more responsibility (*Eaton v Nuttall* (1977)) will justify a difference in pay as long as this happens throughout the working year (*Redland Roof Tiles v Harper* (1977)). If there are differences between the woman's case and the man's, the tribunal must look at how frequently they occur in practice. In Vicky's case, Steve's work appears to be the same but Coronation will argue that there is a difference in that Steve works overtime and Vicky does not.

In *Dugdale v Kraft Foods Ltd* (1977), the men and women were doing the same work, but the men were paid at a higher basic rate because they worked night shifts and some Sundays. The EAT held that this was not a difference of practical importance, although it pointed out that an employer can pay a higher rate when the unsocial hours are worked, but not a higher basic rate. If Steve worked all of his hours at an unsocial time, therefore, this would render the work not broadly similar (*Thomas v NCB* (1987)), but, given that he appears to work at the same time as Vicky and in addition does overtime, he is doing like work within the definition in s 65(2).

Can Coronation raise a defence to defeat Vicky's claim? Steve's pay is union-negotiated and therefore there are different pay-bargaining structures within the establishment. By s 69 an employer has a defence to an equal pay claim if it shows that the difference in pay is because of a material factor reliance on which does not involve treating Vicky less favourably than Steve because of her sex and does not put women, who are doing equal work to Steve, at a particular disadvantage and Coronation can show that the factor is a proportionate means of achieving a legitimate aim. Do either of these defences apply? In the case of Vicky and Steve, their pay is differently bargained. Can this be a material factor? In *Reed Packaging Ltd v Boozer* (1988), it was held that the defence applied where the applicant and the male comparator were employed under different pay structures where those structures were not discriminatory. This decision, however, must now be subject to the ruling of the ECJ in *Enderby v Frenchay Health Authority* (1994). In that case, the ECJ ruled in relation to one of the questions referred to it by the Court of Appeal – that different non-discriminatory bargaining procedures did not necessarily amount to an objective justification for the different pay rates when the group affected was 'almost exclusively' women. Vicky may therefore seek to defeat both parts of s 69. In respect of s 69(1)(a), as it could be argued that, by discouraging female membership of the union, so that no women are union members, Coronation is treating Vicky less favourably because of her sex. In addition, if there are a larger number of female clerical assistants than men, Vicky may be able to show that the factor of union membership has the effect of putting women clerical assistants at a particular disadvantage under s 69(2). If this is the case, then Coronation would have to show that reliance on that factor was a proportionate means of achieving a legitimate aim (s 69(1)(b)). Coronation does not seem to have identified an aim that it is trying to achieve and as such any defence will fail.

Gail works in the printing shop and wishes to claim equal pay with the paint shop workers. Such workers will be valid male comparators under s 79. From *Pickstone*, above, her choice of male comparator will determine her route to equal pay, but should she choose the paint shop workers, she, at first sight, has a problem. This is because a JES has been conducted. This means that her route to equal pay appears to be that of work rated equivalent in s 1(5) of the Act. However, the JES has given her job a lower value to that of the workers in the paint shop. While s 65(4) allows a woman to claim work rated equivalent under a JES if her work is given an equal value or 'would give an equal value to A's job and B's job in those terms were the evaluation not made on a sex-specific system' (s 65(4)(b)), s 65(5) states that a system is sex-specific if, for the purposes of one or more of the demands made on a worker, it sets values for men different from those it sets for women. This allows the tribunal to adjust the scheme; a tribunal cannot undertake its own JES under s 65(4) (*England v Bromley London Borough Council* (1978). Thus a tribunal can award equal pay if it feels that the claimant's job would have been given an equal rating under a non-discriminatory scheme.

The equal value procedures in the EqA s 131 and the Employment Tribunals (Constitution and Rules of Procedure) (Amendment) Regulations 2004 may be a better route for Gail and state that, where a claimant lodges an equal value claim, there is a presumption (by s 131(6)) in favour of upholding any JES and therefore finding that the work is not of equal value, unless the tribunal has reasonable grounds for suspecting that the JES is sexually discriminatory or it is otherwise unsuitable to be relied upon. This removes the burden from the claimant in showing that a JES is discriminatory.

Section 80(5) of the Act states that a JES must be an evaluation of the job in terms of the demand made on a worker under various headings (for instance, effort, skill, decision). In *Eaton v Nuttall* (1977), the EAT stated that such a study should be 'thorough in analysis and capable of impartial application'. In *Bromley v H and J Quick Ltd* (1988), the Court of Appeal said that such a scheme should not be done on a job-ranking basis and Art 1 of the Equal Pay Directive says that an evaluation study must be fair in that it is based on the same criteria for men and women and so exclude any sexual discrimination. In Gail's case, it appears that a predominantly male characteristic, strength, has been part of the evaluation. Likewise, the dirty conditions have been taken into account, despite the fact that women have not been asked to work in such conditions. It would therefore appear that the study is discriminatory in that a predominantly male characteristic appears to have been given a higher rating and the work conditions have been rated even though the women have no opportunity to work in those conditions. As such, it is open to the tribunal to rebut the presumption of upholding the JES at the stage 1 equal value hearing, and allow Gail to continue her equal value claim.

Coronation Products may raise a defence under s 69(1)(b) of a material factor, which is a difference between her case and that of her comparator. It would appear that women are not allowed to work in the paint shop. Therefore, should the employer argue that this is the reason for the disparity in pay, the policy of not allowing women to work there (and so earn higher wages) is discriminatory. While it is acceptable to pay extra for dirty working conditions, the company policy creates an impact on women and therefore is gender-biased. It does not appear to be imposed to achieve a particular aim and as such the defence will fail.

Sally and Denise job share. They are paid a lower hourly rate than the full-time workers. Their route to equal pay is like work as a man doing the same work full-time is a valid male comparator under s 79. The question again arises whether Coronation can raise the defence of material factor in s 69 of the Act. At one time, it was thought that the fact the woman worked part-time was a material factor (*Handley v H Mono Ltd* (1979)). However, in *Jenkins v Kingsgate Clothing Productions* (1981), the ECJ held that the fact of being part-time can only be a material factor if there is an economic objective that needs to be achieved and the lower rates achieve this objective. In other words, the concept of indirect discrimination was introduced into the area of equal pay with the effect that if the factor discriminates against women, it can only be a defence under s 69(1)(a) and (2) if it can be objectively justified and there is no intention to discriminate. Jenkins was adopted by the House of Lords in Rainey v Greater Glasgow Health Board Eastern District (1987). Jenkins and Rainey have been widened by Strathclyde Regional Council v Wallace (1998). In that case, the House of Lords stated that where the applicant cannot show that the difference in pay is due to a practice that has a disparate impact on women, the employer merely has to show why the difference exists but does not have to justify it objectively. Therefore, in this case, the practice of paying less to staff who were acting as principal teachers as compared to permanent principal teachers affected 81 men and 53 women. The applicant could not therefore show a disparate impact on women and thus the employer did not have to justify the reason of financial constraints.

In the problem, Coronation argues that the full-timers are more productive, presumably because of the gap between midday and 1 pm when the machine lies idle. Such a claim must be investigated, however. If the full-timers have a lunch hour, during which the machines are turned off, and they work from 8 am to 5 pm, it is difficult to see what shortfall in production there can be in relation to Sally's and Denise's machine. It could be that Coronation could argue that administrative costs are such that it needs to encourage full-time working rather than part-time working, but it has not argued this point. As such, if, in reality, there is little difference between the output of the machines, and production is the only argument raised by the employer, it is difficult to see that the employer has the defence under Jenkins and s 69(1)(b) and (2) and Sally and Denise will be entitled to the full-time hourly rate.

On the other hand, Wallace may have an impact. Sally and Denise will have to show that the practice of paying job sharers less has a disparate impact on women. Clearly, there is a difference in treatment, in that the question states that job shares are paid a lower rate and thus any men job sharing will get paid the same as the claimants. However, if this equally affects men (that is, there are a number of men who job share in the factory), then the employer can simply point to why the difference exists without objectively justifying it (Wallace). If, on the other hand, only women are in reality affected by this practice, then Coronation Products must objectively justify the practice, presumably, given its arguments, on the basis of reduced production, which, as stated above, it will have to prove. Should this argument be unsuccessful, Sally and Denise will be entitled to the full-time hourly rate.

Employment Protection

INTRODUCTION

Employment protection rights are often mentioned in employment law courses, but very few go through them in a large amount of detail. In the context of this book, employment protection rights are taken to mean those rights that are derived from statute: originally the Employment Protection Act 1975, now the Employment Rights Act (ERA) 1996 and the Trade Union and Labour Relations (Consolidation) Act (TULR(C)A) 1992, both as amended by the Employment Relations Act 1999, and the Employment Acts 2002 and 2004, which create a set of basic minimum rights that the employer cannot contract out of. Some courses deal with these rights at appropriate points in the course: for example, the right to an itemised pay statement is dealt with when looking at the implied duty to pay the employee. However, it is useful for the purposes of this text to separate the rights out and look at them in isolation, as long as students are aware that such rights may permeate throughout other examination questions. In this particular chapter, we will look at rights owed by the employer to the employee, excluding dismissal rights, which are dealt with in Chapter 9. Once these rights are extracted, general rights that the student needs to understand are:

- notice rights;
- rights in relation to payment;
- maternity, adoption and parental rights;
- rights not to suffer a detriment in certain cases;
- time-off provisions.

It has already been mentioned that often these rights are dealt with in other areas of an employment law course and therefore may come up in a problem in almost any other area. The questions in this chapter, therefore, aim to ensure that students fully understand the rights.

In particular, students should be familiar with:

- the minimum notice provisions in s 86 of the ERA 1996;
- rights in relation to itemised pay statements;

❖ guaranteed weeks;
❖ pay during lay-offs and short-time working;
❖ medical suspension pay;
❖ maternity rights, in particular, time off for ante-natal appointments, maternity leave, the right to return, suspension on maternity grounds and statutory maternity pay;
❖ parental rights, in particular, parental leave, paternity leave, adoption leave, paternity pay, adoption pay;
❖ what constitutes a detriment on health and safety grounds – because the employee is an employee representative or a trustee of an occupational pension fund or refusing Sunday working; because the employee took parental leave or time off to deal with an emergency involving a dependant; because the employee made a protected disclosure; because the employee exercised rights to be accompanied at a disciplinary or grievance hearing or took action in respect of recognition or derecognition of a trade union; or because the employee requested flexible working;
❖ the rights to time off for trade union duties, public duties, trade union activities, health and safety duties, trustees of occupational pension funds, employee representatives, time off to look for work if under notice of redundancy, time off to deal with an emergency involving a dependant and time off for union learning representatives.

Finally, a knowledge of all the above rights can impact particularly on the area of dismissal, as a refusal on the part of the employer to allow the employee to exercise these rights may lead to a finding of constructive dismissal.

Checklist ✔

Students should be familiar with the following specific areas:

■ the minimum notice the employer must give and receive;
■ details within the itemised pay statement and remedies for breach of the provisions;
■ what constitutes a guaranteed week;
■ what constitutes a lay off or short-time working;
■ what are the rights in relation to medical suspension;
■ the implementation of the **Pregnant Workers Directive (92/85/EC)**;
■ parental rights, paternity rights, adoption rights and rights to request flexible working;
■ the protection from suffering a detriment.

- the rights in the **Work and Families Act 2006**; and
- what constitutes reasonable time off and, in particular, the ACAS Code of Practice, *Time Off for Trade Union Duties and Activities* (revised 2003) and the new Code on Union Learning Representatives.

QUESTION 25

Martin, Ronnie and Phil work as teachers for Middlewich School. The recognised union in the school is the National Union of Teachers (NUT).

Martin has been a member of the governing body of the local university for the past four years. During that time, he has had, on average, 14 days off to attend meetings during term-time. Due to a recent scandal involving the university vice chancellor, the governing body has met frequently in the past three months and Martin has had 21 days off to date. The chair of the governing body has just informed him that he will be required to attend meetings for at least another 15 days during the rest of this academic year. Martin's headmaster has refused to allow him any more time off, saying it is unfair to other colleagues who cover his classes. Martin has never been paid for his time off.

Ronnie is the union health and safety representative at the school. Given that the school has just opened a chemistry department, Ronnie has had three weeks off over the past six months to attend training courses in the handling of chemicals. He now requires a further seven days off to train the chemistry teachers. The headmaster has refused to allow Ronnie the time to train the teachers and has said that Ronnie must train them during the vacation. In addition, Ronnie's class size has doubled recently and he has been given extra classes to teach, to make up for the time he has been out of the school.

Phil is a member of the NUT. The union has held regional meetings in the past to discuss action against the national curriculum. These meetings are normally held at lunchtime or in the evenings and Phil has always attended them. He has just been informed that the next two regional meetings will be held on two separate mornings when classes are on and that the union wishes him to be a member of a party that is being sent down to London for a week, during term-time, to lobby Parliament. The headmaster has refused to allow Phil to attend the regional meetings or to join the lobby.

▶ Advise Martin, Ronnie and Phil.

Answer Plan

This question deals with time off rights in relation to all of the parties. In each case, the reason for the time off is different and students should be careful to distinguish whether the issues raised are in relation to time off for duties or activities.

Particular issues to be considered are:

❖ whether Martin's appointment to the governing body is a public duty within s 50(2) of the Employment Rights Act (ERA) 1996;
❖ the balance between the employee's rights and the employer's needs;
❖ the right to time off for health and safety duties under the Safety Representatives and Safety Committees Regulations 1977 and the Code of Practice issued by the Health and Safety Executive;
❖ the right to time off for trade union activities;
❖ what is a trade union activity;
❖ what constitutes reasonable time off; and
❖ the provisions relating to time off for trade union activities in the ACAS Code of Practice.

ANSWER

The Employment Protection Act 1975 created a series of basic time-off rights for employees. These rights are now contained in the ERA 1996. Some of the rights allow paid time off and some allow unpaid time off. In addition, both ACAS and the Health and Safety Executive have issued codes of practice in this area to provide guidance for employers and tribunals and the courts.

Martin has been a member of the governing body of a local university for the past four years. In the past, he has averaged only 14 days off in the performance of these duties, but to date he has had 21 days and will be required for a further 15, totalling 36 in all. By s 50(2) and (9) of the ERA 1996, membership of the governing body of a higher education corporation such as a university is deemed to be a public duty and the subsection requires the employer to allow an employee time off during working hours to perform those duties. Section 50(4), however, states that the amount of time off an employee is permitted to take and any conditions attached to the time off must be reasonable in all the circumstances, and a tribunal must have regard to how much time off is required to perform the duties, how much time off the employee has already received under s 50, the circumstances of the employer's business and the effect of the employee's absence on that business. In the case of a dispute, the tribunal cannot substitute a figure if it considers that reasonable time off has not been allowed (*Corner v Buckinghamshire County Council* (1978)). It can merely make a declaration that the complaint by the employee is well founded and in a suitable case make an award of compensation. In *Corner*, however, Slynn J suggested obiter that a failure to pay during the time off could be construed as a failure to pay. As such, Martin may have two lines of argument: the refusal to allow any more time off and the fact that the time off already taken has been unpaid.

In relation to the refusal to give more time off, the tribunal is required to consider the time off Martin has already had and the effect of his absence on the employer's business. In *Borders Regional Council v Maule* (1992), the EAT stressed that the tribunal had to achieve a balance between the needs of the employer and the rights of the employee. On the facts of the case, the fact that the employer had allowed the employee time off to perform her duties as a member of a social security tribunal did not mean that the employer was acting unreasonably in refusing her time to attend a training session in relation to such membership, and there was a duty on the employee to moderate the activities to fit in with the employer's business needs. Safety considerations may, for example, mean that it is dangerous for the employee to have time off because of dangerous manning levels (*Walters v British Steel Corp*). On the other hand, the time off must be allowed. In *Ratcliffe v Dorset County Council* (1978), it was held that rearranging a lecturer's classes so that they did not conflict with his public duties was not allowing him time off.

In Martin's case, there has been no problem until this year when a problem at the university necessitated a great many more meetings. To date, he has had more time off this year than in the past and, if he attends all the future meetings, he will have nearly tripled the time he has had off in the past. What effect is this having on the employer's business, however? It appears that his classes have been covered by colleagues, and there is nothing in the facts to suggest that they are now complaining, merely that the employer does not think it is fair. In addition, the time off for this year has only occurred because of a problem at the university and there is nothing to suggest that this will be repeated in future years. There appears to be no safety risk attached to Martin's absence and nothing to suggest that it causes problems for the employer. In *Corner v Buckinghamshire County Council*, the employer allowed the employee 15 days off but refused to allow any more. Despite the fact that the tribunal was overruled on a jurisdictional point, it felt that 19 days was not unreasonable. In *Emmerson v Inland Revenue Commissioners* (1977), it was held that 30 days' absence was not unreasonable, given that the employee was prepared to use 12 days' holiday as part of his time off. On the other hand, 36 days during term-time is just over seven weeks and this is a considerable proportion of time in relation to an academic year. Taken in context, therefore, it may be that the tribunal feels that the employer's refusal is not unreasonable. If, on the other hand, the tribunal in Martin's case picks up on the obiter by Slynn J in *Corner* in relation to unpaid leave, it could be that it makes the necessary declaration in Martin's favour on the basis that he has been refused time off full stop. This is unlikely, however, as s 48 does not require that such time off be paid.

Ronnie is the union health and safety representative and the NUT is the recognised union. The Safety Representative and Safety Committees Regulations 1977 were made under the authority of s 2(4) of the Health and Safety at Work, etc Act 1974. These provide in reg 4(2) that an employer shall allow paid time off for representatives appointed by recognised trade unions to perform functions listed in reg 4(1), and to undergo training in relation to those functions. In addition, the Health and Safety Executive has issued a code of practice entitled *Time Off for Training Safety Representatives* (1978). The functions listed in reg 4(1) include representation of employees in consultations with the employer and the enforcement authorities, and the investigation of complaints. The Regulations do not include time off to train other employees, although the employer is under a duty under reg 11 of the Management of Health and Safety at Work Regulations 1992 to ensure that employees are periodically trained with regard to health and safety matters. In relation to the employer's refusal to allow Ronnie time off to train the employees, however, such time off does not appear to fall within the 1977 Regulations and therefore the tribunal has no jurisdiction.

Ronnie, however, may have another action that he may pursue against the employer. In *Ratcliffe v Dorset County Council* (1978), it was held that a reorganisation of a lecturer's classes amounted to a refusal of time off. If it could be argued that, in essence, the employer is obtaining the same amount of work from Ronnie, there is a possibility under *Ratcliffe* that the tribunal will grant the declaration. Could the employer's action, however, be construed as subjecting Ronnie to a detriment?

Section 44 of the ERA 1996 creates the right not to suffer a detriment by the employer on the basis that the employee was a designated health and safety representative and the detriment was suffered because the representative was carrying out activities in connection with preventing or reducing risks to the health and safety of employees at work (s 44(1)(a)). The employee must present a claim to an employment tribunal, which can award such compensation as it considers just and equitable should it find the complaint well founded. The onus is on the employer to show the ground on which the act was done (s 48(2)). In Ronnie's case, he has had additional pupils in his classes and additional classes to teach. If there is no economic reason for this, the inference appears to be that the employer is imposing the extra work on Ronnie because he has taken time off in relation to his health and safety duties. The provision is closely modelled on the provisions protecting trade union members from having action short of dismissal taken against them because of their trade union membership or activities. In *Carlson v Post Office* (1981), the EAT held that the equivalent section encompassed any action that subjected the employee to a disadvantage and refusing the employee a parking space was held to be sufficient to create liability. On the basis of this decision, it would appear that Ronnie has suffered a detriment and can sue for compensation.

Phil is a member of the NUT and has, in the past, attended union meetings outside working hours. The employer has now refused to allow him time off to attend two meetings within working hours and a week off to participate in the lobby of Parliament. By s 170 of the Trade Union Labour Relations (Consolidation) Act (TULR(C)A) 1992, an employer must allow an employee who is a member of an independent recognised trade union unpaid time off during working hours to take part in trade union activities or any activities in relation to which the employee is acting as a representative of the union. The ACAS Code of Practice on *Time Off for Trade Union Duties and Activities (revised 2003)* gives examples in paras 21 and 22 of those activities for which time off should be given, and they include workplace and regional meetings. Such time off should be reasonable in all the circumstances (s 170(4) of the TULR(C)A 1992). Paragraph 39 of the ACAS Code stresses, however, that time off does not have to be permitted for activities that consist of industrial action. While the regional meetings Phil wishes to attend fall within the activities listed in the Code, it is debatable whether the lobby would do so. In *Luce v Bexley London Borough Council* (1990), the EAT held that a parliamentary lobby was not a trade union activity within the meaning of the Act and, therefore, the employer had not refused time off for trade union activities. Following this, it would appear that Phil may get a declaration in respect of the refusal to allow him time off to attend the regional meetings, but not in respect of the refusal to allow him time off to participate in the parliamentary lobby.

Think Point

1 Students should note that action short of dismissal because of trade union membership is often part of an unfair dismissal question.

QUESTION 26

Brookside Ltd is a company that produces widgets for the aircraft industry.

Terry is employed as a quality controller. Due to the loss of a major order, the company temporarily sold from stock that had accumulated rather than produced any new widgets. Terry and other employees were laid off for a period of six weeks as a result. For the first two weeks, the union held a protest and pickets prevented entry to the works. The lay-off ended two weeks ago. During the lay-off, Terry received no pay. Terry has now heard that there may be another lay-off in two weeks' time.

Barry works in the shop that sprays the widgets. The paint used contains lead. He was suspended in November due to the high levels of lead in his bloodstream. He was paid his full salary until Christmas. In January, he was ill with shingles but got over the illness by the end of January. In February, Brookside offered him work loading vans, which Barry refused. He returned to work on 1 March, having received no pay since Christmas.

Jimmy has worked for Brookside for six months; before that he was unemployed. Three weeks after starting the job, Jimmy was ill. He returned to work last week. During his illness, he received no pay. Three weeks into his illness he was examined by the company doctor but Brookside refused him access to the doctor's report.

▶ Advise Terry, Barry and Jimmy in respect of their statutory employment protection rights.

Answer Plan

In this question, the student is asked to advise the parties in respect of statutory employment protection rights only. In relation to all three parties, the main issues to discuss are statutory rights in relation to pay in certain circumstances.

Particular points to discuss are:

- the right to a guarantee payment under ss 28–32 of the Employment Rights Act (ERA) 1996;
- the exclusions that operate in relation to such a right;
- the right to claim redundancy in certain periods of lay-off under s 148;
- the right to pay during medical suspension under s 64;
- when the right to pay during medical suspension does not arise;
- loss of entitlement to medical suspension pay;
- the employee's rights to access to his medical records; and
- the right to Statutory Sick Pay under the Social Security Contributions and Benefits Act 1992.

ANSWER

The question requires advice as to the statutory rights of the parties involved. In all cases, it will be assumed that the contract is silent as to pay in the situations given and that the employee's only rights to pay will come from statute.

Terry has been laid off temporarily for six weeks due to the loss of an order. Under ss 28 and 29 of the ERA 1996, an employee who has been continuously employed for at least one month and who is not on a fixed-term contract of three months or less is entitled to a guarantee payment in respect of a whole day when he is not provided with work because there is a diminution in the requirements of the employer's business for work of the kind the employee is required to do or any other occurrence affecting the normal working of the employer's business (s 28(1)). The section is designed to protect employees in relation to occurrences outside the employer's control; thus, in *North v Pavleigh Ltd* (1977), it did not cover the days when the owner of the factory closed because of Jewish holidays. In Terry's case, it appears that the workless days are due to an 'occurrence' that is outside the employer's control and therefore, on the face of it, he is entitled to a guarantee payment. There are exclusions to the right, however, contained in s 29. By s 29(3), an employee is not entitled to a guarantee payment in respect of a workless day if the failure to provide work occurs in consequence of any industrial action.

In *Garvey v Maybank (Oldham) Ltd* (1979), there was a national lorry drivers' strike, and pickets at the factory refused to allow lorries to enter or leave. The employer ordered his lorry drivers to cross the picket lines but they refused. As a result, there were insufficient supplies entering the factory and Garvey was laid off. It was held that he was not entitled to a guarantee payment as the lay-off was a consequence of the picket outside the factory.

In Terry's case, the union has objected to the lay-off, and consequently has picketed the factory for the first two weeks. On the facts, it appears that the trade dispute was a consequence of the lay-off rather than the other way around. On the wording of s 29(3), therefore, Terry has not been laid off as the result of a trade dispute but because of the loss of an order. As such, Terry is entitled to a guarantee payment under s 28(1), and does not fall within the excluded classes of employees.

Having said that, the amount of payment is not large. By s 31(3), Terry is entitled to five one-day payments in any three-month period. Any contractual entitlement to remuneration in relation to a day when no work is provided is set off against the statutory payment and any contractual payment per day counts as payment in the statutory calculation of the five days (*Cartwright v G Clancey Ltd* (1983)). In the problem, Terry was laid off for six weeks. He is therefore entitled to five one-day payments and will not be entitled to any further payments for another six weeks. Should another lay-off occur before that time, Terry will not be entitled to further statutory payments until the three months have elapsed.

Terry has not received any pay. He can ask Brookside for his statutory entitlement and, should Brookside refuse to make the guarantee payments, Terry can complain to an employment tribunal within three months of the failure to pay. Terry may have an additional remedy, however. If the contract provides a right on the part of the employer to lay-off, such a lay-off is not a breach of contract. If such a right does not exist, however, the employer is in repudiatory breach, which will justify the employee in resigning and claiming constructive dismissal. This prejudices the employee when there is a contractual right to lay-off, because should he leave because he has no pay, he has resigned and will have no protection. To provide such protection, s 148 of the ERA 1996 provides that if an employee is laid off for four consecutive weeks or six weeks in any 13, he may claim a redundancy payment. Lay-off means that he receives no remuneration under his contract. He must give written notice to Brookside that he intends to claim a redundancy payment within four weeks of the end of the lay-off and must terminate his contract by giving the contractual notice (s 148(1) and (2)). Brookside may challenge the claim of redundancy by giving a written counter-notice within seven days of the receipt of Terry's notice, giving evidence that within four weeks of the receipt of the employee's notice Terry will be employed for 13 consecutive weeks without lay-off or short-time working (less than half a week's pay being earned). The question is decided by the tribunal, but if, after the hearing, the tribunal discovers that in the four weeks after the employee's notice the employee was laid off or on short time, this conclusively decides the case against the employer (s 152(2)).

Barry was suspended from work when the lead content in his bloodstream became too high. The lead appears to come from the paint he uses to spray the widgets and, thus, Barry has been suspended on medical grounds under s 64. Sections 64 and 65 provide that an employee who has been continuously employed for more than one month and who is not on a fixed-term contact of three months or less is entitled to remuneration if he is suspended from work in consequence of a requirement imposed by certain statutory provisions or a recommendation made under a code of practice issued or approved under s 16 of the Health and Safety at Work, etc Act 1974. The statutory regulations are contained in s 59(3) and include provisions relating to lead (the Control of Lead at Work Regulations 1980). The employee is entitled to be paid for a period of up to six months from the day on which the suspension begins.

Exclusions to payment are contained in s 65. These include periods during which the employee was incapable of work due to disease (s 65(3)), or periods during which the employee was offered suitable alternative employment by his employer, whether or not it was work that the employee is required to do under his contract, and the employee unreasonably refused to perform that work (s 65(4)).

Barry was suspended in November and received pay until Christmas. During January, he had shingles and was therefore unable to work, but this appears to be due to the shingles as well as to the lead content in his bloodstream. Medical suspension pay is only payable if the employee is fit to work but is unable to do so because of the suspension. In *Stallite Batteries Co Ltd v Appleton* (1988), the applicant became ill after falling into a skip containing lead paste. No medical suspension certificate was issued by the company doctor, although his own doctor considered him unfit to work. It was held that he was not entitled to medical suspension pay as he was unavailable for work due to sickness and was therefore excluded by s 65(3). Similarly, it would appear that, in Barry's case, during the whole of January he was unable to work because he had shingles. He will therefore fall within the provisions of s 65(3) and is not entitled to medical suspension pay for the period of his illness.

In February, Brookside offered Barry alternative work loading lorries, which he refused. Section 65(4) excludes the employee from payment if he refuses suitable alternative work, whether such work is what he is required to do under his contract or not. Clearly, Barry is not employed to load lorries but, by virtue of s 65(4), this does not mean that the employer has not offered suitable alternative work. Whether the work is suitable is a question of fact for the tribunal, taking into account the employee's skill and aptitude. Similarly, the reasonableness of the employee's refusal is also a question of fact for the tribunal, which will look at the circumstances of Barry's case. Barry must present his claim to the tribunal within three months of the failure to pay, although the tribunal can extend the three-month period if it feels that it was not reasonably practicable for the applicant to present his claim in time. While Barry will not be able to claim payment for January, he may have a claim for February.

Jimmy was unemployed until he began working for Brookside six months ago. He worked for three weeks and then fell ill and returned to work last week. This indicates that the period of his illness was five months. During his illness, he received no remuneration. The question that needs to be asked is whether Jimmy should have received Statutory Sick Pay (SSP) from his employer. The scheme was introduced by the Social Security and Housing Benefits Act 1982 (now the Social Security Contributions and Benefits Act 1992) and is designed to put the administrative burden of sickness benefit on the employer who can, at present, reclaim some or all payments from the state. There is a statutory obligation on all employers to pay SSP in respect of their qualifying employees (s 151). In order to qualify, the employee must claim in respect of a day that is part of the period of incapacity for work (that is, a period of four consecutive days or more); the day must fall within a period of entitlement (that is, the end of the illness or the expiry of 28 weeks); and the day claimed for must be a qualifying day (that is, a day on which the employee would normally work). Certain employees are disqualified from receipt of SSP (Sched 2, para 2). One of these exclusions is where the employee's first date of sickness is within 57 days of a claim in receipt of other state benefits, such as Incapacity Benefit or Jobseeker's Allowance if there has been a previous entitlement to Invalidity Benefit. Jimmy was unemployed before starting work for Brookside, and presumably in receipt of Jobseeker's Allowance. His illness began within 57 days of his starting the job, but this will not disentitle him to SSP unless there was a previous entitlement to incapacity benefit. Unless this is the case, Jimmy is entitled to SSP for the whole of his period of illness and, because of Brookside's failure to pay, he may refer its failure to the local insurance officer and any decision made in his favour may be enforced in the county court.

In addition to his lack of payment, Jimmy is also concerned that he has not been allowed to see the company doctor's medical report. The Access to Medical Reports Act 1988 gives the employee the right to refuse permission to his employer who is seeking to examine his medical records, or the right to see the report beforehand and refuse to give consent to allow it to be sent to the employer, or request that the doctor amend the report before transmission to the employer. A medical report is defined in s 2(1) as 'a report . . . prepared by a medical practitioner who is or who has been responsible for the clinical care of the individual'. As such, these rights apply only to reports written by the employee's own doctor and, as such, Jimmy has no legal right to see the report written by the company doctor or to prevent its transmission to Brookside.

QUESTION 27

Bet, Vicky and Emily work for Street Ltd. All of them recently became pregnant.

Bet has worked for the company for six years as a stock controller. She took maternity leave 20 weeks ago and, until recently, had no intention of returning to work. Her partner is now unemployed, however, and Bet wants to return at the end of her maternity leave. She has raised the matter with Street Ltd, who has told her that she cannot return to work because the job of stock controller has now been amalgamated with that of stock organiser and the existing stock organiser (who has been at the company for 18 months) now performs both jobs.

Vicky had been employed for eight months when she became pregnant. She works on the factory floor where a great many of the workers smoke. Vicky is asthmatic and her asthma has worsened since her pregnancy and is now causing a risk to the baby. As a result, Vicky has been off work for ten weeks and is now three weeks from her expected date of confinement. Street Ltd has refused to pay her anything apart from SSP for the first two weeks of her illness and has told her she must return to work within one week of the birth.

Emily also works on the factory floor and has been employed by Street Ltd for one year. Her maternity leave period finished three weeks ago. She is, however, breast feeding the baby and, due to her obsessive concern about the smoky atmosphere in which she works and the effect on her baby, she had a doctor's certificate stating that she was incapable of work for four weeks after the end of her maternity leave. Today, the employer terminated her contract.

▶ Advise Bet, Vicky and Emily of their statutory maternity rights against Street Ltd.

Answer Plan

It is obvious from the problem that this deals exclusively with the maternity rights available to women. It is important to note that the law changed on 1 April 2007 giving women the right to 12 months' maternity leave irrespective of length of service. However, Statutory Maternity Pay (SMP) will still be determined by the requirement of 26 weeks' service ending with the week immediately preceding the 14th week before her expected week of confinement. Since April 2007, SMP is payable for 39 weeks with an intention to extend it to 52 weeks eventually.

Specific points to discuss are:

❖ the right to return to work under s 73(4)(c) of the Employment Rights Act (ERA) 1996;
❖ any notice requirements in relation to the exercise of the right;
❖ the provisions in relation to redundancy before the right to return is exercised;
❖ the right to 52 weeks' maternity leave;
❖ when maternity leave begins in relation to sickness during pregnancy;
❖ suspension from work on maternity grounds; and
❖ dismissal on maternity grounds after maternity leave.

ANSWER

All the parties in the question require advice in relation to their maternity rights. This right to maternity leave is irrespective of length of service but the right to statutory maternity pay varies depending upon the length of employment and has been extended by the Employment Relations Act 1999, the Maternity and Parental Leave Regulations 1999 (as amended by the MPL (Amendment) Regulations 2002) and the Work and Families Act 2006. The original rights were brought in to give effect to the Pregnant Workers Directive. The basic rights are now governed by ss 71–75 of the ERA 1996.

Bet has been employed for six years. By s 73 of the ERA 1996 and reg 4(1) of the 1999 Regulations (as amended by the Maternity and Parental Leave and Paternity and Adoption Leave (Amendment) Regulations 2006), a woman, irrespective of hours of work or length of service, is entitled to 52 weeks' maternity leave and has a right to all the benefits under her contract (excluding pay) and a right to return to the job in which she was employed before her absence. Bet therefore has the right to 52 weeks' maternity leave.

Should she wish to return at the end of her maternity leave, no notice is required unless she wishes to return early. In that situation, she must give eight weeks' notice to her employer (reg 11). Should she wish to return later than the agreed date, she must give her employer eight weeks' notice ending with the original date. After maternity leave, she has a right to return to the job in which she was employed before her absence, or a similar job (reg 18(1)). However, by reg 10, if a redundancy has arisen during her ordinary maternity leave, which makes it impracticable for the employer to continue to employ her under her original contract of employment, she is entitled to be offered alternative employment. Failure to offer such employment renders the dismissal automatically unfair (reg 20(1)(b)). She may only exercise her rights (and thus gain protection) if she has satisfied the notice requirements. She must have informed her employer at least 15 weeks before her expected week of childbirth (EWC): (a) that she was pregnant; (b) the EWC; and (c) the date on which she intended to start her leave. If she gave birth before she had notified a date or before the notified date, she should have informed her employer of the actual date (in writing if requested) as soon as reasonably practicable. On receipt, the employer must have informed her of the date on which her maternity leave would end. There is no longer a requirement that she must give her employer notice of her date of return unless she wishes to return early, in which case she must give eight weeks' notice (reg 11(1)).

Bet is entitled to return on terms and conditions that are no less favourable than those before she left (reg 18); if the terms are less favourable, then the employer is refusing her the right to return (McFadden v Greater Glasgow Passenger Transport Executive (1977)). Her continuity is preserved for statutory purposes.

The reason for Street's refusal to allow Bet to return appears to be that she is redundant in that Street no longer requires a stock controller. If the redundancy occurs before she returns, she has the right to be offered a suitable vacancy if one is available (reg 10). If suitable work is available and she is not offered it, she is treated as unfairly dismissed. In *Community Task Force v Rimmer* (1986), the EAT ruled that a redundancy dismissal was unfair, even though the only vacancy could be filled only by an unemployed person under the rules of the Manpower Services Commission funding.

In Bet's case, there appears to be a redundancy situation, but the employer has chosen to keep on a person with much less continuity than Bet. If Bet can establish that the reason for her redundancy was her pregnancy or taking of maternity leave, or any other reason in reg 20(3), her selection for redundancy will be automatically unfair (s 99 and *Brown v Stockton-on-Tees Borough Council* (1988)).

Vicky has eight months' continuity. Since April 2007, all women, regardless of length of service or hours of work, are entitled to 52 weeks' maternity leave. By s 71(4) of the ERA 1996 (as amended), she is entitled to all the benefits of her contract, excluding pay. To some extent, a woman may choose when her maternity leave starts, but she cannot choose a date earlier than the beginning of the 11th week before the EWC (reg 4(2)(b)). Her ordinary maternity leave will automatically be triggered, however, by any day she is absent wholly or partly because of pregnancy or childbirth after the beginning of the fourth week before the EWC (reg 6(1)(b)). As with Bet, Vicky must have complied with the notification requirements in relation to her leave. She has the right to return to her job (s 71(4)).

Vicky has now been off for ten weeks, and it is three weeks to her EWC. Given that her illness is related to her pregnancy, her maternity leave will have started at the beginning of the fourth week before the EWC – that is, one week ago – unless she informed Street of an earlier date. If one week ago is the start of her maternity leave, she has a further 51 weeks to go – that is, she can take 48 weeks after the birth and not the one week on which Street is insisting.

Vicky has only received sick pay during her time off. In order to qualify for SMP: she must be earning more than the lower rate for making National Insurance contributions; she must give her employer medical evidence of the EWC; she must give it at least 28 days' notice of the date on which she expects its liability to pay SMP will begin; she must have been employed by her employer for at least 26 weeks ending with the qualifying week (that is, the 14th week before the EWC); and she must have reached the 11th week before the EWC (or recently have given birth) and she must have stopped work. If she satisfies these conditions, she will be entitled to six weeks at the higher rate of pay (nine-tenths of her week's pay) and the further 20 weeks at the lower rate, which is fixed by regulations.

If Vicky is earning less than the lower rate for making National Insurance contributions, she will not fit into the conditions for SSP. Street has only paid her SSP for two weeks. By s 153 of the Social Security Contributions and Benefits Act 1992, SSP is not payable to a pregnant woman during the disqualifying period – that is, for 26 weeks beginning with the 11th week before the EWC. As such, Street is not obliged to pay her SSP and, unless there is a provision in her contract, she will be unable to sue, although she may be entitled to the state maternity allowance.

Emily has given birth. Although her maternity leave has ended, she has a medical certificate covering the period afterwards. Her contract has now been terminated. Section 99 of the ERA 1996 and reg 20 of the 1999 Regulations provide that a dismissal is automatically unfair if the principal reason for her dismissal is, amongst other reasons, a maternity reason. No continuity period is required to enter a complaint of unfair dismissal on these grounds. Emily appears to have been signed off because of her obsession about the effect of the atmosphere in which she works on her breast milk. Regulation 20(3) states that a dismissal is unfair if the reason for the dismissal is connected with the pregnancy of the employee or the fact that the employee has given birth. Her obsession appears to be due to her pregnancy and the birth of her child and, if the dismissal is due to her extra time off, this could be due to her having recently given birth. If this interpretation is correct, Emily has therefore been unfairly dismissed and can pursue a claim in the employment tribunal.

Aim Higher ✕
- Often students don't think that articles are relevant to problem-type questions, but often articles discuss the interpretation of particular provisions.
- On maternity rights, see, for example, James (2007) 36 ILJ 315.

QUESTION 28

The present government, in the 1998 White Paper, *Fairness at Work*, stated that its proposals were intended to create a framework for the future. One of the elements of this framework was to introduce provisions that enhanced family life.

Critically assess whether changes introduced since 1998 are, in reality, family-friendly.

Common Pitfalls

❖ Merely writing down all the family-friendly provisions is only answering half the question.
❖ The question asks the student to assess whether, together, they enhance family life, and thus the student must discuss the provisions and then assess if in reality they do what the last government intended.

Answer Plan

The question requires the student to discuss a number of rights from a number of different sources and missing some out will not answer the question or allow the student to engage in an adequate assessment to answer the question. As such, it is a question to answer only if the student knows all of the sources.

Issues to be considered include:

❖ the Part-Time Workers (Prevention of Less Favourable Treatment) Regulations 2000;
❖ parental leave and the protection of the right;
❖ the right to time off for dependants and protection of the right;
❖ the new maternity leave and maternity pay provisions;
❖ the new rights for paternity leave, paternity pay, adoption leave and adoption pay;
❖ the Fixed-Term Employees Regulations 2002;
❖ the right to request flexible working in the Employment Act 2002;
❖ changes made by the Work and Families Act 2006.

ANSWER

Since 1998, there have been a number of provisions that could be described as 'family-friendly'. It could be argued that the Working Time Regulations 1998 and the National Minimum Wage Act of the same year started this policy, in that the former restricted the number of hours a week an employer could require its employees to work, and the latter introduced the right to three (now four) weeks' paid holiday. However, it is the protection of workers who do not work full-time, the introduction of a number of rights to time off for family reasons, increased maternity rights and the new right to flexible working that, when looked at together, could be said to create family-friendly policies.

The start of family-friendly policies came with the Employment Relations Act 1999 and regulations made thereunder. This extended the right to ordinary maternity leave to all pregnant employees, irrespective of length of service, and increased the period of leave from 14 to 18 weeks to bring the leave period in line with Statutory Maternity Pay (SMP). In April 2003, the leave period was further increased to 26 weeks. In April 2007, the leave was further extended to 52 weeks by the Maternity and Parental Leave and the Paternity and Adoption Leave (MPLPAL) (Amendment) Regulations 2006, for all women, regardless of length of service. The same Regulations extend SMP to 39 weeks if the employee satisfies the qualifying conditions. The right to leave is accompanied with a right to return to her old job unless this is not reasonably practicable, and is protected by the right not to be unfairly dismissed or selected for redundancy on the grounds that leave was taken. In addition a new reg 12A allows a woman to carry out up to ten days' work for her employer without her maternity leave coming to an end. 'Work' means contractual work or training or any activity undertaken for the purposes of keeping in touch with the workplace (reg 12A(3)). However, the regulation makes it clear that an employer cannot require the employee to undertake the work or training, and she is protected from suffering a detriment or being unfairly dismissed for undertaking or refusing to undertake such work.

The Employment Relations Act 1999 also implemented the Parental Leave Directive. This created two new rights. First, it introduced a right to take parental leave, now found in the Maternity and Parental Leave Regulations (MPLR) 1999 (as amended). This allows an employee who has or expects to have parental responsibility for a child and who has one year's continuity of service the right to up to 13 weeks' unpaid leave to care for that child. This right lasts until the child's fifth birthday and applies to every child, so that if an employee has two children under the age of 5, that employee is entitled to a maximum of 26 weeks' parental leave. The employee taking such leave has the right to return to his or her old job and there is the usual protection from unfair dismissal and redundancy, in addition to the right not to suffer a detriment because parental leave has been taken (ERA 1996, ss 99 and 47C; MPLR 1999, reg s 20, and 19).

The second right introduced by the Employment Relations Act 1999 was the right to request unpaid time off to care for dependants. The Act inserted a new s 57A into the ERA 1996 (as amended), and gave employees the right to request reasonable time off to cope with a family emergency, such as a dependant falling ill or childcare arrangements falling through. Again, this right is protected by the right not to suffer a detriment because the right has been exercised, and protection against unfair dismissal and redundancy for the reason that the right has been exercised. To exercise these rights, the employee must inform the employer as soon as is reasonably practicable the reason for and length of the absence. In *Qua v John Ford Morrison Solicitors* (2003), the EAT held that the right is to request time off to deal with an immediate crisis. There are the remedies of a declaration and compensation if the employer unreasonably refuses to grant time off (ERA 1996, s 57B).

While these rights, without doubt, help those employees with children, the government has gone further. Many women work part-time, often because of childcare or other responsibilities. While legislation such as the Sex Discrimination Act (SDA) 1975 provided some protection against less favourable treatment of part-time workers, litigation under this Act is expensive and can take a long time. As such, in 2000, the government introduced the Part-Time Workers (Prevention of Less Favourable Treatment) Regulations implementing the Part-Time Workers Directive 97/81/EC. These provide a remedy where a part-time worker is treated less favourably than a full-time worker employed by her employer engaged in the same or broadly similar work, unless the employer can objectively justify the less favourable treatment. While the regulations operate on a pro rata basis, they prevent an employer paying reduced hourly wages to part-timers (the majority of whom are women) and provide an environment in which women who wish to work part-time can do so without suffering a disadvantage.

The Paternity and Adoption Leave Regulations 2002 introduced the right to paternity and adoption leave. These rights have been considerably extended from April 2007. The Work and Families Act 2006 inserted a new s 80AA into the ERA 1996. This gives the Secretary of State the power to make regulations to allow for paternity leave of up to 26 weeks, which must be taken before the end of a period of 12 months beginning with the birth. The new regulations will also provide for Statutory Paternity Pay (SPP), at the rate of SMP, where the leave is taken when the mother has taken action that is treated as constituting a return to work. This means in reality that the parents of a child can share leave and pay so that if, for example, the mother returns after 26 weeks, her partner can claim the other 26 weeks, of which 13 weeks will be on SPP. When SMP is increased to 52 weeks, it is likely that SPP will also be increased. At present, in order to qualify, the father must have been continuously employed for 26 weeks at the 14th week before the EWC, be either the child's biological father or the mother's husband or partner, and have responsibility for the child's upbringing (reg 4). The employee must inform his employer (in writing if requested) of his intention to take leave by the 15th week before the EWC and tell the employer the week of the child's birth, amount of leave he wishes to take and the date on which he wants his leave to start (reg 6). It is likely that the new regulations will have similar qualifying conditions.

Similar provisions exist when a child is adopted. Section 4 of the Work and Families Act 2006 allows the Secretary of State to make regulations allowing the father of an adopted child to take up to 26 weeks' paternity leave and receive paternity pay (at the same rate as SMP). As with the new Paternity Leave Regulations, these rights are interchangeable with the right of the other partner to take adoption leave (below) and means that adoptive parents can share both the leave and the statutory pay. In addition, in respect of an adopted child, the Employment Act 2002 introduced the concept of adoption leave, which is based on maternity leave provisions. The length of the leave has been extended to 52 weeks by the MPLPAL (Amendment) Regulations 2006 (reg 13) and similarly a new reg 21 allows an employee to work for up to ten days without affecting his or her adoption leave. As with changes to the maternity leave provisions introduced by the Regulations, the adoptive parent must give eight weeks' notification of his or her return to work. Either adoptive parent can take the leave, the other being entitled to paternity leave. While similar to maternity leave in notification provisions, unlike maternity leave, an employee must be employed for 26 weeks by the time of notification of being matched with a child, for both ordinary and additional adoption leave. Statutory Adoption Pay is available for the same length of time as SMP and at the same rate. As with maternity leave, there is protection against dismissal or detriment for exercising rights to paternity or adoption leave.

While these rights will allow new parents the right to time off to be with their new offspring, perhaps the most important new right is the right to request flexible working, introduced by the Employment Act 2002 by the insertion of s 80F into the ERA 1996. This allows qualifying employees the right to apply to that employers for a change in the terms and conditions of employment in order to care for a child for whom the employee is responsible. Examples of such changes can be to hours of work, times of work or place of work to enable them to care for a child. To qualify, the employee must have 26 weeks' continuous service at the date of application. The changes must be requested before the 14th day before the child reaches the age of 6, or, if the child is disabled, 14 days before the child reaches the age of 18. The employer may reject the request on specified grounds, inter alia, a detrimental effect on the ability to meet customer demands and the burden of additional costs. There is protection against detriment and unfair dismissal.

The Work and Families Act 2006 (amending s 80F) has increased this right to include other carers. From April 2007 the right to request flexible working extended to any employee who is or expects to be caring for an adult who is married to, the partner or civil partner of the employee, is a near relative of the employee, or who does not fall into those categories but lives at the same address as the employee. 'Near relative' includes parents, parents-in-law, adult child, adopted adult child, siblings (including those who are in-laws), uncles, aunts, grandparents and step-relatives. The former

Department of Trade and Industry estimated that these changes will now mean that the right to request flexible working will extend to 80 per cent of carers.

It is submitted that this right to request flexible working is perhaps the most important, coupled with protection against less favourable treatment now given to part-time workers, and shows a clear commitment by the government to promote family-friendly policies. The extension of maternity leave, paternity leave and adoption leave all help parents at the start of a child's life, but the right to request flexible working will allow more employees to spend time at home discharging domestic responsibilities. The question that must be asked, however, is: do the provisions go far enough?

While on the face of it, the government seems committed to family-friendly policies, the reality may be different. The original parental leave provisions applied only to parents of children born after 15 December 1999, and it was only after a challenge by the TUC (*R v Secretary of State for Trade and Industry ex p TUC* (2001)) that the government extended the right to the parents of all children who were under the age of 5 on that date. The parental leave provisions, the provisions giving leave for dependants and the part-time worker protection were all introduced because of a requirement to implement EC directives and it may be questioned whether the government would have introduced these measures without that compulsion. Furthermore, the right to request flexible working is just that. There is no right to work flexibly, merely a right to request to do so, and a tribunal cannot question the employer's reason for refusal if it falls within the designated categories. Once a request has been rejected, no further request can be made for 12 months. All of this may lead a person to question whether the government does truly see family-friendly policies as central to its employment legislation.

It may also be questioned whether all of these new rights will allow the flexibility of working needed to balance work and family life. For many employees, flexible working will mean working fewer hours. This means the protection afforded to part-time workers is crucial. However, in order to prove less favourable treatment, the part-time worker must have a full-time comparator on the same or broadly similar work. A full-time worker on different work is not a valid comparator for the purposes of the Regulations. It is submitted that this is a major loophole in the Regulations, a loophole that was in the original EPA 1970, which severely restricted the number of women who could claim equal pay and which took some 11 years to remove.

Furthermore, it must be questioned how many employees can afford to exercise the rights above. While from April 2007 anyone with 26 weeks' continuity who takes paternity, maternity or adoptive leave can get the basic SMP rate, this is often far less than an employee's salary and many workers simply will not be able to take it. Parental leave remains unpaid. In addition, while many workers may wish to work more flexibly, the cost of child care while working may make this option prohibitive. While the rights may be in place, without adequate state-funded child care, such as is available in other EC countries, it may mean that the victory for those who wish to see a balance between home and working life is a hollow one.

Aim Higher ★

❖ After the publication of the White Paper and subsequent legislation, a number of articles were written about whether the provisions would be effective. Citing these in your answer would improve your marks – for example, Anderson (2003) 32 ILJ 37, Di Torella (2007) 36 ILJ 318, Dickens (2006) 35 ILJ 445 and James (2006) 35 ILJ 272.

8

INTRODUCTION

The common law rules on termination of an employment contract are important in that they apply to all employees but, more importantly, they are the only form of protection for an employee who does not have the right to sue for an unfair dismissal.

Termination is a large area on its own, but is wider than dismissal because it covers not only termination by the employer but also termination by operation of law and employee termination. In addition, questions relating to common law can arise in the context of statutory rights, particularly in relation to unfair dismissal and redundancy, as we shall see in Chapters 9 and 10. As such, the principles relating to common law termination really need to be understood when answering the type of questions seen in those two chapters.

For questions specifically on this area, general issues that the student needs to understand include:

- the concept of termination by operation of law;
- termination by agreement;
- repudiation;
- resignation;
- common law dismissal;
- reasons for dismissal;
- procedure for dismissal; and
- remedies.

As will be seen from the questions in this chapter, issues often raised are what type of termination has occurred and what are the available remedies. In particular, therefore, students should be familiar with:

- the consequences of finding that there is termination by operation of law or agreement;

❖ the automatic and elective theories in relation to repudiation;
❖ what constitutes a resignation or dismissal;
❖ the types of common law dismissal; and
❖ contractual and public law procedures and remedies.

Finally, as stated above, issues raised in this area need to be understood in relation to unfair dismissal and redundancy. Obviously, an employee cannot sue for unfair dismissal or a redundancy payment unless it can be shown that there is a dismissal. In some questions, therefore, the examiner may be looking for the relationship between common law and statutory termination.

Checklist ✔

Students should be familiar with the following areas:

■ the doctrine of frustration in relation to employment contracts;

■ the reality of termination by agreement – in particular, cases such as *Birch and Humber v University of Liverpool* (1985) *Caledonian Mining Co Ltd v Bassett* (1987) *Igbo v Johnson Matthey Chemicals Ltd* (1986)

■ repudiation – in particular, cases such as *Marshall (Thomas) (Exports) Ltd v Guinle* (1978) *Gunton v Richmond upon Thames London Borough Council* (1980) *London Transport Executive v Clarke* (1981) *Rigby v Ferodo Ltd* (1988);

■ the reality of resignation;

■ the concepts of summary dismissal and dismissal with notice;

■ the differences between common law and statute in relation to reasons and procedure for dismissal;

■ the difference between a breach of contractual procedures and natural justice, and the resultant remedies.

QUESTION 29

'These complications arise, and only arise, if there is grafted on to the old common law rule that a repudiated contract is only terminated by acceptance, an exception in cases of contracts of employment. In my view, any such exception is contrary to principle, unsupported by authority binding on this court and undesirable in practice.'
(Templeman LJ in *London Transport Executive v Clarke* (1981))

▷ Consider whether any such exception exists and the advantages of applying the
     orthodox elective approach to contracts of employment.

Answer Plan

This question falls into two separate parts: whether there are any cases in which
the automatic approach has been applied in cases of repudiation of an
employment contract and the advantages of applying the elective approach.

Particular points to discuss are:

❖   the normal common law doctrine (*Howard v Pickford Tool Co* (1951));
❖   cases in which the automatic theory has applied (particularly the
       judgments of Shaw LJ in *Gunton v Richmond upon Thames London Borough
       Council* (1980) and the House of Lords in *Rigby v Ferodo Ltd* (1988));
❖   the reinforcement of the common law position by statute;
❖   the advantages in adopting the elective approach, particularly in relation to
       continuity and statutory rights.

ANSWER

A repudiatory breach is a breach going to the root of the contract. Such a breach,
however, may have a variety of consequences. It may be a rejection of the original
contract, and bring into operation new terms – for example, a reduction in pay. In this
situation, the innocent party has two options. First, he can treat the breach as
terminating the contract and leave. In an employment context, in which the innocent
party is the employee, then in this situation, if he does not have the protection of
statute, he has resigned and can only sue for damages if the change was introduced
without the necessary notice being given. Second, he can treat the breach as a
variation in his terms and agree to continue the contract working under the new
terms. In this situation, there is a variation and, as such, no termination. In both of the
above situations, it is the innocent party who makes the choice and the contract will
not terminate until he accepts this as a consequence of the breach.

Such is the normal situation under contractual principles. Asquith LJ in *Howard v
Pickford Tool Co* (1951) said: 'An unaccepted repudiation is a thing writ in water and of
no value to anybody; it affords no legal rights of any sort or kind.' The problem in the
field of employment contracts, however, is that in some cases there is no real choice
on the part of the innocent party. If an employer wrongfully dismisses its employee,
for example, in practical terms the employee has no real choice as to whether to work
or not. In addition, at common law, the courts will not force parties to continue with a

contract for personal services (a position adopted by s 236 of the Trade Union and Labour Relations (Consolidation) Act (TULR(C)A) 1992). As such, it would appear that a repudiatory breach, such as a wrongful dismissal, terminates the contract immediately as acceptance by the employee is irrelevant.

Such an interpretation goes against established contractual principles and can have unfortunate consequences for the employee. For some time, however, the idea of automatic termination was accepted by the courts and contracts of employment were seen as the exception to the normal contractual rule. This view was expressed by Viscount Kilmuir LC in *Vine v National Dock Labour Board* (1957), and in *Sanders v Ernest Neale Ltd* (1974), Sir John Donaldson P stated that repudiation of a contract of employment 'terminates the contract without the necessity for acceptance by the injured party'.

Later cases have challenged the theory of automatic termination. Megarry VC, in *Marshall (Thomas) (Exports) Ltd v Guinle* (1978), argued that the automatic theory would give the guilty party the right to decide when the contract came to an end and so allow him to benefit from his wrongdoing (for example, an employer could wrongfully dismiss an employee to avoid him acquiring continuity to claim unfair dismissal). In *Gunton v Richmond-upon-Thames London Borough Council* (1980), the majority of the Court of Appeal favoured the elective theory, but stressed that, in reality, there may be little difference between the two theories, as often the employee has no option, in reality, but to accept the repudiation and that the rule of practice that contracts of employment should not be specifically enforced means that the employee is merely left with an action in damages, as he would be on an automatic termination. Shaw LJ, in *Gunton*, tried to find a middle ground by arguing that, in some situations, the nature of the repudiatory act was such that it automatically destroyed the contract and acceptance would be unnecessary. This appears to leave the way clear to say that in other situations, in which the contract has not been destroyed, acceptance would be necessary before the breach brought the contract to an end. The House of Lords, in *Rigby v Ferodo Ltd* (1988), limited cases to where an automatic termination could occur to a wrongful dismissal by the employer or a walkout by the employee who fails to return, although their Lordships declined to consider whether or not acceptance was required in other cases. In *Smith v Phil's TV Service* (1991), an employee walked out after a dispute with the employer. When he failed to show up for work the next day, the employer assumed he had resigned and wrote a letter accepting the resignation. The Employment Appeal Tribunal (EAT) held that a repudiatory breach by the employee would only terminate the contract when the employer had accepted it as such. The employer had accepted the termination of the contract by his letter and therefore there was a dismissal as this ended the relationship.

It will appear, therefore, that whether the automatic or elective theory applies to an employment contract is still undecided. It is, however, vitally important for the employee in relation to his statutory rights. First, if the elective theory applies, then the employee may be able to increase his continuity and so bring himself within the requirements to claim unfair dismissal or redundancy. While this may be beneficial, it can cause problems in determining the effective date of termination for the purposes of ensuring that a claim is presented to a tribunal in time, in that it can create uncertainty for both sides as to the date on which the relationship ended. On the other hand, if the automatic theory applies, this supports the idea of a constructive resignation – in other words, the employee behaves so badly that his contract terminates automatically because of his conduct. Such an interpretation would appear to go against statute for two reasons. In *London Transport Executive v Clarke* (1981), the Court of Appeal refused to accept that an employee's failure to return to work on a set date constituted a constructive resignation or self-dismissal. The argument of the Court was that statute, by s 95(1)(c) of the **Employment Rights Act (ERA) 1996**, created the concept of a constructive dismissal (where the employee resigns due to a repudiatory breach by the employer) but had not created the corollary. Furthermore, by that section, it is only when the employee resigns (that is, accepts the breach as terminating the contract) that a constructive dismissal takes place, so supporting the elective theory.

In addition, ss 238 and 238A of the TULR(C)A 1992 give certain protection from unfair dismissal for strikers. Such protection would not be available if the strike (repudiatory conduct by the employee) were to automatically terminate the contract. Adopting an elective theory gives further advantage in that it allows the party in breach to withdraw the breach before it is accepted and to restore the status quo. This may be favourable to either party. The employee who resigns in a temper can withdraw his resignation before it is accepted by the employer. Likewise, an employer can withdraw a fundamental change in terms before it is accepted by the employee, as in *Norwest Holst Group Administration Ltd v Harrison* (1985), and the employee will retain his job with no change in terms.

It would appear, therefore, that the elective theory has a number of advantages for the employee. This still leaves concern, however, as to the uncertainty it can cause in relation to the date of the dismissal and the limitation period on presenting a claim. While Clarke favoured the elective theory to avoid the concept of self-dismissal, the EAT, in *Brown v Southall and Knight* (1980) and *Robert Cort and Sons Ltd v Charman* (1981), refused to use the elective theory when determining the effective date of termination because of the wording of the (then) **Employment Protection (Consolidation) Act 1978** and the need for certainty in this area. McMullen ('A Synthesis of the Mode of Termination of Contracts of Employment' [1982] CLJ 110) suggests that this different approach, depending on the issue before the court, is the most logical. It would appear, therefore, that there are exceptions to the general rule that a repudiatory breach must be accepted as such by the innocent party before the contract will terminate. On the whole, however, the courts prefer the elective approach and, as seen above, this can act to the advantage of the innocent party.

QUESTION 30

The following has recently occurred at Mucktown Secondary School: Mr Logan, the PE teacher, was recently convicted of theft and sentenced to two years' imprisonment. During the time of the police investigation, Mr Logan was off sick for three months prior to his trial. At an appeal against sentence held one month later, his sentence was reduced to six months' imprisonment. His post had not been filled at the time of his release from prison and he is claiming a redundancy payment. The school argues that Mr Logan is no longer on the books. Mr Francis, a caretaker at the school, was recently found to have borrowed money from the school's petty cash box, although he returned the money the very next day. On one previous occasion, when he had done a similar thing, he was spared from disciplinary action on the signing of a statement, which read 'I understand that should I borrow or take money from my employers on any future occasion that my contract of employment will automatically terminate'. The school contends that by this recent act of borrowing from the school, Mr Francis has terminated his contract by agreement. Mr Francis is now claiming unfair dismissal.

▶ Advise Mr Logan and Mr Francis only on the issue of whether they have been dismissed.

Common Pitfalls ✗

◆ The main thing to note about this question is that while one party is claiming redundancy and the other unfair dismissal, the question is only asking the students to come to a decision as to whether the two parties have been dismissed and does not require any other discussion. This is a prime example of making sure that you read the question properly.

◆ Don't ignore other forms of termination that may be relevant.

Answer Plan

As the question is only looking at different forms of termination, topics that will need to be considered are:

- ❖ frustration and how the doctrine is applied to an employment contract;
- ❖ the judicial discussion on self-induced frustration and imprisonment;
- ❖ termination by agreement; and
- ❖ s 203 of the Employment Rights Act (ERA) 1996.

ANSWER

The question asks us to advise the two parties in relation to whether the situations in which they find themselves can be deemed to be a dismissal, and so allow Mr Logan to claim a redundancy payment and Mr Francis to claim an unfair dismissal. In situations of both redundancy and unfair dismissal, the employee must show he has been dismissed before he can enter a claim in an employment tribunal. The fact that there has been a dismissal does not necessarily mean that the employee is entitled to a redundancy payment or that the dismissal is unfair; establishing a dismissal merely opens up the tribunal jurisdiction.

Mr Logan was ill for three months and imprisoned for six months. The school argues that Mr Logan is no longer on the books and appears to be arguing that because of his illness, imprisonment or both, the contract has now been frustrated. Frustration occurs when, in the words of Streatfield J in *Morgan v Manser* (1948):

> ... there is an event or change of circumstances which is so fundamental as to be regarded by the law as striking to the root of the contract as a whole, and as going beyond what was contemplated by the parties.

Should an employment contract be frustrated, the contract terminates immediately on the happening of the frustrating event, with no liability on either party, as the law regards that neither party is at fault. The employee is not entitled to any pay after the frustrating event has occurred and, as frustration ends the contract automatically, the employee is not dismissed nor has he resigned. Two major events that may occur and frustrate the contract are illness and, potentially, imprisonment. The test to establish whether illness has led to a frustration was formulated by Donaldson P in *Marshall v Harland and Wolff Ltd* (1972) when he said that tribunals had to ask 'whether the nature of the employee's incapacity was such that further performance of his obligations was impossible or radically different from that originally intended when he entered the contract'. He then gave a list of factors that tribunals should consider when looking to see if frustration had occurred. These factors were added to in the later case of *Egg Stores Ltd v Leibovici* (1977) and have now been summarised and approved by the EAT in the case of *Williams v Watsons Luxury Coaches Ltd* (1990):

the court must be careful not to use the doctrine too easily; the date the frustration occurred; there are a number of factors which should be considered, which include the length of employment prior to the frustrating event and the length of future foreseeable employment; the nature of the job and the terms of employment; the nature, length and effect of illness and the prospect for recovery; the employer's need for a replacement; the risk of the employer incurring statutory liability to a replacement; the conduct of the employer; whether wages or sick pay have been paid and whether in all the circumstances a reasonable employer would have waited longer; the frustrating event has not been caused by the party seeking to rely on it.

In *Hart v AR Marshall and Sons (Bulwell) Ltd* (1977), the employee was a key worker, who was ill for 20 months and was replaced during his illness. The EAT held that his contract had been frustrated. By contrast, in *Hebden v Forsey and Sons* (1973), an employee was off for two years with the employer's agreement. There was insufficient work for him to do while he was sick and it was held that the contract had not been frustrated.

Applying the above to Mr Logan, while there are no facts as to how long he had been employed, there is no evidence that he intended to leave in the near future. He was not replaced and presumably sick pay would have been paid. Taking these factors into account, it is unlikely that the court would argue that his contract had been frustrated because of his three-month illness. In relation to his imprisonment, the court's attitude towards this has changed over the years. The problem that used to arise was whether imprisonment could be classed as self-induced frustration and therefore no frustration at all. In *Hare v Murphy Bros* (1974), Lord Denning said that where an employee had been imprisoned for 12 months, the contract was clearly frustrated and that it was not self-induced as the frustrating event was the imposition of the sentence and not the criminal behaviour. Later EATs, however, were in disagreement and, in *Norris v Southampton City Council* (1982), the EAT decided that, as the imprisonment had been caused by the employee's own misconduct, there could be no frustration and that the employee was guilty of repudiatory conduct that, if accepted by the employer as ending the contract, would lead to an employer termination and therefore a dismissal. The Court of Appeal resolved the issue in *Shepherd (FC) v Jerrom* (1986) when it decided that a six-month prison sentence could frustrate a four-year contract of apprenticeship. Balcombe LJ accepted Denning's argument in *Hare* that it was the imposition of the sentence that was the frustrating event; Lawton LJ and Mustill LJ argued that a self-induced frustration only had no effect on the contract when a party was seeking to rely on his own misconduct. Given that it was the employer in *Shepherd* arguing that there had been a frustration, this could not be self-induced.

Where does this leave Mr Logan? While *Shepherd* establishes that imprisonment can be a frustration, it may be possible to distinguish Mr Logan's situation. In *Shepherd*, a six-month prison sentence frustrated a four-year contract, but we have no evidence that Mr Logan was on a fixed-term contract. In Shepherd, the sentence was one-eighth of the employment period, but Mr Logan may have been employed for some years before his misdeeds and intended to stay for some time afterwards. It is also important to know when Mr Logan was imprisoned. If this was during the summer vacation, given that he would probably not have served the full six months, then the imprisonment may have had little or no effect on the performance of his duties. It is suggested, therefore, that *Shepherd* can be distinguished and that this particular imprisonment will not frustrate the contract.

This leads to one final question. Could the illness and imprisonment together frustrate the contract? Mr Logan was ill for three months and then served his sentence. If he served the whole of his sentence, he would have been away from work for nine months. In *Chakki v United Yeast Co Ltd* (1982), it was held that an 11-month prison sentence could frustrate a contract (although not proved on the facts). It is submitted that if Mr Logan was off for nine months and this affected the performance of his work, the attitude and actions of the employer must be examined. If the employer had no intention of allowing him to return and did not maintain contact with him, it is possible to distinguish *Hebden*, although no replacement was appointed. Such a question would be for the tribunal to decide.

In respect of Mr Francis, Muckton is arguing that there is a termination by agreement. While the courts are prepared to recognise such terminations, Donaldson P in *McAlwane v Broughton Estates Ltd* (1973) said that tribunals should be careful when finding an agreement to terminate and ensure that the employee was aware of the financial implications of doing so. In cases in which the employee has received some financial consideration, the courts are more prepared to find that there is a genuine agreement. For example, in *Birch and Humber v University of Liverpool* (1985), two employees who volunteered for early retirement and acquired certain financial advantages were deemed to have mutually agreed to terminate their contracts and they had not been dismissed for redundancy even though their posts were not filled. A similar conclusion was reached in *Scott v Coalite Fuels and Chemicals Ltd* (1988). On the other hand, an employee who resigned because he was told by his employer that he would be made redundant was held to be dismissed because his employer's conduct made it clear that he would be dismissed in the near future (*Caledonian Mining Co Ltd v Bassett* (1987)).

The problem in Mr Francis's case is that, before he borrowed the money, he appeared to sign a document agreeing that his employment would end should there be a repetition of his previous conduct. In the early case of *British Leyland (UK) Ltd v*

Ashraf (1978), an employee signed a similar document when he was given five weeks' unpaid leave to visit his family in Pakistan. He agreed that should he fail to return on the due date, his contract would terminate automatically. The EAT held that there had been an agreement to terminate. Later cases tried to distinguish *Ashraf*, but the challenge came in the Court of Appeal in *Igbo v Johnson Matthey Chemicals Ltd* (1986). The Court held that a document similar to that in *Ashraf* was contrary to s 203 of the ERA 1996, and was therefore void. On the basis of *Igbo*, therefore, it would appear on the face of it that the agreement Mr Francis signed is contrary to s 203 and, as such, Muckton has terminated his contract and so dismissed him.

Muckton may try and argue on the basis of *Logan Salton v Durham County Council* (1989). In this case, the employee had been redeployed as a result of disciplinary proceedings. Further disciplinary proceedings were to be initiated, with a recommendation that the employee be dismissed. Prior to this, the union representative negotiated with the employer that the employment be terminated and a car loan waived out. After the agreement, the employee sued for unfair dismissal on the basis that the agreement was contrary to s 203. The EAT distinguished *Igbo* on the basis that there was a separate agreement to terminate that did not depend on the happening of some future event, which was supported by consideration. The parties had therefore mutually terminated their contract. On the facts of Mr Francis's case, the agreement did depend on the occurrence of some future event, but there was consideration in that he was spared from disciplinary action on the first occasion. While in *Logan*, there was financial consideration in wiping out the car loan, the employee was also spared disciplinary action and dismissal and it could be that the tribunal will hold that Mr Francis's case can be distinguished from *Igbo* and that the agreement is not void. If this is the conclusion, Mr Francis will have agreed to terminate his contract and has not therefore been dismissed. His only possibility is to rely on the comments of Donaldson P in *McAlwane* and argue that the agreement was entered into under pressure and that he was not aware of the financial consequences of signing the agreement. This may sway the tribunal to find that Mr Francis signed the agreement because of the fear of the consequences (that is, potential dismissal) and, as such, there is no real agreement at all.

QUESTION 31

Remedies for wrongful dismissal are limited by the restricted measure of damages recoverable in many cases. There are, however, a number of exceptions that mitigate this harsh general rule and thus the common law provides sufficient protection for those employees unprotected by unfair dismissal provisions.

▶ Critically evaluate this statement.

Answer Plan

This type of question can be dangerous if not read properly because it is the sort of question in which students use the 'shovel' approach – that is, write all they know about the exceptions with no critical analysis. The question is asking for a discussion of the exceptions to the general rule that damages are restricted in a wrongful dismissal claim, and asks the student to evaluate the statement that therefore the common law provides adequate protection for employees. To merely list the exceptions is insufficient.

Issues that need to be considered are therefore:

❖   the definition of a wrongful dismissal;
❖   the restrictions on the award of damages in respect of a wrongful dismissal claim;
❖   the exceptions to the general rule; and
❖   an evaluation of whether the exceptions give employees sufficient protection.

ANSWER

A wrongful dismissal is a dismissal that is in breach of contract, in that either no notice has been given or short notice has been given in circumstances under which the employer has no right to ignore the employee's notice rights. Until the employee has the continuity to claim unfair dismissal (normally one year), his only rights are in contract and therefore should that contract be broken, he has the right to sue for damages for his loss. His loss, however, is restricted by the notice he is entitled to receive under his contract. If an employee is entitled to three weeks' notice and is dismissed with one week's notice, his loss is two weeks' net pay, because his employer at common law has the right to terminate the contract with three weeks' notice and his breach has only caused the employee to lose two of those weeks. As such, the employee's damages are restricted to his actual loss.

In some cases, the courts have argued that the employee's actual loss is greater than his notice period. Therefore if, for example, the employee has a contractual disciplinary procedure that has not been observed, his damages may reflect his wages for the length of time it would have taken the employer to observe the procedure in addition to his notice period (*Boyo v Lambeth LBC* (1995)). How far this will be an argument in wrongful dismissal claims since the introduction, in 2004, of statutory disciplinary and grievance procedures has yet to be seen, although the government, in introducing those procedures, did not avail itself of the opportunity to make the statutory procedures contractual, arguably because of the fear of breach of contract claims. In addition, where the employee has also been deprived of a benefit for which he would have qualified had he been given the correct notice, he may also be compensated for that loss. For example, in *Silvey v Pendragon plc* (2001), if the employee had been given the correct notice he would have reached the age of 55, which had an effect on his pension, and his damages reflected this loss. Until recently, this principle did not extend to loss of discretionary benefits (*Laverack v Woods of Colchester Ltd* (1967)); however, *Laverack* has since been departed from. In *Clarke v BET plc* (1997), Clarke was a chief executive on a fixed-term contract. His salary was subject to discretionary pay rises and bonuses. He was wrongfully dismissed and the question for the EAT was whether the discretionary pay rises and bonuses should form part of the award for damages. On the basis of *Laverack*, the answer should have been in the negative; however, the EAT said that, given that such payments had been made in the past, damages should be calculated on what he would have been paid if the employers had continued to exercise their discretion in good faith. Similarly, in *Clarke v Nomura International plc* (2000), a highly successful trader, who received large discretionary bonuses based on his trading, was dismissed and received no bonus for his final year, even though he had continued to be successful. Burton J held that the bonus should be part of his award of damages (despite the fact that the dismissal was lawful). However, unlike the EAT in *Clarke v BET plc*, he did not base his argument on the duty of trust and confidence but on the principle of perversity, arguing that no reasonable employer would have failed to exercise its discretion and not pay the bonus. This argument was adopted by the Court of Appeal in *Mallone v BPB Industries plc* (2002), in which an executive who was lawfully dismissed had his rights to share options cancelled by the company (a right the company had under the terms of the contract). The Court of Appeal granted damages for the loss of the share options on the basis that the company had acted irrationally in cancelling them, particularly as it could provide no evidence of the basis on which the decision had been made.

The introduction of perverse or irrational conduct on the part of the employer almost seems akin to the requirement of reasonableness in an unfair dismissal claim. Whereas traditionally an employer in a common law dismissal situation merely has to give the required notice (or wages in lieu), this importation of looking at the employer's conduct appears to restrict the previous unfettered actions by the employer. It is submitted that there is a vast difference between perverse and unreasonable actions, but the Court of Appeal in *Mallone* made two important points that could be developed further. First, the Court found the employer's action to be irrational, not perverse. It is submitted that this is a lower standard than that in *Clarke v BET plc*, and is arguably more akin to the requirement of reasonableness.

The Court also made the point that it had reached this decision because of the lack of evidence showing how the employer's decision had been reached. If these two strands are developed, it could mean that case law in the area of unfair dismissal, which creates requirements for the employer to show evidence to support its decision to dismiss and to treat the employee reasonably in terms of a hearing, may be transposed into the common law. Arguably, this may already be the case given the introduction of the statutory procedures, despite the fact that the government declined to make them contractual.

In addition to the discussion above, there are other situations in which the employee may get damages in excess of notice provisions. On the basis of *Silvey* above, where the employer's breach of contract prevents the employee from gaining sufficient continuity for statutory protection, continuity that he would have acquired if the contract had not been broken, his damages should reflect this loss. After a number of cases questioning whether this should be the case, the EAT in *Raspin v United News Shops Ltd* (1999) allowed an award representing the loss of his potential claim for unfair dismissal. While this is in line with previous cases, such as *Silvey*, it will apply only in two situations: first, where if the employer had given the correct notice, the employee would have acquired the correct continuity; and second, where a contractual disciplinary procedure has not been observed and such observance would have meant that the employee would have the required continuity at the time of his dismissal. As stated above, the impact of the statutory procedures on such claims has yet to be seen. It should also be noted that such a claim cannot lie where the employer has a contractual right to pay wages in lieu as he is not in breach but exercising a contractual right.

There are two other potential exceptions to the rule that an employee is entitled only to damages to represent his lack of notice. If the employee is on a fixed-term contract, where there is no express contractual notice clause, it is likely that the courts would hold that the intention of the parties was that the contract should run its full term and not imply into the contract the statutory minimum notice period under s 86 of the Employment Rights Act (ERA) 1996. In that case, the employee's loss is the full term of the contract and his damages would reflect this.

A further potential exception lies where damages may be awarded in respect of the manner of the dismissal. The House of Lords, in *Addis v Gramophone Co Ltd* (1909), held that an employee was not entitled to damages for injury to feelings nor for the fact that the manner of his dismissal had damaged his reputation and made it difficult for him to find another job. However, in *Malik v BCCI* (1997), the BCCI bank collapsed, owing $6 billion. It had been having problems for some time, but these problems had been hidden by the fraudulent dealings of the senior officers of the bank. These facts became public knowledge. As a result of the collapse, all 1,400 employees lost their jobs and two sued claiming damages for injury to their reputation and their employment prospects as a result of their association with a dishonest and corrupt employer. The House of Lords upheld their potential claim on the basis that the conduct of the employer was a breach of the duty of trust. This was despite the fact that the employees did not know of the breach until after the employment ended. *Addis* was distinguished on two grounds: first, it was a claim relating to the manner of dismissal, whereas *Malik* was a claim for future loss; and second, *Addis* was decided before the development of the duty of trust and confidence.

Malik appeared to be opening up the way for additional claims in wrongful dismissal cases – that of so called 'stigma' damages – in that the manner of dismissal breached the duty of trust and confidence. (The claim, in fact, eventually failed on the basis of causation – *BCCI SA (in liquidation) v Ali* (2002)). This, however, was stopped by the later House of Lords' decision in *Johnson v Unisys Ltd* (2001). In this case, an ex-employee sued for damages in respect of a nervous breakdown and consequent inability to work, caused by the manner of his dismissal. The House of Lords said that such damages were not available for two reasons. First, the decision in *Malik*, that there had been a breach of the duty of trust and confidence, related to breaches that had occurred during the employment, but such a duty did not survive the termination of the contract and therefore the manner of dismissal could not be a breach. The second reason was that the law should not circumvent the statutory rights of unfair dismissal for which there are compensation limits. Unfair dismissal, according to Lord Hoffman, is the proper action in which to claim compensation for the manner of dismissal.

While *Johnson* raises issues of when the contract actually terminates, the present law is demonstrated by the Court of Appeal in *McCabe v Cornwall County Council* (2004). In that case, the Court said that the issue is to see if there is any damage flowing from the breach of the duty, which is separate from the damage flowing from the manner of the dismissal. The latter cannot be compensated for.

So do the exceptions to the general rule provide adequate protection at common law? While *Raspin* provides some protection, it will apply only in limited circumstances, and the same can be said for many of the other exceptions. The developments seen in the *Clarke* and *Mallone* cases show that the equivalent of statutory principles may be imported into the common law, but, it is suggested that these cases are based on unusual facts and the principles may be limited to such facts and unlikely to aid the average employee. *Malik* opened up potential claims for damages, but *Johnson* clearly stemmed the flow. As such, the average employee, suing for wrongful dismissal, will still only get the wages owed under his notice and, as such, the common law does not provide sufficient protection.

Aim Higher

❖   There have been a number of articles discussing remedies for wrongful dismissal and for those who do not have protection from unfair dismissal. These critique the existing remedies and thus can add to your discussion – for example, Fredman and Lee (1986) 15 ILJ 15 and Fredman and Morris (1991) 107 LQR 298.

QUESTION 32

Robert, Tom and David work for Prior Products Ltd, a company specialising in garden furniture. Recently, the following events took place.

Robert, who has worked for Prior Products for six months, was given two days' notice of dismissal and was told that he was being sacked for incapability. He was never warned that he was incapable of doing the job. During his notice period, Robert sabotaged some machinery, a fact not discovered by Prior Products until three weeks after he had left.

Tom, who worked for the company for nine months, has always been a practical joker. Last week, he had an argument with his manager, during which the manager said: 'I can't stand you joking around any longer and neither can the bosses, just clear off.' Tom replied: 'If you think I'm staying where I'm not wanted, you've got another think coming.' With that, Tom left. The next day, Tom received his P45 with a note from the company accepting his resignation. The works rules state that all resignations must be in writing.

David has been employed for 11 months. His contract entitles him to four weeks' notice and contains a disciplinary procedure, entitling him to a hearing and an appeal. He was given two weeks' notice of dismissal last week. The reason given for his dismissal is bad timekeeping. He feels that this is unjustified and has asked to exercise his right of appeal contained in the contractual disciplinary procedures, but this has been refused.

▶   Advise Robert, Tom and David.

Common Pitfalls ✗

❖ Note that none of the parties has the required continuity to claim unfair dismissal and thus the question is about common law dismissal and not unfair dismissal.

❖ Another common pitfall is that the concept of constructive dismissal only applies where the employee is protected by unfair dismissal, and therefore generally if the employee has less than 12 months' continuity and leaves, it will be considered resignation.

Answer Plan

All of them have been employed for less than one year and so the question relates to the common law and not the statutory provisions. The question also raises the issue of remedies, particularly in relation to David.

Issues which the student should consider are:

❖ statutory notice provisions in s 86 of the Employment Rights Act (ERA) 1996;
❖ the effect at common law of misconduct during notice;
❖ what action by the employer constitutes a dismissal;
❖ what action by the employee constitutes a resignation;
❖ the effect at common law of a breach of contractual disciplinary procedures; and
❖ remedies – particularly the availability of an injunction.

ANSWER

None of the employees at present have the necessary one-year continuity of employment to claim an unfair dismissal, so all of their rights will arise under common law. At first glance, it would appear that all the employees will wish to sue for damages for wrongful dismissal. A more detailed examination of the individual cases is necessary, however, to determine whether claims for wrongful dismissal lie.

Robert has been employed for six months. There is no evidence in the problem that there is a notice provision in his contract and therefore the statutory minimum notice provided by s 86 of the ERA 1996 applies. Section 86(1)(a) provides that for a person employed for more than four weeks, but less than two years, the statutory minimum notice period is one week. If Robert's contract gives a longer notice period, then the contractual notice applies. If the contractual notice is shorter than the statutory notice, the statutory notice applies and the contractual provision is void. This means that, whatever may or may not be in Robert's contract, by giving him two days' notice, Prior Products is in breach of the relevant notice provision and, on the face of it, it would appear that Robert has been wrongfully dismissed. Robert, however, sabotaged some machinery during his two-day notice period.

At common law, the employer does not have to have a reason to dismiss, but merely has to give the correct amount of notice. In certain situations, however, the employer does not have to give notice and this is where the employee is guilty of gross misconduct or gross neglect. Furthermore, whereas under unfair dismissal provisions, the employer must have a reason that justifies the dismissal at the time he dismissed, the same is not true at common law and an original wrongful dismissal can be retrospectively made lawful if the employer discovers a reason after dismissal that would justify it dismissing instantly.

In the old case of *Ridgway v Hungerford Market* (1835), an employee, while under notice of dismissal, committed an act of gross misconduct. It was held that while the original dismissal had been wrongful because insufficient notice had been given, his misconduct justified instant dismissal and therefore rendered the original wrongful dismissal lawful. In a similar case, *Boston Deep Sea Fishing and Ice Co v Ansell* (1888), the misconduct was not discovered until some time after the dismissal had taken effect, but again the original wrongful dismissal was retrospectively rendered lawful. Applying these cases to Robert's situation, without doubt, his act of sabotage is gross misconduct and, therefore, while originally his dismissal was wrongful because of insufficient notice, his actions have now made his dismissal lawful and he will be unable to sue for damages.

The question in Tom's case is, first, whether the words of the manager constitute a dismissal. The problem here is that the manager has not used normal words to signify a dismissal, but told Tom that he and the bosses are fed up and that he should clear off. In situations like these, the tribunal will look at the intention behind the words. Cases such as *Futty v Brekkes Ltd* (1974) and *Davy v Collins Builders Ltd* (1974) show that swear words used in the heat of an argument do not necessarily constitute a dismissal when the intention of the employer is looked at, together with the situation in which they are spoken and the working environment the employee comes from. In *Tanner v Kean* (1978), the employer lost his temper with an employee and said: 'That's it, you're finished with me.' The EAT decided that these words were spoken in anger and not intended to be a dismissal. Likewise, in *Martin v Yeoman Aggregates Ltd* (1983), an employer told the employee to leave after he refused to obey an order, but within five minutes, he recanted his words and suspended the employee instead. The employee insisted on treating himself as dismissed. Kilner Brown J said that it was a matter of common sense, vital to good industrial relations, that either party should be able to retract words spoken in the heat of the moment. On the basis of the above, therefore, it is unlikely that the tribunal would interpret the words 'clear off' as a dismissal, particularly as they appear to have been spoken in anger and Tom left without giving the manager time to withdraw them.

This leads to the second question. Do Tom's words and actions constitute a resignation? The works rules state that resignations must be in writing and therefore it would appear that a verbal resignation will be insufficient, although the employee can always waive the right to a written resignation if he wishes. In Tom's situation, he appears to have reacted in the heat of the moment and it is debatable whether he intended to resign. As such, it could be argued, at best, that his words were ambiguous. In such situations, the tribunals again apply a common sense approach. In *Kwik Fit (GB) Ltd v Lineham* (1992), the employee, Mr Lineham, a manager, used the depot toilet on the way home from the pub one night. This was not contrary to any rules and he reactivated the alarm. The security staff reported him and a director gave him a written warning in front of a junior colleague. Lineham threw down his keys, walked out and did not return to work the next day, so the employer sent him a letter confirming termination of the employment. In a subsequent unfair dismissal claim, the employer argued that Lineham had resigned. The tribunal found that there was an ambiguous resignation and the burden therefore fell to the employer to establish the intention of the employee. The EAT held that the employer was not under such a heavy burden unless there were special circumstances, but where these existed, the employer should wait a reasonable time before accepting the resignation at face value. In Lineham's case, special circumstances existed and therefore the employee had not resigned; the contract had been terminated by the employer.

In Tom's case, the words are not specific. He did not say, for example, 'I am resigning', but merely appeared to react angrily to the words spoken by the manager. As such, on the basis of *Lineham*, it could be argued that the words were spoken in anger and that there were special circumstances. The employer should have waited a reasonable time to establish Tom's intention. In Tom's case, the employer sent his P45 the next day (as in *Lineham*). It is submitted that this is not a reasonable time and that the sending of the P45 constituted an employer termination and thus a dismissal. As with Robert, Tom is entitled to at least one week's notice, unless his conduct in joking around can be construed as gross misconduct. If he is not guilty of gross misconduct during his employment and the court feels that his reaction to the manager's words is not gross misconduct, then Tom is entitled to one week's pay as damages.

David, by the time his notice expires, will be two weeks short of continuity for unfair dismissal. In his case, there are two potential breaches of contract on the part of his employer: the short notice that he has been given and the refusal to allow him to pursue a contractual disciplinary procedure. In David's case, unlike Robert and Tom, the contract gives better notice rights than s 86 of the ERA 1996 and therefore the contract will prevail. On the assumption that David's conduct during his employment does not amount to gross misconduct, David is entitled to four weeks' notice and therefore can sue for two weeks' pay.

This leads to the second breach. David is entitled to pursue an appeal against dismissal by his contract and the employer has refused to let him exercise his contractual right. If he had been given the correct amount of notice, he would have the continuity to claim unfair dismissal. Likewise, if he had been given a hearing and allowed to pursue his contractual right of appeal, it could be that the process would not have been completed before David had been employed for 12 months, although if the appeal confirmed his dismissal, then the date of termination would be the original date of dismissal and not the date of the appeal (*Sainsbury (J) Ltd v Savage* (1981)).

If there is no evidence to support the employer's argument that David is a bad time-keeper, this could affect the remedies he can claim. In *Jones v Lee and Guilding* (1980), the employee was dismissed without being allowed to exercise his contractual right to a hearing. The Court of Appeal granted him an injunction restraining the employers from purporting to dismiss the employee until the hearing had been granted. In contrast, in *Gunton v Richmond upon Thames London Borough Council* (1980), the employee was dismissed with one month's notice although his contractual disciplinary procedure had not been fully implemented. The Court of Appeal held that his loss included a reasonable period in which it would have taken his employer to implement the disciplinary procedures fully and, in *Robert Cort and Sons Ltd v Charman* (1981), it was stated obiter that damages may include a sum to cover the loss of unfair dismissal compensation, if the nature of the dismissal was such that the employee had been excluded such protection. The later case of *Raspin v United News Shops Ltd* (1999) confirms that this is the case.

In David's case, it would appear that he has had no hearing whatsoever, despite the right in his contract. The court may therefore adopt the approach taken in *Jones v Lee and Guilding* and issue an injunction to prevent the employers from dismissing him until he has been granted a hearing, provided that the criteria necessary for an injunction exist – that is, that damages are an inadequate remedy and that there is no loss of trust and confidence in the employee (*Wadcock v London Borough of Brent* (1990)). Alternatively, the court may award damages in excess of two weeks' pay either on the basis that it would take longer than two weeks to instigate the procedures (*Gunton*) or to compensate for the loss of unfair dismissal protection (*Raspin*).

Unfair Dismissal

INTRODUCTION

There can be few employment law examination papers that do not contain at least one question on unfair dismissal. Sometimes, essay-type questions are set in this area, but more often than not the questions are problems. There is a very simple way to break down unfair dismissal problems, which leads the student through the question logically and should help to identify which particular area the problem concentrates upon.

Thus, students should ask themselves the following questions:

❖ has the employee the required continuity?
❖ is the employee excluded from the statute?
❖ has the employee been dismissed?
❖ has the employer got a statutory fair reason to dismiss?
❖ has the employer acted reasonably?

If students work through the above questions in relation to each party, there should not be too many problems. Questions in this area can concentrate on any of the issues above.

Therefore, students should understand:

❖ issues relating to continuity;
❖ the effective date of termination;
❖ exclusions under the statute;
❖ the definition of dismissal in s 95 of the Employment Rights Act (ERA) 1996;
❖ the statutory fair reasons for dismissal;
❖ the automatically unfair reasons for dismissal;
❖ the concept of reasonableness; and
❖ remedies.

It should be noted that, when considering the question of dismissal, the common law concepts dealt with in Chapter 8 are just as applicable in this area. An employee can hardly claim unfair dismissal if he has not been dismissed. It is necessary, therefore, to understand the different forms of termination before tackling an unfair dismissal question.

Checklist ✔

Students should be familiar with the following areas:

- weeks that do/do not break continuity;
- the effect of a change of employer on continuity;
- classes of excluded employees – particularly cases relating to normal retirement age;
- the meaning of dismissal, including constructive dismissal;
- the six statutory fair reasons – capability and qualifications, conduct, redundancy, redundancy, statutory restriction and some other substantial reason;
- the concept of a fair decision and procedural fairness;
- automatically unfair dismissals; and
- the remedies of reinstatement, re-engagement and financial compensation.

QUESTION 33

Until recently, Bill was a senior manager at Gaumont Restaurants, a company that operates restaurants in hotels. He had worked for the company for three years. Four weeks ago, after a company function, Bill, who was staying in the Dandelion Hotel for the night, invited two of his colleagues back to the hotel for a drink. Gaumont operates the restaurant in the Dandelion. A security guard, who worked for Dandelion, told Bill and his colleagues to leave the bar as it was closing. Bill said they would just finish their drinks, whereupon the guard removed their drinks and threatened to call the police. Bill's two colleagues left the bar, but Bill remonstrated with the guard about his behaviour to customers. There were no witnesses to that conversation. Bill then complained to the hotel deputy manager about the guard's behaviour.

The next day, Bill's employer received a complaint about the incident. In the complaint the guard stated that Bill had said he was a big boss in Gaumont, and would ensure that the guard lost his job and that Gaumont would pull out of the contract with Dandelion. He also stated that Bill was very drunk and very abusive. Bill's boss immediately suspended him and set a disciplinary hearing for three days later. The suspension letter said he was being suspended for alleged gross misconduct and included a copy of the alcohol policy, which states that anyone who is drunk on company premises is guilty of gross misconduct. Bill received copies of interviews conducted with certain parties. Both of his colleagues stated that the guard was very rude. The deputy manager stated that the guard had told him that Bill was drunk and abusive and had threatened to lose him his job. The deputy manager further stated that Bill had complained to him about the guard's behaviour and that, at the time of the complaint, Bill was not drunk. The guard, when interviewed, said that he was very polite to Bill and his colleagues, that Bill was very drunk, and that Bill had said he was a manager of Gaumont and would lose him his job.

At the disciplinary hearing, Bill's boss told him he was being disciplined for gross misconduct, and when Bill asked for an explanation, his boss told him he should know. He also refused to let Bill call any witnesses (in breach of the company disciplinary procedures). He told Bill he would make a decision after further investigation. Bill has now received a letter dismissing him for gross misconduct.

▶ Advise Bill.

Answer Plan

This is a question that goes to the heart of unfair dismissal. It is a complex question that needs to be broken down into its constituent parts, and raises questions on whether the employer had a reason to dismiss and whether the dismissal was procedurally fair.

Particular issues to be considered are:

- ❖ whether the employer had already concluded that Bill was guilty;
- ❖ the implications of *British Home Stores (BHS) v Burchell* (1980);
- ❖ the effect of the ACAS Code of Practice on Disciplinary and Grievance Procedures 2009.

ANSWER

Bill has the necessary continuity to claim unfair dismissal, and it is clear that he has been dismissed. In order for an employer to fairly dismiss an employee, he must have a statutory fair reason under s 98 of the Employment Rights Act (ERA) 1996. In addition, the tribunal must be satisfied that an employer has acted reasonably or unreasonably in treating that reason as sufficient reason to dismiss (s 98(4) of the ERA 1996). The interpretation of the predecessor of s 98(4) was given by Browne-Wilkinson J in *Iceland Frozen Foods v Jones* (1983), which introduced the 'band of reasonable responses' test. In other words, if dismissal is one of the sanctions a reasonable employer would have employed, the dismissal is fair. While this was doubted as a correct interpretation in *Haddon v Van Den Bergh Foods* (1999), the Court of Appeal restored the test in *Post Office v Foley*, and *HSBC v Madden* (2000). As such, this means that whether the employer is acting reasonably falls to two issues: is the decision to dismiss a fair sanction based on the employee's conduct, and did the employer act in a way that was procedurally fair in line with the ACAS Code of Practice on Disciplinary and Grievance Procedures 2009? While the Code is not legally enforceable, by s 207 of the Trade Union and Labour Relations (Consolidation) Act (TULR(C)A) 1992, a tribunal is required to take the provisions of the Code into account.

On the face of it, Bill's employer appears to have a statutory fair reason under s 98(2)(b) – that is, the conduct of his employee; however, *BHS v Burchell* (1980) has stated that the employer must have a genuine belief, based on reasonable grounds after a reasonable investigation, that the employee is guilty. If we analyse what happened in Bill's case it can be argued that the employer does not satisfy the *Burchell* test. A complaint has been made about Bill's behaviour. This relates to: (a) his being drunk; and (b) the comments he made to the security guard.

In relation to the allegation that Bill was drunk as stated by the security guard, this was refuted by the hotel manager and neither of Bill's colleagues mentioned it in their interviews. The suspension letter stated that Bill was being suspended for gross misconduct and included mention of the alcohol policy, but apart from the allegation of the security guard, there is no evidence that Bill was drunk, nor was he on company premises. It is in the policy that being drunk on company premises is gross misconduct and the Dandelion Hotel is not owned by Gaumont. Furthermore, there is evidence that the security guard has lied. First, he said he was polite to Bill and his colleagues. This is rebutted by not only Bill but also the colleagues with whom he was drinking. Second, the guard stated in his complaint that Bill had said he was a big boss in Gaumont and that he would lose him his job and pull the contract between Gaumont and Dandelion. However, he did not mention this second point when he spoke to the hotel deputy manager, and when interviewed, he said Bill had told him he was a manager. Third, he stated that Bill was drunk and abusive. But, as already mentioned, this was rebutted by the hotel manager and was not mentioned by Bill's colleagues. Even if Bill was drunk, he was not on company premises and thus not in breach of the alcohol policy. As such, in relation to the first aspect of the complaint, it cannot be said that the employer has a genuine belief, based on reasonable grounds, of Bill's guilt.

In relation to the second part of the complaint, again it can be argued that the employer cannot have a genuine belief based on reasonable grounds. Bill's two colleagues did not overhear the conversation that Bill had with the guard after they left, but said that even though the guard was very rude, Bill was polite back to him. Thus, while the conversation was not witnessed, the evidence of Bill's colleagues suggests that he would not have been abusive. Furthermore, the differences between the guard's complaint and his interview also suggest that he was lying. The contradictions between his complaint, his later statement and the comments of both the hotel deputy manager and Bill's colleagues were never pursued. This suggests that the investigation was, at best, perfunctory. As such, given that the conversation was not witnessed, given that the inconsistencies in the guard's complaint and interview were not examined, nor the inconsistencies with his version of events and those of the deputy manager and Bill's colleagues, it is argued that in relation to the allegation about Bill's abusive behaviour, the employer cannot have a genuine belief, based on reasonable grounds after a reasonable investigation. Thus the employer does not have a statutory fair reason for dismissal under s 98 of the ERA 1996.

In addition, from *Burchell*, any investigation must be reasonable and the Code states that good disciplinary procedures should require management to investigate fully before any disciplinary action is taken. To conduct a full investigation, the employer must gather all the evidence so that it can make a reasoned and fair decision (*Scottish Daily Record and Sunday Mail* (1986) and *Ltd v Laird* (1996)). As has already been discussed above, it is unlikely that a tribunal would find the investigation in Bill's case to be a full one and one where all the evidence has been obtained.

The Code states that at any hearing the employee should know what he is being disciplined for, the evidence against him should be gone through and the employee should be given an opportunity to present his side of the case. In addition, an employee should also be allowed to ask questions, present evidence, call witnesses and be given an opportunity to raise points about any information provided by the witnesses. In Bill's case, it was unclear from the letter whether he was being investigated for a breach of the alcohol policy or because of the alleged conversation with the security guard. Further, although he had the statements made by the witnesses he was not allowed to call any or call the guard to challenge him about the contradictions in his complaint and subsequent statement. This was not only a breach of the Code, but also a breach of the company disciplinary procedures. Furthermore, Bill has been dismissed without any notification of his right of appeal and, although this is not clear, it appears that the employer may have carried out further investigation of which Bill has not had any detail. Should the decision to dismiss have been made on new evidence, of which Bill has no knowledge or been given the opportunity to refute, this is again a breach of the Code.

It therefore appears that Bill has a strong case for unfair dismissal. The employer has not conducted an adequate investigation, which leaves doubt as to whether it has a reason under s 95. It did not explain to Bill the conduct that had led to the disciplinary action being taken, it did not allow Bill to call witnesses in breach of both the Code and the company's own procedures, it appears to have made a decision to dismiss based on evidence that Bill has not been given an opportunity to rebut and it has denied Bill a right of appeal in breach of the statutory discipline and grievance procedures. Bill has therefore been unfairly dismissed.

QUESTION 34

Rita and Mavis both worked for Alec Machine Tools Ltd.

Rita was the machine shop floor supervisor. She was dismissed when she missed a shift because she was visiting her sick mother in hospital. After an internal appeal, she was reinstated at a lower grade, with a consequent reduction in salary, after consideration had been given to the fact that:

(a) she had worked there for 15 years;
(b) she had an exemplary work record; and
(c) she had arranged for another supervisor to cover her shift and no disruption to the business occurred.

Rita resigned after the appeal.

Mavis worked on the shop floor for five years. Due to foreign imports, Alec had been striving to produce more products in less time and the workers were ignoring safety procedures – such as fencing machinery – to meet targets Alec had set. Mavis refused to remove the fence on her machine and therefore could not work as quickly as the others. Alec warned her that if she could not meet her targets, he would reduce her wages. Because of the stress placed upon her, she resigned.

▶ Ignoring the issue of fairness under s 98(4) of the **Employment Rights Act (ERA) 1996** advise Rita and Mavis whether they may claim unfair dismissal.

Common Pitfalls ✗

◆ This is another question to read carefully. It specifically tells the student to ignore the issue of fairness and therefore is asking for the question to be focused on whether the parties have been dismissed.
◆ Going into fair reasons and reasonableness will not gain any marks.

Answer Plan

Going through the questions posed at the beginning of the chapter when faced with an unfair dismissal problem, we know that the persons are employees, we know that they have the requisite continuity and there is nothing to suggest that either of them is excluded from unfair dismissal protection. The question therefore concentrates on the issue of dismissal and asks whether the parties have been dismissed at law or whether one or both have resigned. Given that, on the face of it, both the parties have terminated their own contracts, we can see that the question is more focused and requires a discussion of one type of dismissal (constructive dismissal).

Issues that need to be discussed are therefore:

❖ the definition of constructive dismissal in s 95(1)(c) of the Employment Rights Act (ERA) 1996;
❖ the test in *Western Excavating (ECC) Ltd v Sharp* (1978);
❖ whether the imposition of a lesser sanction than dismissal can be a breach of contract;
❖ whether insisting on breaches of health and safety procedures can be a breach of contract;
❖ whether threatening a potential breach of contract can set up a constructive dismissal claim;
❖ whether causing an employee stress is a breach of contract.

ANSWER

The question asks us to advise the two parties as to whether they can claim unfair dismissal. In both the situations, the parties have terminated their own contracts, but this does not mean that there has not been a dismissal in law. By s 95(1)(c) of the ERA 1996, once an employee is protected by unfair dismissal provisions, a dismissal can occur where the employee terminates the contract 'with or without notice, in circumstances such that he is entitled to terminate it without notice by reason of the employer's conduct'.

A resignation in these circumstances is known as a constructive dismissal. From the definition in s 95(1)(c), however, it can be seen that not all conduct on the part of the employer entitles the employee to resign. In *Western Excavating (ECC) Ltd v Sharp* (1978), Denning MR said that, for the employer's conduct to amount to a constructive dismissal, the conduct had to be 'a significant breach going to the root of the contract of employment, or which shows that the employer no longer intends to be bound by one or more of the essential terms of the contract', thus indicating that the essence of a constructive dismissal is a fundamental or repudiatory breach by the employer. Unreasonable conduct per se on the part of the employer will normally not establish a constructive dismissal claim. In all the cases in the problem, therefore, it is necessary to establish whether the employees have terminated their contracts due to a fundamental breach of contract by Alec.

Rita resigned after an appeal reinstated her after her original dismissal, but at a lower grade and on a reduced salary. As previously stated, given that Rita resigned, her resignation will only be a constructive dismissal for the purposes of the ERA 1996 if Alec was in fundamental breach of the employment contract. The first question that must be asked is: did Alec have a right to demote Rita as part of his disciplinary procedures and were such procedures part of Rita's contract?

Disciplinary procedures may become contractual, particularly if they are given to the employee at the same time as the contract and the contract refers to them. Many employers make such procedures contractual because if one of the sanctions within the procedures is a reduction in wages, for example, by a demotion, then the employer must have contractual authority to reduce the wages (or the employee's authority to reduce his pay) to prevent being in breach of contract. If Alec has no contractual authority to demote Rita, then he has unilaterally altered her contract. Such an alteration will involve a change in her job duties and in her term relating to pay.

Whereas, in some cases, it has been held that a failure to pay wages or a pay reduction was not a repudiatory breach (*Adams v Charles Zub Associates Ltd* (1978)), generally, a reduction in pay will be a repudiation by the employer. In addition, in *Millbrook Furnishing Industries Ltd v McIntosh* (1981), the transfer of highly skilled sewing machinists to unskilled work was held to be a breach, for it was to last until work picked up in their normal area and the time this would take could not be predicted. In *Adams*, there was no breach by the employer because there was a temporary cash flow problem and the employee would be paid in the near future. In Rita's case, it does not appear that either the demotion or the reduction in pay is of a temporary nature and, as such, it is possible to distinguish *Adams* on the issue of her pay reduction and to follow *McIntosh* in relation to the demotion. Thus, if Alec has no contractual authority to demote as a disciplinary sanction, he has committed a repudiatory breach of contract within the terms of s 95(1)(c) of the ERA 1996 and Rita has been constructively dismissed.

This then leads to the following question: what if Alec has the contractual right to demote in disciplinary situations? On the face of it, there appears to be no breach of contract as Alec is merely exercising his contractual rights. Such an approach is subject, however, to the decision in *Cawley v South Wales Electricity Board* (1985). In that case, Cawley was seen urinating out of the back door of a company vehicle. He was originally dismissed, but a subsequent appeal reinstated him but at a new site and with a reduction in salary of £1,400 a year. Cawley resigned. An employment tribunal held that the action by the employer was disproportionate to the employee's conduct and therefore there had been a breach of contract and a constructive dismissal. The tribunal held, however, that the dismissal was fair. Cawley appealed, arguing that the tribunal was using two different standards of reasonableness. By stating that the action by the employer was so unreasonable in the circumstances that there was a breach of contract, it must therefore follow that the dismissal must also be unreasonable and, as such, unfair. The EAT agreed with Cawley and ruled that he had been unfairly dismissed. This means that even if the employer has the contractual right to demote or reduce salary, it is subject to the proportionality principle: in other words, the sanction imposed must not be out of proportion to the conduct of the employee. If the sanction is excessive, following *Cawley*, its very excessiveness is a breach of contract because it is a breach of the implied duty of mutual trust and confidence and the ensuing constructive dismissal is unfair.

If we apply this to Rita's case, she did not work one shift because she was visiting her sick mother. Her absence did not disrupt the business as she had arranged for a replacement and she had never been disciplined before in 15 years of employment. Given these facts, it would appear that a demotion and a reduction in salary is a harsh sanction to impose for a first disciplinary offence, particularly one that did not affect the business. Following *Cawley*, it can be argued that the employer's sanction was disproportionate and unreasonable and that this unreasonable action constituted a repudiatory breach because it was a breach of the implied duty of mutual trust and confidence. This means that Rita has been constructively dismissed and, further, that her dismissal must be unfair.

Mavis has resigned due to pressure put upon her to meet targets set by Alec. The only way she can meet these targets appears to be by ignoring safety procedures in relation to the fencing of machinery. While Alec has not actually appeared to have told her to break safety procedures, given that the other workers were removing the fences to meet targets suggests that this is the only way that the targets can be met.

Mavis resigned when Alec threatened to reduce her wages if she failed to meet the targets. As yet, at the time of her resignation, Alec had not told her to remove the fence or reduced her wages. Allowing the use of machinery without a fence when one is required by law is a breach of the common law implied duty of safety that an employer owes to all its employees – in particular, the requirement to provide a safe system of work. In addition, lack of fencing is contrary to s 14(1) of the Factories Act 1961 unless the lack of a fence does not make the machinery unsafe.

Furthermore, under s 7 of the Health and Safety at Work, etc Act 1974, Mavis is under a statutory duty to take reasonable care for the health and safety of herself and others who may be injured by her acts and omissions at work and as regards any duty or requirement imposed under any statutory provision. In short, Mavis will be in breach of her statutory duty if, by law, the machinery should be fenced, and Alec is in breach of both common law and statutory duties by allowing the workers to operate the machinery without the fences on. If the implication of Alec's warning is that Mavis must remove the fence, he is giving an unlawful order. While an employee must obey all lawful, reasonable orders issued by the employer, there is no duty to obey any order that is unlawful (Morrish v Henlys (Folkestone) Ltd (1973)) or unreasonable (Ottoman Bank Ltd v Chakarian (1930)). Thus, if in essence this is what Alec requires Mavis to do, she can refuse, and her refusal will not be a breach of contract. If, however, it is possible to meet the targets complying with safety procedures and Mavis is merely slower than the rest, Alec is not in breach of contract by trying to get her to work to target.

Alec threatened to reduce Mavis's wages if she could not make the target set. At the time Mavis resigned, this remained as a threat that had yet to be carried out. This will not necessarily defeat Mavis claiming dismissal, as it is possible to have an anticipatory breach (Norwest Holst Group Administration Ltd v Harrison (1985)). The question that arises, however, is whether a reduction in wages is within Alec's contractual rights as part of a disciplinary procedure for not meeting targets. The discussion above on Rita, and the contractual status of disciplinary procedures, is pertinent here. Even if Alec was acting within his contractual rights, if the targets can only be made by removing the fences, imposing a sanction for refusing to act contrary to statute is unreasonable and, on the basis of Cawley v South Wales Electricity Board, Alec is in anticipatory breach of contract; as such Mavis can claim constructive dismissal. If, on the other hand, the targets can be met legally and there is a contractual right to reduce wages in these circumstances, unless it could be argued that threatening the sanction without training or giving an opportunity to improve falls within the ambit of the decision in Cawley (which is doubtful), there is no breach of contract on the part of the employer.

A final issue in relation to Mavis is whether Alec is in breach of the duty of mutual trust and confidence by putting so much pressure upon her that stress causes her to resign. The duty is a fairly recent innovation from the courts and has still to be fully developed. Cases such as Bliss v South East Thames Regional Health Authority (1985) show that the employer must not act in such a way as to destroy the trust and confidence necessary to make the relationship work. In *Meikle v Nottinghamshire CC* *(2004)*, a failure on the part of the employer to make reasonable adjustments for a disabled employee was treated as a breach of the duty, and in *Horkulak v Cantor Fitzgerald International (2005)*, it was held that an employee who was subjected to a campaign of bullying and intimidation, and as a result resigned, had been constructively dismissed. If Alec's conduct can be construed as destroying that trust and confidence, particularly as Mavis has resigned because of stress, then this would be a repudiatory breach and, as such, again Mavis could claim constructive dismissal.

QUESTION 35

The test for determining whether a termination of a contract of employment by an employer amounts to a constructive dismissal is not a reasonableness but a contractual test. Courts and tribunals deny the existence of a duty upon employers to act reasonably towards their employees. Nevertheless, in practice, the difference between the two tests is minimal if not illusory.

▶ How far do you consider this statement to be an accurate reflection of the law?

Answer Plan

The question is asking for a discussion of the definition of a constructive dismissal and the interpretation of that definition by the courts. It is easy to think that this is all the question demands, but it also requires a discussion of cases in which tribunals have refused to imply a term that the employer shall act reasonably and cases in which in reality the contractual and reasonableness tests seem to have been used interchangeably. The question therefore calls for a detailed knowledge of a number of cases and the student to come to his or her own conclusion on the accuracy of the statement.

Issues that need to be considered are therefore:

❖ the contractual test in *Western Excavating (ECC) Ltd v Sharp* (1978);
❖ the reasonableness test in *United Bank Ltd v Akhtar* (1989) and *Cawley v South Wales Electricity Board* (1985);
❖ limits on the reasonableness test in cases such as *White v Reflecting Roadstuds Ltd* (1991) and *Courtaulds Northern Spinning Ltd v Sibson* (1988);
❖ the effect of the development of the duty of mutual trust and confidence in this area; and
❖ areas in which a strict contractual approach is used.

ANSWER

The definition of a constructive dismissal is found in s 95(1)(c) of the Employment Rights Act (ERA) 1996. This section provides that an employee is to be treated as dismissed by his employer if the employee terminates the contract 'with or without notice, in circumstances such that he is entitled to terminate it without notice by reason of the employer's conduct'. The key word in the statutory definition, however, is 'entitled'. What conduct on the part of the employer entitles an employee to resign and claim he has been dismissed?

In early cases, courts and tribunals took the view that unreasonable conduct by the employer justified the employee in resigning and claiming constructive dismissal (*George Wimpey Ltd v Cooper* (1977)). This reasonableness test was rejected for a narrower contractual test by the Court of Appeal in *Western Excavating (ECC) Ltd v Sharp* (1978).

Lord Denning MR said:

> If the employer is guilty of conduct which is a significant breach going to the root of the contract of employment, or which shows that the employer no longer intends to be bound by one or more of the essential terms of the contract, then the employee is entitled to treat himself as discharged from further performance.

In the case, an employee was suspended without pay for taking unauthorised time off. Due to the fact that he had no money, he asked the employer for his holiday pay to date or alternatively for a loan. The employer refused both requests and the employee resigned and claimed constructive dismissal on the basis that the employer's conduct was so unreasonable that he was entitled to resign. The employment tribunal upheld his complaint, but the employer's appeal was allowed in the Court of Appeal, which stated that the true test under s 95(1)(c) was whether the employer had broken a fundamental term of the contract. In that case, the employer was not contractually obliged to pay accrued holiday pay or grant the employee a loan. As such, there was no breach of contract by the employer and therefore no constructive dismissal.

The Court gave three main reasons for adopting the contractual approach. First, the statute distinguished between dismissal and unfairness and therefore the same test of reasonableness could not apply to both. This may now be in doubt since the decision of *Cawley v South Wales Electricity Board* (1985). Second, the words in the section were 'entitled to terminate' and these had a legal and therefore contractual connotation. Third, unreasonableness as a test was too indefinite and imprecise.

While Lord Denning enunciated that the test was contractual, however, Lawton LJ obviously envisaged a flexible approach. He said:

> Sensible people have no difficulty in recognising such conduct (needed to entitle the employee to terminate the contract) when they hear it . . . what is required for an application of this provision is a large measure of common sense.

It would therefore seem that at least one judge in the *Western Excavating* case intended a much more flexible approach.

While the Court of Appeal has since reiterated the contractual test in cases such as *Courtaulds Northern Spinning Ltd v Sibson* (1988), it is arguable that the reasonableness test in reality is being applied in recent cases. There are two reasons why this is suggested. First, in recent years, the EAT, in particular, has developed what has become known as the duty of mutual trust and confidence as an implied term in the contract of employment. To some extent, this can be seen as the corollary of the employee's duty of faithful service. In *British Telecom plc v Ticehurst* (1992), the Court of Appeal appeared to resurrect *Secretary of State for Employment v ASLEF (No 2)* (1972) and allowed an employer to refuse to permit an employee to work if she was not prepared to sign a document saying that she would work normally and take no further industrial action. In other words, the employer could prevent an employee from working if it no longer had trust in that employee because it feared that she would work to rule. Likewise, it appears that if the employer is guilty of conduct that destroys the trust that the employee has in the relationship, the employer is in breach of contract (see, for example, the judgment of Browne-Wilkinson P in *Woods v WM Car Services (Peterborough) Ltd* (1981)).

While this would at first sight merely support the contractual test, its importance lies in the fact that the duty can be seen as what Smith and Baker (*Smith and Wood's Employment Law*, 10th edn, 2010, Oxford) describe as an 'overriding term' that can override the express terms of the contract. The essence of the term means that the employer must exercise its contractual rights reasonably. This was first propounded by the EAT in *United Bank Ltd v Akhtar* (1989). In *Akhtar*, there was an express mobility clause in the contract allowing the employer to move the employee anywhere in the UK. The employer ordered the employee to move from Leeds to Birmingham, giving him six days' notice, and refused the employee's request for more time because of personal circumstances. The employee resigned and the EAT held that he had been constructively dismissed. This was despite a previous decision by the same tribunal (*Rank Xerox v Churchill* (1988)), which held that the courts will not imply an element of reasonableness where the term is clear and unambiguous. The essence of the judgment in *Akhtar* is seen from the quote from Knox J. He said:

there may well be conduct which is either calculated or likely to destroy or seriously damage the relationship of trust and respect between employer and employee which a literal interpretation of the written words of the contract might appear to justify, and it is in this sense that we consider that in the field of employment law it is proper to imply an overriding obligation which is independent of, and in addition to, the literal interpretation of the actions which are permitted to the employer under the terms of the contract.

The later EAT decision of *White v Reflecting Roadstuds Ltd* (1991) may appear to go against *Akhtar* and so refute the reasonableness test, but in reality, this is not the case. In *White*, an employee resigned after he had been transferred to a lower paid job at another site, a move for which the employer had contractual authority. Wood P said that *Akhtar* did not establish such a sweeping principle that an employer must always exercise its contractual rights reasonably. *Akhtar* lays down the principle that an employer, when exercising its rights under a mobility clause, should not exercise them in such a way as to render it impossible for the employee to do his job. In *Akhtar*, the employee could not commute from Leeds to Birmingham. In *White*, the site was within easy travelling distance of the employee's home. Furthermore, Wood P in *White* stated that a capricious decision to move an employee would not be within the ambit of an express mobility clause and that, as a result of *Woods*, there is an overriding implied term of mutual trust and confidence.

As mutual trust and confidence is now a term of the contract, breach of such can establish a constructive dismissal within the decision of *Western Excavating*. The importance of this term, however, lies in its overriding nature. From both *Akhtar* and *White*, it would appear that the term means that the employer must not act capriciously – that is, it must act reasonably, otherwise it is in breach of contract. The reality therefore appears to be that by imposing the term of trust and confidence on the employer, there is little difference between acting reasonably and treating the employee in such a way that it does not destroy the trust and confidence the employee has in the relationship.

The second reason for stating that the reasonableness test is, in reality, one of the tests applied is the decision in *Cawley v South Wales Electricity Board* (1985), in which an appeal against dismissal reinstated the employee but at a lower salary and at another site. The reduction in salary was £1,400 per annum. The EAT held that the demotion was an excessive sanction in the light of the employee's conduct and, as such, the employee's resignation was a constructive dismissal, which was unfair. The reasoning behind the decision was that there was an implied term in the contractual disciplinary procedures that the employer would impose a sanction proportionate to the conduct. If the sanction was out of proportion, the employer's conduct was unreasonable and the employee was entitled to resign. If the employer's conduct was so unreasonable that it was a breach of contract, it followed that the constructive dismissal must be unfair as there could not be different standards of reasonableness in relation to dismissal and fairness. This interpretation goes against the reasons given by Lord Denning MR for his decision in *Western Excavating* and the Court of Appeal decision in *Savoia v Chiltern Herb Farms Ltd* (1982). What is important, however, is that, yet again, the EAT has introduced a concept of reasonableness into the way in which the employer exercises its rights, albeit it is arguable that *Cawley* is merely another demonstration of the duty of mutual trust and confidence.

It would appear, therefore, from the above discussion, that there is little difference in reality between the reasonableness test and the contractual test and that the differences are minimal and illusory. It is arguable, however, that there are two important situations in the area of constructive dismissal in which the contractual test prevails and in which a reasonableness test would give a different result. The first of these is where there is an anticipatory breach. Following the strict contractual approach, in *Norwest Holst Group Administration Ltd v Harrison* (1985), it was held that where the employer is in anticipatory breach of contract, he can rectify the breach before the employee accepts it as repudiatory and any later resignation by the employee after the breach has been withdrawn is not a dismissal. This requires the employee to make a decision before he is certain that the breach will occur or lose his rights to claim unfair dismissal. The second situation is where there is a dispute as to the terms of the contract. In *Frank Wright and Co (Holdings) Ltd v Punch* (1980), the employee resigned when he was not paid cost-of-living expenses. His contract issued in 1973 said that he was so entitled, but a statement issued in 1978 was silent as to the expenses. The employer genuinely believed that the expenses were not payable. The EAT said that the conduct of the employer in carrying out the contract in accordance with its own erroneous interpretation of its terms was not repudiatory. This shows that there must be an intention to commit a repudiatory breach and, while the decision is in line with normal contractual principles, it can work harshly against an employee who can only claim dismissal if he can show that the employer's belief is not genuine.

From the discussion above, it can be seen that in a great many situations in which constructive dismissal is alleged, the test used by courts and tribunals can arguably be called a reasonableness test, and that there is little difference between this test and the contractual test in reality. In the two areas, however, of anticipatory breach and disputed terms, the strict contractual test is used, showing the vast difference in these two areas between the two tests – a difference that often works against the employee.

Aim Higher ★

❖   Rubenstein (1991) IRLR 321 gives an interesting opinion on the EAT decision in *Ahktar* and the concept of reasonableness.

❖   Reynold and Palmer wrote an interesting article on constructive dismissal, which can be found at (2005) 34 ILJ 96.

QUESTION 36

Brahms and Liszt work for the Legless Brewery Company. Brahms took a week off work without permission and without telling his manager the reasons for his absence. (In fact, Brahms' wife had left him.) He has worked for the firm for 20 years but of late has shown little interest in his job. The manager told him yesterday that, because of his attitude, he was being taken off his job as supervisor and put back to working the machinery. Brahms told his manager to 'stuff' his job and left saying: 'See you in court.'

Liszt was employed as a sales representative for ten years. He was employed under a contract that required him to work 35 hours a week. Two weeks ago, on 1 April, the company announced that it would require all sales representatives to work up to five hours' compulsory overtime a week from 1 May. Staff were not consulted about this change. Although most of the sales representatives have accepted this change, Liszt has refused to do so and has resigned with effect from 30 April. Legless has introduced the change because of an anticipated increase in competition.

▶   Advise Brahms and Liszt whether they may sue for unfair dismissal.

Answer Plan

This is a fairly common type of unfair dismissal problem and demonstrates that employment law cannot be separated into neat little boxes. The question raises issues in respect of the employee's duty to obey lawful, reasonable orders discussed in Chapter 4. It also raises issues to relation to the establishment of a reason and procedures in relation to a conduct/capability dismissal.

❖   what constitutes a constructive dismissal under s 95(1)(c) of the Employment Rights Act (ERA) 1996;

❖   the relevance of the knowledge of the employer at the time of the dismissal and *British Home Stores v Burchell* (1980);

* the procedure in a conduct/capability dismissal;
* what constitutes a lawful, reasonable order;
* some other substantial reason as a potential fair reason for dismissal; and
* the impact of the ACAS Code of Practice 2009.

ANSWER

In both of the cases in the problem, the parties have the necessary continuity to claim unfair dismissal. Both parties appear to have resigned: Brahms by his walking out and Liszt because of the imposition of overtime. It is necessary in both cases to see if the resignations can be treated as constructive dismissals under s 95 (1)(c) of the ERA 1996.

The problem states that Brahms walked out when his manager told him he would be demoted. The manager's reason for the demotion was Brahms's attitude. In order for Brahms to be able to claim unfair dismissal, by s 95(1)(c) he must establish that he has resigned and that resignation was prompted by the employer's conduct. Since *Western Excavating (ECC) Ltd v Sharp* (1978), the conduct that entitles Brahms to resign and claim constructive dismissal must be a breach of contract by the employer.

Does Brahms's walking out constitute a resignation? The court will look at Brahms's intention. It may be that he walked out in the heat of the moment and intended to go back when he had calmed down. If, on the other hand, he intended to leave permanently, he will have terminated his contract – that is, he has resigned. It is obvious from the facts that the reason for his resignation is the fact that the manager told him he had been demoted. If there is no contractual right to demote, then the employer is in breach and Brahms has been constructively dismissed (*Western Excavating (ECC) Ltd v Sharp*). If there is a contractual right to demote, it may still mean that the employer is in breach of contract. In *Cawley v South Wales Electricity Board* (1985), an employee was initially dismissed after a member of the public complained that he had been seen urinating out of a company van. After an appeal, the dismissal was substituted for a demotion, resulting in a reduction in his salary of £1,400. He resigned and the EAT upheld his claim of unfair dismissal on the basis that the employer had imposed too harsh a sanction in respect of his misconduct and that in itself was a breach of the duty of mutual trust and confidence. If the action by the manager, therefore, is seen as too harsh a sanction, on the basis of *Cawley* the employer is in breach and Brahms is entitled to resign and claim constructive dismissal. In addition, given that the manager has acted unreasonably and hence breached the duty, such a dismissal must be unfair as the employer will be unable to satisfy the reasonableness test. Given that Brahms has worked for the company for

20 years and it is only of late his work has been poor, a tribunal may well hold that demotion is too harsh a sanction.

The problem states that the reason for the employer's actions was Brahms's attitude. The problem also states that his absence was because his wife had left him. By *British Home Stores v Burchell* (1980), if the employer wishes to dismiss under s 98(2)(b) of the ERA 1996, the employer must have a genuine belief, based on reasonable grounds after a reasonable investigation, that the employee is 'guilty'. To conduct an investigation, the employer must gather all the evidence so that it, he can make a reasoned and fair decision (*Scottish Daily Record and Sunday Mail* (1986) *Ltd v Laird* (1996)). Here, it appears that no investigation has been conducted; indeed, if it had, it may have revealed that the reason for Brahms's conduct was his problems at home. As such, given that the employer has not really investigated why Brahms has changed, a tribunal may find that the employer has not established conduct as a reason. The same reasoning will apply if the employer raises capability (s 98(2)(a)) as a reason for dismissal.

If an employer establishes to the satisfaction of the tribunal that a reason under s 98(2) existed, s 98(4) requires the tribunal to consider whether the employer acted reasonably in treating the reason as sufficient to dismiss. Reasonableness falls into two categories: fairness of the decision and procedural fairness.

In relation to fairness of the decision, a tribunal will look for consistency, taking past work record into account and whether the employer has considered alternative employment in respect of a redundancy or incapability dismissal. In relation to consistency, the employer has to treat truly identical cases the same; therefore, the decision can only be challenged on the ground of consistency if, in the past, an employee with the same length of service and with a similar performance problem was not demoted. It is not inconsistent to treat employees with different work records differently (*Sherrier v Ford Motor Co* (1976)). In relation to his past work record, there is nothing in the problem to suggest that until recently there has been any problem in the 20 years of his employment, and tribunals expect employers to treat long-serving good employees more leniently than those of shorter lengths of service or blemished work records (*Johnson Matthey Metals Ltd v Harding* (1978)). As such, demoting someone with Brahms's work record may be unreasonable and thus an unfair dismissal. The employer has offered alternative employment, but, it is suggested, it is some way removed from his job as supervisor. In *Hall v Lodge* (1977), a manager who had been over-promoted was demoted to sales assistant in another branch. Given her incapability to do the manager's job, and the fact that she had been removed from the branch where she had been manager, the constructive dismissal was held to be fair. In Brahms's case, however, there is no suggestion that he is permanently incapable of doing the job, merely that his personal problems have affected him temporarily; as such, the offer may in itself be unreasonable.

The ACAS Code of Practice on Disciplinary and Grievance Procedures (2009) suggests that an employer should investigate before making the decision to start disciplinary action. Although the Code is not legally enforceable, tribunals are required to take its provisions into account (s 207 of the Trade Union and Labour Relations (Consolidation) Act (TULR(C)A) 1992). Here, there has been no such investigation. The Code also recommends that dismissal should not be a sanction for a first disciplinary offence and that a warning (albeit a final warning in this case, warning of the consequences of the continued conduct) is more appropriate. As such, the employer has not complied with the Code or the common law.

Should the employer argue capability as the reason for dismissal, the Code states that the employer should investigate the reason for the incapability, tell the employee the standard to be achieved, give him a reasonable opportunity to improve and tell him the consequences of a failure to improve. None of this seems to have happened in Brahms's case, further enforcing the decision that this is an unfair dismissal.

Liszt has been told that the employer is unilaterally altering his contract to include compulsory overtime. As a result, Liszt has resigned. By *Western Excavating (ECC) Ltd v Sharp*, this will be a constructive dismissal only if the employer is in breach of contract. Here, the employer appears to have unilaterally altered the terms and is therefore in breach and, as such, Liszt has been constructively dismissed.

The employer may try to argue one of two reasons for the dismissal. It may first try to argue that, given the anticipated increase in competition, the order to work compulsory overtime is reasonable and Liszt is in breach of the duty to obey lawful reasonable orders and as such is guilty of misconduct. Given that the change in terms is a breach by the employer in that it is a permanent unilateral variation in the terms of the contract, it is submitted that a tribunal would not regard this as a reasonable order and this reason would fail. It is more likely that the employer would argue some other substantial reason under s 98(2)(e) of the ERA 1996. Changing business needs has been recognised as falling under this head – in particular, a need to change hours (*Johnson v Nottinghamshire Combined Police Authority* (1974)) – and, as such, it is likely that the employer has a fair reason to dismiss.

The tribunal, however, also has to decide whether the employer has acted reasonably. In situations such as this, the tribunal will first ask itself if the changes were necessary. Originally, the test appeared to be that, without them, the business would be brought to a standstill (*Ellis v Brighton Co-operative Society Ltd* (1976)). But the test is not so stringent today and all a tribunal should ask is whether there is a sound business reason behind the changes (*Hollister v National Farmers' Union* (1979)). *Chubb Fire Security Ltd v Harper* (1983) states that, in seeing whether the employer acted reasonably, a tribunal might consider the advantages to the employer and weigh them against the disadvantages to the employee. Other factors are whether other employees have accepted the change and the attitude of the union, if there is one (*Catamaran Cruisers Ltd v Williams* (1994); *Bowater Containers Ltd v McCormack* (1980)). Given that most of the other sales representatives have accepted the change, a tribunal may hold that the needs of the employer may still be met without insisting that Liszt change his hours (*Martin v Automobile Proprietary Ltd* (1979)), although in *Robinson v Flitwick Frames Ltd* (1975), the fact that all the other employees had agreed to the change made the dismissal fair. Trivial changes are likely to result in a fair dismissal for refusal (*Baverstock v Horsley Smith and Co*, unreported), although it is submitted that in Liszt's case the change is not trivial. In addition, a reasonable employer consults with its employees before making the changes, although lack of consultation has not in the past always been fatal to an employer's claim (*Hollister*). It is suggested that if Liszt is the only one who refuses to accept the change, the employer's needs will still be achieved and thus the employer's insistence is unreasonable. If this is found to be the case, Liszt's dismissal will be unfair.

Aim Higher ★

◆ At the time of writing, the impact of the abolition of the statutory disciplinary procedures and the effect of the ACAS Code is unknown.

◆ It would be useful to read and incorporate what some authors think will be the impact of the abolition of the statutory procedures – for example, Sanders (2009) 38 ILJ 30.

QUESTION 37

Pinch, Nick and Swipe are all employed by Triggerhappy Ltd. Pinch and Nick have been employed for ten years and Swipe has been employed for two years. During their periods of employment, only Swipe has any disciplinary sanctions against him. This is a warning issued six months ago for bad timekeeping.

Last bank holiday, only Pinch, Nick, Swipe and another employee, Sneak, were at work. During that working day, Sneak had a radio-cassette player stolen while at work. The company was of the opinion that one of the three other employees was responsible for the theft. In fact, Sneak has repeatedly told the company that he has severe reservations about Swipe's honesty, but the company has failed to investigate his complaints.

All three employees were dismissed. Their dismissal notices contained the following statement: 'You are aware, of course, that you are obliged to report instances of theft by fellow employees to the management promptly.'

All the employees had a contractual right to an appeal. All the employees appealed against their dismissals. The appeals consisted of a review of the evidence. The dismissals of Nick and Swipe were confirmed for theft, that of Pinch for failing to report theft by a fellow employee. Nick and Swipe had threatened Pinch that if he reported what had really happened, he would be hurt, but the company are unaware of this because in all the disciplinary hearings, the employees were merely allowed to answer 'yes' or 'no' to questions put to them by the manager.

▶ Advise Pinch, Nick and Swipe who have all entered complaints of unfair dismissal.

Answer Plan

While this appears to be a fairly straightforward question, there is in fact a great deal in it. It is essentially about procedure and therefore students need to be aware of what constitutes an adequate investigation, the rules of a fair hearing, consistency of decisions and how far past work record is relevant.

Issues that need to be considered are:

❖ the test in *British Homes Stores v Burchell* (1978);
❖ the elements of a reasonable investigation;
❖ dismissal of a group of employees (*Parr v Whitbread plc t/a Threshers Wine Merchants* (1990));
❖ the constituents of a fair hearing;
❖ the confirmation of dismissal for a reason other than the original reason;
❖ the band of reasonable responses test in *Iceland Frozen Foods v Jones* (1983).

ANSWER

In any unfair dismissal complaint, the burden on the employer is to prove that it had a statutory fair reason to dismiss the employee within s 98(1) and (2) of the Employment Rights Act (ERA) 1996. Once this has been established (s 98(4)):

the determination of the question of whether the dismissal was fair or unfair, having regard to the reasons shown by the employer, shall depend on whether in the circumstances (including the size and administrative resources of the employer's undertaking) the employer acted reasonably or unreasonably in treating it as a sufficient reason for dismissing the employee; and that question shall be determined in accordance with equity and the substantial merits of the case.

Thus, Triggerhappy must prove only that it had a fair reason to dismiss the three employees and then the tribunal, looking at all the circumstances, will decide whether dismissal was reasonable or unreasonable.

When only the three dismissed employees were working, a theft occurred. Under the test in *British Home Stores v Burchell* (1978), it was held that in an unfair dismissal case, the employer must have a genuine belief, based on reasonable grounds after a reasonable investigation, that the employee is 'guilty'. Thus, Triggerhappy must show that the three points in the *Burchell* test have been met. Without doubt, it appears that a theft has occurred, but, on the facts presented, it appears that the *Burchell* principles have not been complied with. First, Sneak has told the company that he has reservations about Swipe's honesty, but the company has never investigated the complaints. While it is accepted that Sneak's accusations may be unfounded, it would appear that the company has not reacted to this in the present case, as allegations of dishonesty could naturally lead the company to suspect Swipe rather than the other two employees.

However, cases of blanket dismissals – that is, dismissal of a group of employees, all of whom could have been guilty but, after an investigation, the employer cannot pin down which one is – can be fair despite the fact that the employer cannot have a genuine belief in the guilt of all the employees.

In the leading case of *Monie v Coral Racing Ltd* (1980), the employee was an area manager with responsibility for 19 shops. Only he and his assistant knew the combination of the safe at headquarters. While Monie was away, his assistant discovered that £1,750 was missing from the safe. As there was no sign of a break-in, the company concluded that one or both were involved in the theft and dismissed them. The Court of Appeal confined the *Burchell* principles to cases in which only one employee is suspected. *Parr v Whitbread plc t/a Thresher Wine Merchants* (1990) has confirmed this in relation to the dismissal of four suspected employees, but stressed that the employer must do a thorough investigation to limit the group to only those who definitely could have committed the theft. Therefore, while Triggerhappy does not have to show that it genuinely believes all three are guilty, it must show that its investigation revealed that any one of the three employees must be guilty. Here, Triggerhappy already has suspicions that Swipe is dishonest and appears at the appeal to decide that Pinch is not. This suggests that the original investigation that preceded the dismissals was inadequate and therefore not reasonable. If this is the case, then it will be difficult for Triggerhappy to argue that it has a genuine belief that all of the employees could be guilty based on reasonable grounds. The grounds and the belief can only form a reasonable investigation that, on the facts, does not appear to have happened.

In looking at reasonableness in s 98(4), a tribunal will look to both the fairness of the decision to dismiss and procedural fairness. While the rules of natural justice do not apply in unfair dismissal cases, the employer must give the employee a fair hearing.

These rules are contained, in the main, in the ACAS Code of Practice on Disciplinary and Grievance Procedures (2009). The rules of a fair hearing are first that the employee should know the case against him (*Hutchins v British Railways Board* (1974)). In the problem, it is not stated that the employees were told that their dismissals were for theft, but it appears that they were told that their dismissals were for failing to report theft by fellow employees. It is also unclear what was said in the appeal, but even if theft were mentioned at the appeal, the employees thought that they would be putting their case in relation to a failure to report theft, and to discover that they are accused of theft in the hearing has not given them adequate opportunity to prepare their case.

The second rule of a fair hearing is that the employee must be given an opportunity to put his side of the case. On the facts in the problem, it seems highly debatable that this occurred. The employees were only allowed to answer 'yes' or 'no' to questions put to them by the manager conducting the appeal and it would appear that the employees' versions were not given, nor were any of them given the opportunity to put forward mitigating circumstances. This is very pertinent in Pinch's case, as he had been threatened by the other two employees if he revealed what had happened. It is relevant that this fact was not known by the company, and further supports the argument that an inadequate investigation was conducted, and that the employees were not given the opportunity to give their versions of the facts.

Another rule of a fair hearing is that the hearing should be unbiased, in that the person who chairs the hearing should not already have been involved in the case and formed an opinion (*Moyes v Hylton Castle WMC* (1986)). While the problem gives no details as to the manager who conducted the hearing, this may be another challenge available to the employees.

Two further comments should be made about the hearing. The problem states that the hearing merely reviewed the evidence. An appeal that is a complete rehearing of the case can rectify earlier deficiencies in procedure (*Whitbread and Co plc v Mills* (1988)). It is unknown how this will be affected by the statutory procedures but it is submitted that *Mills* will only be relevant where the employer has contractual procedures that are in excess of the statutory ones – for example, where an employee has two rights of appeal. However, in this case, as it appears that the employees have never put their side of the case and the hearing did not give them that opportunity, the defective investigation has not been rectified by the later appeal. In addition, it appears that originally the dismissals were for failing to report theft by a fellow employee. While an employer is entitled to lay down its own rules and state what he regards as gross misconduct, it cannot act autocratically. It appears from the facts that this rule of reporting has just been told to the employees in their dismissal letters. Therefore, the employees were originally accused of a breach of a rule of which they were unaware.

In addition, Swipe and Nick had their dismissals confirmed on the basis of theft. It would appear from the facts that they thought that they were dismissed for failure to report theft and then dismissed for a totally different reason, which they discovered after the appeal. Referring to the rules of a fair hearing above, this means that they went to the hearing not knowing the case against them and having been given no opportunity to answer any allegations. As such, this is yet further evidence of an unfair hearing, as an appeal cannot confirm a dismissal for a different reason from that originally alleged without the whole process of investigation, hearing and appeal being conducted (*Monie v Coral Racing* (1980)). On the basis of the arguments presented, therefore, it would appear that all the dismissals are procedurally unfair.

Tribunals also look to the fairness of the decision to dismiss. In other words, was dismissal a fair sanction in the circumstances? Browne-Wilkinson J in *Iceland Frozen Foods v Jones* (1983) said that the task of a tribunal was:

> to determine whether in the particular circumstances of each case the decision to dismiss the employee fell within the band of reasonable responses which a reasonable employer might make.

This does not mean that the tribunal should find the dismissal unfair if it would not have dismissed, but it should ask itself if a reasonable employer would have dismissed. Substituting its own decision for that of the employer will lead to a finding that the tribunal decision is perverse. This means that the tribunal will look for a consistent approach by the employer, in that it must treat truly comparable cases the same and, particularly in conduct cases, will look to see if the employer took into account factors such as the employee's past work record and length of service. It is not inconsistent to treat two employees who have committed the same offence differently if there is a considerable difference in their length of service and their work record.

In *Sherrier v Ford Motor Co* (1976), two employees were caught fighting. Despite an investigation by the employer, it could not discover who had instigated the fight. One of the employees had a 15-year unblemished record and the employer suspended him for five days without pay. Sherrier, on the other hand, had been employed for two years and had had six disciplinary sanctions imposed upon him, and so the employer dismissed him. It was held that the dismissal was fair.

In the problem, Pinch and Nick have ten years' unblemished service and it could be argued that to dismiss one for suspicion of theft and the other for failing to report theft by fellow employees is too harsh, given their work record. In *Johnson Matthey Metals Ltd v Harding* (1978), an employee with a 15-year unblemished record was dismissed when the missing watch of a colleague was found in his possession. The EAT held that the dismissal was unfair in the light of the length of his previous good service. Given the facts in the problem, a tribunal may hold that, in the case of Pinch and Nick, a reasonable employer would not have dismissed them and that, therefore, dismissal was not within the band of reasonable responses. Given Swipe's shorter length of service, his previous disciplinary record and the allegations against his honesty, on the other hand, a tribunal may feel that the decision to dismiss Swipe was a reasonable one. It would appear, therefore, that, in all the cases, the dismissals were procedurally unfair and, additionally, the decision to dismiss may also be unfair in the case of Pinch and Nick, but probably reasonable in the case of Swipe. Thus, all three employees have good claims for unfair dismissal. It may be, however, particularly in the case of Swipe, that compensation is reduced due to the employee's conduct by s 122(2) of the ERA 1996, which allows a tribunal to reduce compensation to an amount that is just and equitable due to the employee's conduct before the dismissal. This does not mean conduct that contributed towards the dismissal but any conduct that the tribunal feels should be taken into account.

In the light of the above discussion, the dismissals are likely to be procedurally unfair because of breaches of the rules of a fair hearing and the ACAS Code.

QUESTION 38

Jack, Ken and Sally work for Rover Ltd. Jack and Sally have worked for the company for ten months. Ken has worked for the company for ten years.

Jack works in the factory. Recently, one of the machines got very hot and Jack felt there was a danger that it would cause a fire. He panicked and immediately pressed the fire alarm and, while other employees were leaving the premises, he threw what he thought to be a bucket of water over the machine. In fact, the bucket contained inflammable cleaning fluid and the machine caught fire, causing serious damage to the factory and halting production for a week. The bucket of cleaning fluid should not have been there, but had been left there accidentally by another employee. Jack has now been dismissed because of his actions.

Ken is one of 30 salesmen. The company wishes to reduce the sales force by 20. The managing director, after discussions with the recognised trade union, decided that selection for redundancy would be on the basis of an employee's contribution to the company's future viability, based on criteria such as efficiency and management potential. Ken, who is the longest serving salesman, was today told that he has been selected for redundancy and given wages in lieu of notice.

Sally is pregnant. She suffers from severe arthritis but can work with painkillers. Since she has been pregnant, however, she cannot take the painkillers and therefore cannot work. She is three months' pregnant and has been off work for ten weeks. Today, she received a letter of dismissal and a cheque to cover her notice period.

▶ Advise Jack, Ken and Sally if they have any claim for unfair dismissal against Rover Ltd.

Common Pitfalls ✘
- This is the sort of question that can catch a student out because two of the parties do not appear to have the continuity to claim unfair dismissal, but in both cases, if the reason is proved, no continuity is required.
- Also the question in relation to Sally is about unfair dismissal, so it is important not to get sidetracked into sex discrimination.

Answer Plan

This is a problem that brings together procedure and potentially automatic unfair dismissal.

Issues that need to be considered are:

❖ dismissal in health and safety cases under s 100 of the Employment Rights Act (ERA) 1996;

❖ redundancy as a fair reason to dismiss;
❖ procedure for a redundancy dismissal and the guidelines in *Williams v Compair Maxam Ltd* (1982); and
❖ dismissal in cases of pregnancy under s 99 of the ERA 1996.

ANSWER

All the employees in the problem require advice in relation to unfair dismissal. At first sight, it would appear that Jack and Sally will have no claim because neither has the requisite one year's continuity that is required by s 108(1) of the ERA 1996. However, in some circumstances, an employee may pursue an unfair dismissal claim even if he or she has not been employed for one year and it is possible that Jack and Sally may fall within these provisions.

Jack saw a machine getting hot and, worried that it would catch fire, took certain precautions with somewhat disastrous consequences. As a result of his actions, he has now been dismissed. Protection in relation to dismissal on health and safety grounds is found in s 100(1) of the ERA 1996. This was introduced to comply with the Framework Directive on the introduction of measures to encourage improvements in the health and safety of workers. Section 100(1)(e) provides that a dismissal is automatically unfair if the principal reason for the dismissal was that the employee:

in circumstances of danger which he reasonably believed to be serious and imminent, took, or proposed to take, appropriate steps to protect himself or other persons from the danger.

By s 100(2), whether the steps taken are appropriate is judged by reference to all the circumstances, including the employee's knowledge and the facilities and advice available to him at the time. However, by s 100, the employer has a defence to a claim under s 100(1)(e), if it can show that it was so negligent for the employee to take the steps that he took that a reasonable employer might have dismissed him in the circumstances. There is no continuity period necessary to claim on this ground (s 108(3)(c)).

For Jack to be able to pursue a claim for unfair dismissal, therefore, he must show that he reasonably believed that danger was serious and imminent, that the steps he took were appropriate in the circumstances and that a reasonable employer would not have dismissed him.

The problem states that the machine was getting hot and that Jack thought that there was a danger of a fire. The problem then states that he panicked and pressed the fire alarm. The starting point for a tribunal would be to look at any training Jack has received, particularly what training he may have received in relation to machines getting hot. If he has received none, a tribunal may think that his belief that the machine would catch fire was reasonable in the circumstances. If, however, Jack has received training that he did not comply with, or his experience is such that he should have known to switch the machine off, the tribunal may reach the conclusion that, in all the circumstances, Jack's belief that danger was serious and imminent was not reasonable and the first part of s 100(1)(e) has not been made out.

If Jack's belief is deemed to be reasonable, Jack then has to show that his conduct was appropriate in the circumstances and, again, his training and knowledge will be relevant. Jack doused the machine with what he believed to be water. If his training is such that this is inappropriate conduct, then the second part of the section is not made out. If, however, dousing the machine is the correct action or if he has received no training appropriate to the circumstances and it was reasonable to try and cool down the machine with water, it was not Jack's fault that the bucket contained inflammable fluid that had been accidentally left there. This would then raise the question of whether it was reasonable in the circumstances to expect Jack to check the contents of the bucket before he threw them. It is submitted that such checking would not be unreasonable if he expected the bucket to contain water and this expectation was reasonable.

Even if the action was not appropriate, this does not mean that the dismissal is fair. The employer must show that Jack's actions were so negligent that a reasonable employer might have dismissed. In other words, was the action so negligent that dismissal was within the band of reasonable responses from *Iceland Frozen Foods v Jones* (1983)? If it is proved that Jack was trained and experienced, that water should never be thrown over a hot machine in any circumstances, and that Jack would know this and merely panicked, then it is submitted that the defence will have been made out. On the other hand, if Jack has no training and throwing water was a reasonable response, then the defence is not made out and it is likely that Jack's dismissal will be found to be unfair.

Ken has been employed for ten years and his contract has been terminated by reason of redundancy. Redundancy is a fair reason for dismissal, but may be unfair in some circumstances. The first is where an employee is selected for a variety of reasons such as trade union membership or activities, health and safety reasons or maternity reasons. In these circumstances, if the reason for the selection is proved, the selection is automatically unfair and the dismissed employee does not require one year's continuity to claim. None of these reasons apply to Ken. It would appear, therefore, that Ken cannot argue that his redundancy is automatically unfair. While redundancy is a fair reason for dismissal, the employer must still act reasonably.

A tribunal will look at whether the employer has a fair unit of selection, whether the selection criteria are reasonable, whether the procedure the employer adopted was reasonable and whether the employer looked for alternative employment for his redundant employees. In Ken's situation, a fair unit of selection is the sales staff unless work is interchangeable, in which case the unit of selection should be broader and cover all of those involved in the work (*Gilford v GEC Machines* (1982)). If the union has agreed the unit, it is more likely that a tribunal will hold it to be fair. In Ken's case, it appears that all the sales staff have been considered and there is no evidence that work is shared with another group of employees. It would therefore seem that the unit of selection is fair.

The criteria used for selection should also be fair. This means that they should be objective and measurable and leave no room for subjective opinions. A criterion such as 'employees who in the opinion of management will keep the company viable' was frowned upon by the EAT in *Williams v Compair Maxam Ltd* (1982) as being too heavily reliant upon individual opinion. 'Last in, first out' (LIFO) is always a good starting point and if the employer departs from LIFO, he should use objective criteria such as experience, skill and attendance.

In Ken's case, the employer wishes to retain those employees who will contribute to the future viability of the company. While this is similar to the words frowned upon in *Williams*, if such conclusions are drawn using objective criteria, then the selection procedure could still be fair. The criteria adopted by Rover is efficiency and management potential. While efficiency is objective and can be measured, management potential is subjective and is likely to be based on individual opinion. As such, the selection criteria can be challenged as non-objective and unfair.

The *Williams* case laid down guidelines for a fair procedure after selection where there is a recognised trade union. The guidelines are:

❖ the employer should give as much warning as possible to the union and employees concerned;
❖ the employer should seek the agreement of the union with regard to selection criteria and the means of achieving the necessary result;
❖ the employer should consider representations made by the union with regard to selection; and
❖ the employer should consider alternative employment.

It would appear in Ken's case that Rover did consult with the recognised union. Failure to do so would not only make Ken's redundancy potentially unfair, but would also be a breach of s 188 of the Trade Union and Labour Relations (Consolidation) Act (TULR(C)A) 1992. This section requires Rover to consult with appropriate employee representatives, which includes independent recognised union representatives, at least 30 days before the first dismissals occur as Rover is making 20 workers redundant, and further requires Rover to give certain information in writing to the union representatives. Failure to comply with s 188 entitles the union to apply for a protective award (s 189(1)(b)). To act fairly, however, consultation with the employee must take place, even if there has been consolidation with the union (Hough v Leyland Daf (1991) and Rolls Royce Motor Cars Ltd v Price (1993)). The problem states that Ken was told of his selection for redundancy and given wages in lieu of notice. It would therefore appear that he was neither consulted nor warned of his selection as he was dismissed immediately. Nor would it appear that the employer considered whether there was alternative employment that would suit Ken. As such, Rover has used unfair selection criteria and has not consulted or warned Ken, in breach of the guidelines in Mills, and his redundancy is therefore unfair. Rover cannot argue that even if it had consulted Ken, he would have been selected for redundancy and that the breach of a fair procedure has, therefore, had no effect on the final outcome, since the House of Lords' decision in Polkey v AE Dayton Services Ltd (1987).

Sally is another employee who appears not to have the requisite one year's continuity. In 1994, however, new provisions were introduced to protect women who are dismissed on maternity grounds and render such dismissals automatically unfair (now s 99 of the ERA 1996). Maternity grounds include pregnancy, or any reason connected with pregnancy and the amendments enacted in 1994 removed the need for one year's continuity when dismissal was under this head. Before the amendments, the employer could dismiss if it could show that pregnancy made the woman incapable of doing the job – for example, because she could no longer lift anything. Such exceptions have been removed, although if to continue working would be a breach of statute, the woman now has the right to be suspended on maternity grounds under ss 66–68. To satisfy the provisions, however, the dismissal must be causally connected with the pregnancy. It is insufficient that the woman be dismissed when she is pregnant. 'Any reason connected with her pregnancy' was given a broad interpretation pre-1994 in Brown v Stockton on Tees Borough Council (1988), when the House of Lords ruled that a supervisor, who was selected for redundancy because she was pregnant, was dismissed in breach of (the now) s 99. In other words, her pregnancy was the reason for her dismissal and not the redundancy. By analogy with Brown, it could be argued that Sally was dismissed for a reason connected with her pregnancy because her pregnancy meant that she could no longer take painkillers and therefore could not work. On such an interpretation, Sally's dismissal is automatically unfair.

QUESTION 39

Hissan is a Japanese car company with two plants, one in Leicester and one in Birmingham. The company recently dismissed three employees.

Bill was the spokesman for a group of workers at the Leicester plant who had a grievance with the company. He was a member of an independent trade union and had worked for the company for six months at the date of his dismissal. He had arranged meetings and organised a petition in support of the grievance, which had been vetted by the union. It was these activities, all conducted during working hours, which resulted in his dismissal.

Wally was one of the group of workers at Leicester who took strike action recently in respect of a pay rise. The union had authorised the strike. He had worked for the company for ten years. The strike began on 1 October and, on 7 October, Hissan wrote to all of the employees who were not at work saying that, if they did not return on 10 October, they would be dismissed. Some employees did return, but Wally was one of 20 employees who remained on strike on 10 October. All 20 employees were sent letters of dismissal on 12 October.

Dick worked at the Birmingham plant. He had worked for the company for three years. During the time of unrest at Leicester, the employees at Birmingham organised a work-to-rule to put pressure on the employer to grant the pay rise. The union also authorised this action. On 1 October, the company locked the employees out. On 7 October, the company sent letters to all the Birmingham employees stating that the factory would reopen on 10 October and that they should return to work on that date. Some employees did return, but Dick did not. The next day, he was sent a letter of dismissal.

▶ Advise Bill, Wally and Dick whether a tribunal has jurisdiction to hear their claims for unfair dismissal.

Common Pitfalls

❖ Read the question! This is asking about tribunal jurisdiction only and not whether the dismissals are fair.
❖ This question requires a detailed knowledge of a few statutory provisions and the relevant case law. Without that detailed knowledge, it cannot be answered effectively.

Answer Plan

This problem is looking at dismissal for trade union activities, for which no continuity is required, and the exclusion of tribunal jurisdiction in situations of dismissals during a lockout. The problem looks quite complicated because it covers two sites and a number of dates. However, you will see that the dates of the strike and lockout are the same and this should make things easier.

Particular issues to consider are:

- ❖ the continuity period for dismissal for taking part in trade union activities;
- ❖ the meaning of 'at the appropriate time' in s 152(1) of TULR(C)A 1992;
- ❖ the definition of strike and lockout in s 235(4) and (5) of ERA 1996;
- ❖ the protection under s 238A of TULR(C)A 1992 as amended by the Employment Relations Act 2004; and
- ❖ the definition of relevant employee and exclusion of tribunal jurisdiction by s 238 of TULR(C)A 1992.

ANSWER

By s 152(1) of TULR(C)A 1992, a dismissal is automatically unfair if the principal reason for the dismissal was membership or non-membership of a trade union, or because the employee 'had taken, or proposed to take, part in the activities of an independent trade union at an appropriate time'. By s 154 of the same Act, dismissal for this reason does not need the normal one-year continuity period before the employee is protected by unfair dismissal provisions. If, therefore, Bill can show that the reason for his dismissal fell within s 152(1), it is irrelevant that he had only been employed for six months at the time of his dismissal.

To fall within s 152, Bill must show that he was taking part in the activities of an independent trade union at the appropriate time. The problem states that he is a member of an independent trade union, but that leaves two questions to be answered: what are trade union activities for the purpose of the statute and what constitutes an appropriate time?

Trade union activities are not defined but appear, from the cases, to be given their ordinary meaning. The statutory protection therefore covers union meetings, recruitment, elections, etc. In Bill's case, he has become a spokesperson for a group of employees who had a grievance against the company and had organised a meeting and a petition supporting the employees' grievance. While such activities may be legitimate trade union activities, the question that must be asked is whether Bill was acting on behalf of the union. In *Chant v Aquaboats* (1978), the employee was dismissed for organising a petition about an unsafe machine. Although he was a union member, he was not an official nor was he organising the petition on behalf of the union. It was held that his dismissal was not for trade union activities. The EAT stated that:

> ...the mere fact that one or two employees making representations happen to be trade unionists and the mere fact that the spokesman happens to be a trade unionist does not make such representations a trade union activity.

Furthermore, in *Stokes and Roberts v Wheeler Green* (1979), it was held that the fact that trade union officers felt that the course of conduct was in the interests of their members did not make the conduct trade union activity. On the basis of these cases, it would appear that even though the union had vetted the petition organised by Bill, as he is not an official and the union did not ask him to organise the meeting or the petition, these activities are unlikely to be seen as trade union activities.

Should this not be the case, Bill will still only be protected if he is taking part in trade union activities 'at the appropriate time'. Section 152(2) defines 'appropriate time' as 'outside working hours or within working hours which, in accordance with arrangements agreed with, or consent given by his employer, it is permissible for him to take part in the activities'. In *Zucker v Astrid Jewels Ltd* (1978), an employee who, while she was working, tried to persuade other workers to join the union, was held to be taking part in trade union activities at the appropriate time. On the other hand, in *Marley Tile Co Ltd v Shaw* (1980), a union meeting held during working hours, where the employer had not given its consent but merely remained silent when informed it was taking place, was not held with the employer's consent and thus not protected. In *Robb v Leon Motor Services Ltd* (1978), it was held that, despite a term in the employee's contract that he would be allowed to take part in trade union activities at the appropriate time, there was no agreement on the part of the employer because the term in the contract was too vague and did not define which times were appropriate. In Bill's case, it appears that there has been no express or implied consent or agreement on the part of the employer that the meeting be held or the petition signed. It would therefore appear, on the basis of *Marley Tile Co* and *Robb*, that even if Bill was engaged in trade union activities, he was not doing so at an appropriate time and therefore does not have the protection of s 152. As such, he cannot present a case for unfair dismissal as he does not have the requisite continuity of one year.

In respect of both Wally and Dick, it is assumed that because the union authorised both the strike and the lockout, both actions are official. A tribunal has no jurisdiction to hear a complaint of unfair dismissal, whatever the circumstances, where the dismissals are because of unofficial action (s 237 of TULR(C)A 1992). Where the action is official, Wally may be protected by s 238A of the Act.

In Wally's case, he has been dismissed for taking part in a strike. There is no definition of 'strike' in TULR(C)A, but there is a definition in s 235(5) of the ERA 1996, which states that a strike is:

> ... a cessation of work by a body of persons acting in combination, or a concerted refusal ... to continue to work for an employer in consequence of a dispute, done as a means of compelling their employer ... to accept or not accept terms and conditions of, or affecting, employment.

While the definition in the ERA applies only to that Act, it is useful as a starting point for discussion here. By s 238A(1) of TULR(C)A, which was introduced by the Employment Relations Act 1999 and amended by the Employment Relations Act 2004, any employee who takes part in protected industrial action – that is, action authorised by the union and protected from tortious liability under s 219 – who is dismissed within a period of 12 weeks beginning with the day on which the employee started the protected action shall be regarded as unfairly dismissed. Thus, as long as the union is protected from tortious liability because the action is in contemplation or furtherance of a trade dispute under s 219, which is likely to be the case as a pay rise will come under the definition of trade dispute in s 244(1), Wally's dismissal is unfair and he has the longer period of six months in which to present his claim.

The situation with Dick is different as he has been involved in a lockout. In this case, s 238 applies. This states that where an employee has been taking part in a strike or other industrial action a tribunal will have no jurisdiction to hear a complaint of unfair dismissal unless one or more of the relevant employees have not been dismissed, or a relevant employee has, before the expiry of three months beginning with the date of the employee's dismissal, been offered re-engagement and the claimant has not been offered re-engagement.

The question that first needs to be asked is whether Dick has been taking part in industrial action. The question states that he has been involved in a work-to-rule and this has led to the employer imposing the lockout. Is a work-to-rule industrial action? Where a strike inevitably involves a breach of contract, this does not mean that all industrial action is such a breach. In Power Packing Casemakers Ltd v Faust (1983), employees were involved in a voluntary overtime ban. The employees were threatened with dismissal and all but three lifted the ban. The three employees were dismissed and the Court of Appeal held that the tribunal had no jurisdiction to hear the unfair dismissal complaint as all three were taking part in industrial action at the time of the dismissals. It was irrelevant that the employees were not in breach of contract if the object of the action was to put pressure on the employer or disrupt the employer's business. As such, the work-to-rule will be classed as industrial action because the question states that it was instigated in order to put pressure on the employer to grant the pay rise and it is irrelevant whether the work-to-rule is a breach of contract or not.

By s 238, the tribunal will only have the jurisdiction to hear Dick's unfair dismissal claim if one or more of the relevant employees have not been dismissed. 'Relevant employees' in the case of a lockout means those employees directly interested in the dispute (s 238(3)(a)). This has been interpreted to mean any employees who have been locked out at any time during the dispute. In *Campey and Sons Ltd v Bellwood* (1987), the company, because of a threat of industrial action, closed the factory on 18 October. On 22 October, the employer sent notices to the employees telling them to return on 24 October. Some did not return and were subsequently dismissed. It was held that the relevant employees for the purposes of s 238 were those employees locked out on 18 October. As some of those employees had not been dismissed, there had been selective dismissals and the tribunal had the jurisdiction to see if those who had been dismissed had been dismissed unfairly. In Dick's case, some of the employees who were locked out on 1 October had returned to work and only those who refused to return were dismissed. As such, on the authority of *Campey*, some of the relevant employees were not dismissed and therefore the tribunal has the jurisdiction to decide whether Dick's dismissal is unfair. This does not mean that the dismissal is unfair as with Wally above. It merely means the tribunal has the jurisdiction to hear the claim. The normal rules relating to a fair reason and reasonableness will apply.

Redundancy

INTRODUCTION

Questions on redundancy very often involve other areas discussed earlier in this book. In order to claim a redundancy payment, an employee must show that he or she has been dismissed for reasons of redundancy and therefore previous questions elucidating what constitutes a dismissal are relevant. In addition, there is an overlap between unfair dismissal and redundancy, in that although redundancy may be one of the fair reasons for dismissal, the procedure adopted by the employer may render the redundancy unfair. Some examination questions may deal with this aspect under a general unfair dismissal question, but it is also a likely adjunct to a redundancy question and, therefore, students should be knowledgeable on both areas before feeling sufficiently prepared for either.

General issues that the student needs to understand include:

❖ the definition of dismissal;
❖ the qualifying period;
❖ the definition of redundancy in s 139(1) of the Employment Rights Act (ERA) 1996;
❖ the effect of misconduct during the redundancy notice period;
❖ the concept of suitable alternative employment;
❖ lay-off and short-time working; and
❖ consultation and redundancy.

It has already been stated that questions on this area may also involve a discussion of the procedure involved in redundancy and therefore introduce the added factor of unfair dismissal. Issues relating to unfair selection for redundancy and procedural matters have already been discussed in Chapter 9, above. These questions show how the two areas can interlink.

For specific questions on redundancy, students should be familiar with:

❖ the continuity requirements;
❖ what constitutes an employer ceasing business;

❖ the effect of an employer moving its place of business and the relevance of the employee's contractual terms;

❖ what constitutes a diminution in the employer's requirements and the effect of any flexibility clause;

❖ the effect of a strike or other misconduct during redundancy notice;

❖ what constitutes an offer of suitable alternative employment and a reasonable refusal;

❖ the consultation requirements.

Finally, questions in this area may bring in the Transfer of Undertakings (Protection of Employment) (TUPE) Regulations 2006. These may impact on continuity issues or liability and their interrelationship with s 218 of the ERA 1996 needs to be understood.

Checklist ✔

Students should be familiar with the following areas:

■ what constitutes a redundancy;

■ what constitutes a dismissal for redundancy;

■ the qualification for the right to a redundancy payment;

■ the impact of the **TUPE Regulations 2006**

■ special provisions in relation to lay off and short-time working, misconduct and suitable alternative employment;

■ consultation provisions.

QUESTION 40

Two weeks ago, the following events occurred at Mouldy Productions Ltd, a company manufacturing various types of plastic moulding.

Amy, a married woman with two children, was dismissed after refusing to change from night-shift working to day-shift working. The company was entitled to introduce the change under the terms of her contract. The change was made to maximise profitability, although the company continued to need the same number of workers.

Jack, a maintenance worker, who had always worked at the company's Whitehaven premises, refused to move to its premises at Preston, 100 miles away. The company was moving all the maintenance workers because of a lack of work at the Whitehaven site. He was sacked without notice, having been employed for 103 weeks.

During the latter part of last year, the company conducted a reorganisation during which the company regraded a number of workers. One such worker, Leonard, was regraded downwards and suffered a consequent loss of pay and status. The regrading was on different terms from his original contract and included a provision in relation to compulsory overtime. Leonard rejected the new package and resigned. At his resignation, Leonard had been employed for four years.

▶ All the above parties are now claiming a redundancy payment. Advise Mouldy Productions Ltd as to its liability in respect of such payments.

Common Pitfalls

❖ This question is asking the student to advise the employer in relation to redundancy payments. A redundancy situation can bring in a variety of other issues, such as unfair dismissal, and in the case of Amy, it would be easy to get into a discussion of sex discrimination, but that is not what the question is asking.

❖ Always remember it is the job that is redundant and not the person.

Answer Plan

This particular question, however, is very specific in what it requires the student to discuss and, therefore, the answer must be equally as focused.

Particular points to be considered are:

❖ what constitutes a dismissal for reasons of redundancy;
❖ the definition of redundancy in s 139 of the Employment Rights Act (ERA) 1996;
❖ how far the statutory notice period in s 86 of the ERA 1996 can affect continuity;
❖ what constitutes suitable alternative employment; and
❖ what constitutes a reasonable refusal of suitable alternative employment.

ANSWER

Mouldy Productions Ltd is asking for advice in relation to potential redundancy claims by the three parties. In order to claim a redundancy payment, all the parties must first show that they have been dismissed for reasons of redundancy. Section 163(2) of the ERA 1996 provides a statutory presumption that if an employee is dismissed and claims a redundancy payment, the dismissal is for redundancy, and the burden falls to the employer to rebut the presumption and show that the dismissal was for another reason. In *Willcox v Hastings* (1987), a business was sold with the two employees. The new owner wished to retain only one of the employees because he wished to employ his son. He sacked both of the original employees, however, who both claimed a redundancy payment. The employer argued that only one of the employees was redundant but did not specify which one. The Court of Appeal held that both were redundant as the presumption in s 163(2) arose and this had not been rebutted by the employer. In respect of all three parties, therefore, Mouldy Productions needs to rebut the presumption.

Amy was dismissed when she refused to change from night-shift working to day-shift working. The definition of redundancy is to be found in s 139(1) of the Act. This states that a redundancy has occurred if the dismissal is attributable wholly or mainly to:

(a) the fact that his employer has ceased, or intends to cease, to carry on the business for the purposes for which the employee was employed by it, or has ceased or intends to cease, to carry on business in the place where the employee was so employed; or

(b) the fact that the requirements of that business for employees to carry out work of a particular kind, or for employees to carry out work of a particular kind in the place where he was so employed, have ceased or diminished or are expected to cease or diminish.

In Amy's case, the employer has not ceased to trade nor is there a moving of the place of work; thus, Amy must show that the employer's requirements for the particular work she was employed to do have ceased or diminished. She will therefore try to establish that the change from night work to day work means that Mouldy Productions now requires a different type of work and that the night work has diminished or no longer exists.

Early cases established that a change in hours, rather than a change in the job duties, did not constitute a redundancy for the purposes of s 139(1)(b) if the employer's overall requirement for the work was the same. In *Johnson v Nottinghamshire Combined Police Authority* (1974), two employees were working from 9.30 am to 5.30 pm. The authority altered its hours so that one covered 8 am to 3 pm and the other 1 am to 8 am. Both refused to accept the change and were dismissed. The Court of Appeal held that there was no redundancy. The employer still required two employees doing the same amount of work, albeit at different times. On the other hand, should the employer change the job duties and thus diminish the requirements for part of the job, this will constitute a redundancy. In *Murphy v Epsom College* (1985), the college heating system was replaced, needing new skills to maintain it. The college plumber refused to take on the new duties and was dismissed and replaced by a heating technician. The Court of Appeal held that the plumber was redundant as the employer's need for a plumber had diminished because of a change in the nature of the job.

The question to ask in Amy's case is what particular work is she employed to do? She is employed on night work, but the change to day work is permitted by her contractual terms and conditions. The contractual approach to work of a particular kind has been re-emphasised by *Cowen v Haden Ltd* (1982). In that case, the employee was a divisional contracts surveyor but his contract contained a flexibility clause. The Employment Appeal Tribunal (EAT) held that he had not been made redundant because the test was contractual and therefore there was still work available that he was contractually bound to do. The Court of Appeal reversed the decision on the facts, holding that the flexibility clause had to be interpreted by reference back to the main job duties and therefore the employee was redundant, but, importantly, upheld the tribunal on the contractual approach. The contractual approach was applied in the later case of *Pink v White* (1985). Thus, in *Lesney Products Ltd v Nolan* (1977), the change from a night shift and day shift to a double day shift was not a redundancy.

In Amy's situation, although the change in shifts is permitted by her contract, we are not told whether the job duties have changed or if any other facets of the job have altered. In *Archibald v Rossleigh Commercials Ltd* (1975), it was held that the work of an unsupervised night mechanic was different from that of an ordinary mechanic, and in *Macfisheries Ltd v Findlay* (1985), the EAT held that a change from night shift to day shift could amount to a redundancy if it involved a change in duties and responsibilities. Thus, if there is a change in Amy's job, it could be argued on the basis of *Murphy* and *Findlay* that there is a redundancy situation. It has to be said, however, that on the facts this looks unlikely. It appears that Mouldy Productions Ltd has merely changed when the job is done and Amy is required to work either day or night by her contract. Furthermore, on the facts, it appears that there is no reduction in the workforce and thus Amy is unlikely to be successful in her claim for redundancy. Mouldy Productions can argue that she was dismissed for refusing to obey a contractual order.

Jack has been employed for 103 weeks. In order to claim a redundancy payment, he must have 104 weeks' continuity and thus, on the face of it, appears to be unable to claim. It is possible, however, that the statutory minimum notice period may apply and so bring his continuity period up to 104 weeks. It is therefore necessary to see if Jack potentially has been dismissed for redundancy.

It has already been seen that s 139(1)(a) envisages a redundancy situation when the employer is moving its place of business. This means that Jack appears to have been made redundant. Given that the test is contractual, however (*Cowen v Haden Ltd*), it is necessary to discover whether Jack has a mobility clause in his contract. There does not, on the facts, appear to be an express clause. There also appears to be no evidence on which to imply a clause, given that Jack has always worked at Whitehaven. If, on the other hand, when Jack started the job he agreed to be mobile and the contract envisages this by, for example, providing travelling and lodging allowances, such a clause may be implied (*Stevenson v Teesside Bridge and Engineering Ltd* (1971)). The facts do not say what the content of the contract is and thus, on the basis of *O'Brien v Associated Fire Alarms Ltd* (1969), it could be argued that there is no mobility clause, given that Jack has always worked at Whitehaven and never been mobile. In *O'Brien*, the employees worked from the Liverpool office, which was closing down, and were told to transfer to the Barrow office some 120 miles away. While they travelled around in their jobs, they only did so within a reasonable distance from their homes and thus, while there was an implied mobility clause, the Court of Appeal held it was restricted to being mobile within such reasonable travelling distance; therefore, the employer had no right to require them to move 120 miles away and thus they were dismissed on the grounds of redundancy. While the contractual test was criticised, in *High Table Ltd v Horst* (1997), the Court of Appeal pointed out that in *O'Brien* the employer had dismissed the employees for breach of contract. Once it was decided that the employees were not in breach, the presumption of redundancy applied.

If there is a clause in the contract, however, Jack would be required to move and therefore would not be redundant. Given that such a clause does not appear to be present, can Jack be instantly dismissed for refusing to move? The courts will now only accept instant dismissal in cases of gross misconduct, gross neglect or refusal to obey a lawful reasonable order. In this case, Jack was told to move. Such a move is not part of his contractual terms and therefore it can be strongly argued that Jack is not refusing to obey an order that is lawful or reasonable. As such, the employer is not entitled to dismiss him instantly and Jack's dismissal is unlawful.

There is no mention of a contractual notice period. However, by s 86 of the ERA 1996, Jack will be entitled to a minimum notice period of one week. Although the normal rule is that an instant dismissal terminates the contract on the day the dismissal takes place, s 145(5) provides that, for the purpose of computing the qualifying period for a redundancy payment, if the instant dismissal is unlawful, the date of termination shall be the date on which the statutory notice expires and not the actual date of termination. As such, given that Jack's dismissal was unlawful, s 145(5) will operate to extend his employment by one week, so giving him the required 104 weeks' continuity to claim a redundancy payment. On the basis of *O'Brien* and *Horst* above, the employer's reason for dismissal is unfounded; therefore, the statutory presumption will apply and Jack is entitled to a redundancy payment.

Leonard has been downgraded as part of a reorganisation. He has suffered a loss in pay and status and the new post includes compulsory reasonable overtime. As a result, he has resigned. The first question to ask is: has Leonard been dismissed? While he has terminated his contract, this could be a constructive dismissal if the employer is in breach of contract (*Western Excavating (ECC) Ltd v Sharp* (1978)) by s 136(1). In this situation, it appears that Mouldy Productions has unilaterally altered the terms of Leonard's contract and, in particular, has downgraded him and lowered his pay. This is due to a reorganisation and therefore appears to be permanent. In *Millbrook Furnishing Industries Ltd v McIntosh* (1981), a unilateral alteration in job content was deemed to be a constructive dismissal even though it was temporary and there was a pressing business need. In Leonard's case, it seems that his pay and status have changed. This has been done without apparent contractual authority and without his agreement. As such, his resignation is due to a repudiatory breach on the part of the employer, entitling him to resign and claim constructive dismissal under s 136(1).

In order to be entitled to a redundancy payment, Leonard must show that his dismissal is for reasons of redundancy under s 139. It has already been noted that a redundancy occurs when either the employer ceases or moves its business, or its requirements for work of a particular kind that the employee is employed to do have ceased or diminished. If Leonard's job has changed and overall the requirements of the employer for that type of work have reduced, then there will be a redundancy even if the employer still employs the same number of people doing other work (*Murphy*). If, however, Leonard's job has remained the same and the reorganisation is for cost-cutting purposes, then the requirements of the employer for that particular work have not decreased and a redundancy has not happened. In *Shawkat v Nottingham City Hospital NHS Trust (No 2)* (2001), the Court of Appeal held that the mere fact of a reorganisation, as a result of which the employer requires the employees to do a different job, is not conclusive of redundancy. The tribunal must then decide whether there is a change in the requirements of the employer for employees to do work of a particular kind. If there is a redundancy, Mouldy Productions could try to argue that it has offered Leonard suitable alternative employment, which he has unreasonably refused (s 141). The first question for the tribunal would be whether the offer was of suitable alternative employment. This involves the tribunal looking at the nature of the employment in relation to the employee's skills and capabilities. If the job is the same, the question for the tribunal will be whether the drop in salary and the drop in status makes this unsuitable employment, given that the salary may be made up by the overtime worked. Should the tribunal conclude that the offer is of suitable employment, if it feels that the refusal by Leonard is unreasonable, then he will lose his right to a redundancy payment. It is submitted, however, that the drop in pay and status would make this an offer of unsuitable alternative employment and thus Leonard's refusal would be irrelevant.

Thus, if there has been a redundancy in Leonard's case, he will be entitled to a redundancy payment, but on the facts it seems unlikely that the requirements of the employer have diminished, and therefore no redundancy has occurred. This does not, however, prevent Leonard from taking alternative action against Mouldy Productions and claiming unfair dismissal, arguing that he has not been treated fairly.

QUESTION 41

Contractual issues now dominate all aspects of the decision as to whether an employee was dismissed by reason of redundancy for the purposes of a claim for a redundancy payment.

▶ Discuss.

Answer Plan

This question is a fairly straightforward one but it is important to always bear in mind what it is asking. It talks about all aspects of the decision, therefore it brings in contractual issues in relation to dismissal, as well as in relation to the definition of redundancy, and the answer must constantly refer to the contractual aspects of a redundancy situation.

Particular points to be considered are:

❖ the definition of dismissal in s 136 of the Employment Rights Act (ERA) 1996;

❖ how far contractual issues are relevant in defining dismissal – particularly constructive dismissal and the rest in *Western Excavating (ECC) Ltd v Sharp* (1978);

❖ the definition of redundancy in s 139 of the ERA 1996;

❖ the relevance of the terms of the employee's contract in relation to the definition, looking in particular at cases such as *Cowen v Haden Ltd* (1982); *Chapman v Goonvean and Rostowrack China Clay Co Ltd* (1973); *Johnson v Nottinghamshire Combined Police Authority* (1974); *O'Brien v Associated Fire Alarms Ltd* (1969); *Stevenson v Teesside Bridge and Engineering Ltd* (1971);

❖ contractual issues in offers of suitable alternative employment.

ANSWER

In order to claim a redundancy payment, an employee must first establish that he has been dismissed and, second, that the dismissal is for reasons of redundancy. In *Sanders v Earnest A Neale Ltd* (1974), the employees conducted a work-to-rule and eventually the factory closed down. It was held that the dismissals were not for reasons of redundancy but due to the work-to-rule, which had led to a loss of production that in turn had led to the closure. There is a statutory presumption in s 163(2) of the ERA 1996 that, if an employee is dismissed and claims a redundancy payment, his dismissal is for reasons of redundancy, and the employer must rebut the presumption to escape liability.

The starting point for the employee, therefore, is to establish that he has been dismissed. Dismissal is defined in s 136 of the ERA 1996 as termination by the employer, with or without notice, a fixed-term contract expiring without being renewed, or an employee resigning in circumstances in which he is entitled to do so by the employer's conduct. In addition, by s 136(5), if the employment is terminated by the death, dissolution or liquidation of the employer, or the appointment of a receiver, there is a dismissal for reasons of redundancy. The majority of these situations do not raise contractual issues but, in respect of an employee resigning, contractual issues are vitally important in establishing whether the resignation constitutes a constructive dismissal.

The key part of the definition of constructive dismissal is that the employee must have been entitled to leave. There are two possible interpretations of the word 'entitled'. On the one hand, it could mean that the employer acted so unreasonably that the employee could not be expected to stay. Conversely, it may mean that the employer's conduct amounted to a repudiatory breach that the employee accepted as ending the contract. After a period of uncertainty, the Court of Appeal, in *Western Excavating (ECC) Ltd v Sharp* (1978), decided that the contractual approach was the correct one, Lord Denning stating that conduct that entitled the employee to leave and claim dismissal had to be conduct on the part of the employer that was 'a significant breach going to the root of the contract of employment'. Whereas a breach of an important express term will be the basis of a claim, the test is wider, and a breach of an implied term can lead to a constructive dismissal. Thus, it is important for a tribunal to establish all the terms of the contract to discover if a repudiatory breach has occurred. While the contractual test may appear to be narrow, the development of the implied duty of mutual trust and respect has, in fact, opened up the area so that unreasonable conduct on the part of the employer may in fact be a breach of the implied duty and thus a repudiatory breach (*Bliss v South East Thames Regional Health Authority* (1985)).

The contractual approach, however, can create problems. First, if the breach is a unilateral variation in terms, the employee must decide within a relatively short period of time to resign, otherwise he risks his conduct being seen as acceptance of the variation (*Jeffrey v Laurence Scott and Electromotors Ltd* (1977), although see *Alcan Extrusions v Yates* (1996)). Second, if the breach is anticipatory and the employer rectifies the breach before the employee resigns, there is no constructive dismissal as the employer is no longer in breach (*Norwest Holst Group Administration Ltd v Harrison* (1985)). Third, there can be no repudiatory breach if the employer feels that it is exercising its contractual rights, even if it is mistaken as to the precise terms of the contract (*Frank Wright and Co (Holdings) Ltd v Punch* (1980)). This indicates that where there is a genuine dispute as to the terms, the intention of the employer is relevant.

Should the employee establish that he has been dismissed, in order to claim a redundancy payment, he must further establish that the dismissal is for reasons of redundancy. Should the employer attempt to rebut the presumption in s 163(2), the employee must show his dismissal was for one of the reasons in s 139(1). In other words, he must show that his employer has ceased to trade, that it has moved its business or that its requirements for the particular kind of work the employee is required to do have ceased or diminished or are expected to do so.

While the employer ceasing to trade will normally not raise contractual issues, three points should be mentioned: first, the protection in s 136(5), which states that the death, dissolution or liquidation of the employer constitutes a dismissal for redundancy purposes; second, if the employer is taken over in circumstances in which s 218 of the ERA 1996 applies, if the business is taken over as a going concern, the employee cannot claim redundancy from the old employer, even though there has been a fundamental change in the contract. On the other hand, if merely the assets are transferred, then the employee must claim redundancy from his old employer, otherwise he will lose his employment protection rights as a new continuity period begins with the new employment (*Woodhouse v Peter Brotherhood Ltd* (1972)). Third, if the employer is taken over in circumstances in which the Transfer of Undertakings (Protection of Employment) (TUPE) Regulations 2006 apply, then, despite the change in terms, there is no breach and no redundancy, although the employee has the right, by reg 4(7), to object to the transfer and not move. Should he do this, however, he falls into legal limbo, because the change of employer is not a dismissal and thus he will not be able to claim a redundancy payment.

In relation to the second part of the definition (the employer moving place of business), the question for the tribunal is whether there is a mobility clause in the employee's contract. If there is not, his place of work contractually is where he physically works and, thus, if his employer moves, he will be redundant, unless the move is a short distance away and has no real effect on the employee (*Managers (Holborn) Ltd v Hohne* (1977)). If the employee has a mobility clause in his contract, however, his place of work will be within the content of the clause and thus there is no redundancy. Such a clause may be express or implied. If express, this will cause few problems for the tribunal. Whether such a term is implied, however, will be a question of fact looking at all the circumstances of the case.

In *O'Brien v Associated Fire Alarms* (1969), two electricians worked for a company in Liverpool and had always worked there, although the company operated throughout Britain. The work diminished in Liverpool and they were asked to work in Cumberland. They refused and were dismissed. Their claims for redundancy payments were upheld by the Court of Appeal on the basis that there was no express or implied term requiring them to work anywhere but the Liverpool office. Conversely, in *Stevenson v Teesside Bridge and Engineering Ltd* (1971), a steel erector was not entitled to a redundancy payment when work dried up at the site where he mainly worked, since travelling between sites was found to be an implied term in his contract, given he had accepted this when interviewed and the contract envisaged mobility since it contained provision for travelling and subsistence expenses. Although in *High Table Ltd v Horst* (1997), the Court of Appeal adopted a factual test rather than a contractual one in deciding that an employee, who had always worked at one place, was redundant when work there ceased, this was despite a mobility clause in her contract and was because she had only worked in one place for five years.

The third definition of redundancy is perhaps the one in relation to which contractual issues predominate. Given that the employee is arguing that the work of the particular kind he was employed to do has ceased or diminished, the tribunal must look to his contract to identify the particular work. This contractual approach was taken by the EAT in *Cowen v Haden Ltd* (1982) and was endorsed by the Court of Appeal, although the decision was overturned on the facts.

However, this does not mean that any change of contractual terms is a redundancy (*Chapman v Goonvean and Rostowrack China and Clay Co Ltd* (1973)) and the tribunal must see if, in relation to the contractual terms, the function for which the employee is employed has ceased or diminished. This means that if the work still remains and the amount of work the employer requires remains the same, the fact that it requires the work at different hours does not mean a redundancy has occurred (*Johnson v Nottinghamshire Combined Police Authority* (1974)). On the other hand, if the requirements for the type of work have diminished, there is a redundancy, even if the employer takes on more employees due to an increase in a different type of work (*Murphy v Epsom College* (1985)). Thus, an employer replacing a barmaid with a younger version will not constitute a redundancy because the employer still requires the same function to be performed, albeit by a different type of employee (*Vaux and Associated Breweries v Ward* (1968)), although if it dismisses all its employees and replaces them with independent contractors, then there is a redundancy, because its needs for employees have ceased.

While the contractual test is important, *Horst* and the later case of *Church v West Lancashire NHS Trust* (1998) both talk of a mixture of the factual/function test and the contractual test. This more flexible approach has been endorsed by the House of Lords decision in *Murray v Foyle Meats Ltd* (1999). In that case, employees worked as meat plant operatives. They normally worked in the slaughter hall, but contractually could be asked to work elsewhere and had occasionally done so. As a result of a decline in business, the employer needed fewer employees in the slaughter hall and Murray was made redundant. He argued that the pool of selection (employees in the slaughter hall) was too narrow and that, given that he had worked elsewhere, selection should have been across the whole of the business. The House of Lords held that the requirements of the employer for employees to work in the slaughter hall had diminished and therefore the pool for selection had been correct. However, Lord Irvine LC commented that:

> both the contract test and the function test miss the point. The key word in the statute is 'attributable' and there is no reason in law why the dismissal of an employee should not be attributable to a diminution in the employer's need for employees irrespective of the terms of his contract or the function he performed.

While the contract test is still important, it appears that future decisions will rest on a more flexible approach.

One further aspect of redundancy may give rise to contractual issues and that is where the employer argues that the employee is redundant but that he has been offered suitable alternative work that the employee has unreasonably refused (s 141). While the reasonableness of the employee's refusal will normally involve considerations outside his contract, the question of whether the offer is suitable will entail the tribunal in considering the redundant job and comparing it to the offer to see if the offer matches the employee's skills and capabilities. In *Carron Co v Robertson* (1967), the court held that all factors should be considered such as the nature of the work, hours and pay, the employee's strength and training, his experience and ability, and his status. In *Standard Telephones and Cables v Yates* (1981), it was held that the offer of unskilled assembly work to a skilled card wirer was not an offer of suitable alternative employment. Thus, the terms of the employee's original contract will be the starting point for the tribunal and will be an important factor in deciding if the employee has refused suitable alternative work unreasonably and thus disentitled himself to a redundancy payment.

It can be seen from the above, therefore, that contractual issues permeate all aspects of a dismissal for reasons of redundancy in that they may be a consideration in relation to dismissal, the definition of redundancy and part of the consideration of whether the employer has offered suitable alternative employment to its redundant employee.

QUESTION 42

Express Deliveries Ltd is a freight forwarding firm in the Midlands. At the beginning of the year, it ran into difficulties and carried out a reorganisation. Ron, whose contract stated that he was a credit controller, but that he was obliged to 'carry out any other duties that might be assigned to him', was reassigned to a bookkeeping post, which involved a regrading from Grade 3 to Grade 4, although he remained on the same salary. The change occurred because of a reduction in the need for credit controllers. Ron has resigned and claimed a redundancy payment.

Penny was taken on by the company as a trainee manager to take over from Mr Tibbs who was due to take early retirement. Mr Tibbs changed his mind and therefore the company sacked Penny. Penny is also claiming a redundancy payment.

Wendy is employed by the company as a cashier. Early last month, the company instructed the cashiers that, within six months, they would be required to use the newly installed computers to handle all cash transactions. Wendy has no experience of computers and objects to the change. Last week, she resigned and is now claiming a redundancy payment.

▶ Advise Express Deliveries Ltd.

Answer Plan

This is another question that raises issues in relation to the definition of dismissal for reasons of redundancy and, in particular, in relation to one party, the inherent flexibility within an employment contract.

Particular issues to be considered are:

❖ the qualification requirement to claim a redundancy payment;
❖ the definition of dismissal;
❖ the definition of redundancy in s 139(1) of the Employment Rights Act (ERA) 1996;
❖ the relationship between flexibility clauses and work of a particular kind – in particular, a discussion of *Cowen v Haden Ltd* (1982);

❖   the necessity for a reduction in the employer's requirements for employees;
❖   the inherent flexibility within the contract and how far a change in working methods constitutes a repudiatory breach and can constitute a redundancy situation.

ANSWER

Express Deliveries Ltd has asked for advice in relation to three parties claiming a redundancy payment. All the claims have arisen as a result of a reorganisation caused by the company's financial difficulties last year. In order to claim a statutory redundancy payment, all three parties must have been employed for two years at the relevant date (s 155 of the Employment Rights Act 1996) and must have been dismissed for reasons of redundancy. By s 163(2) of the 1996 Act, if a dismissed employee claims a redundancy payment, there is a statutory presumption that the dismissal was for reasons of redundancy and the burden shifts to the employer to show some other reason for the dismissal. As such, Express Deliveries Ltd can challenge the three parties by first arguing that there have not been any dismissals, and second, if they have all been dismissed, that those dismissals were for reasons other than redundancy.

Ron was employed as a credit controller, but due to the reorganisation has now been downgraded to bookkeeper, although his salary has remained the same. He has resigned and is claiming constructive dismissal. Given the fact that he has a flexibility clause in his contract, the first question to ask is has he been dismissed?

By s 136(1) of the ERA 1996, an employee shall be treated as dismissed by his employer if he terminates his contract, with or without notice, in circumstances in which he is entitled to do so by his employer's conduct. While early cases argued that any unreasonable conduct on the part of the employer set up a constructive dismissal claim, Lord Denning MR in Western Excavating (ECC) Ltd v Sharp (1978) held that the contractual approach is the correct one. His Lordship talked of the employer being guilty of conduct that is a significant breach going to the root of the contract, or which shows that the employer no longer wishes to be bound by one of the essential terms of the contract. Thus, if Ron can argue that Express Deliveries is in breach of an essential term of the contract, he can argue that he has been constructively dismissed.

While it would appear that Ron's contract lays down his specific job duties, it also contains a wide flexibility clause that requires Ron to carry out any other duties assigned to him. Given that Ron's salary has remained the same, the two changes that have occurred are in relation to his duties and his status. If the change in duties is covered by the flexibility clause, then the only potential breach by the employer is the downgrading, and Express Deliveries may further argue that this is impliedly covered by the clause allowing a change in duties. Much therefore hinges on the flexibility clause and how the tribunal will regard it.

In *Nelson v BBC* (1977), the employee was employed as a Grade 3 producer and editor, but had only worked in the BBC's Caribbean service. When that service was cut back, the BBC argued that Nelson had been made redundant, but this was rejected by the Court of Appeal, which said that to come to such a decision would be implying a restriction into a widely drafted express term in his contract. Following this decision, the EAT, in *Cowen v Haden Ltd* (1982), decided that a contracts surveyor had not been dismissed for redundancy because of the wide flexibility clause in his contract. However, this point was reversed by the Court of Appeal, which held that the flexibility clause was an adjunct to his job as a contracts surveyor and not an extra form of employment that allowed his employer to transfer him to a totally different job.

On the basis of this authority, it is necessary to see if Ron's new duties are fundamentally different from his old duties as credit controller. If they are, then the bookkeeping work does not fall within the flexibility clause and Express Deliveries is in repudiatory breach of contract that entitles Ron to resign and claim constructive dismissal (*Western Excavating*). If, on the other hand, the new duties are similar to the old and fall within the flexibility clause, there is still the question of whether the drop in status constitutes a repudiatory breach. It is submitted that the drop would be a repudiatory breach and further that there is no implied contractual right to downgrade within the flexibility clause (*Hall v Lodge* (1977)). Express Deliveries may argue that the changes are only temporary and thus not repudiatory. Such an argument was put forward in *Millbrook Furnishing Industries Ltd v McIntosh* (1981) but was rejected on the facts. On the facts in the problem, there is no evidence that these changes are temporary and they appear to have been in operation for some time. As such, Ron can argue that he has been constructively dismissed.

To a large extent, the arguments used to demonstrate that Ron has been dismissed are also pertinent in relation to the question of whether his dismissal is for reasons of redundancy. By s 139(1)(b) of the 1996 Act, a redundancy exists if the employer's requirements for employees to carry out work of a particular kind have ceased or diminished. *Cowen* demonstrates that the test is the work that the employee was employed to do and for this the tribunal must look to the contractual job duties.

However, in *Shawkat v Nottingham City Hospital NHS Trust (No 2)* (2001), the Court of Appeal held that the mere fact of a reorganisation, as a result of which the employer requires employees to do a different job, is not conclusive of redundancy. The tribunal must then decide if there is a change in the requirements of the employer for employees to carry out work of a particular kind. Furthermore, the cases of *High Table Ltd v Horst* (1997) and *Church v West Lancashire NHS Trust* (1998) state that the test to determine what is work of a particular kind that the employee is employed to do is a mixture of both a contractual and a functional test – that is, the tribunal must look at the work specified in the employee's contract and at the work the employee was actually doing. This more flexible approach was endorsed by the House of Lords in *Murray v Foyle Meats Ltd* (1999), although Lord Irvine in that case stated that there was no reason in law why the dismissal of an employee should not be attributable to the employer's need to reduce its workforce irrespective of the job the employee was employed to do. If, in reality, Ron has only done credit controlling, then the contractual and functional test will produce the same result.

Given that it has already been argued that the work Ron is employed to do is credit controlling and not bookkeeping, if the employer's requirements for credit controllers have diminished, Ron's dismissal is for reasons of redundancy. This will be the case even if the amount of work for credit controllers has increased if, for example, because of new technology, the requirements for employees to do that work has diminished. Likewise, if the amount of credit controlling has diminished, it is irrelevant if the amount of bookkeeping has increased because that was not the work, it has been argued, that Ron was employed to do. The only possible argument for Express Deliveries is to say that Ron was offered suitable alternative work that he unreasonably refused and thus he is not entitled to a redundancy payment (s 141 (2) and (3)). It is unlikely, however, that a tribunal will accept that an offer involving a loss of status will be an offer of suitable alternative work, given the factors a tribunal must consider, as laid down in *Carron Co v Robertson* (1967), and as seen in cases such as *Taylor v Kent County Council* (1969) and *Cambridge and District Co-operative Society Ltd v Ruse* (1993).

Penny was taken on as a trainee manager to take over from another employee who was expected to take early retirement. When this did not materialise, Penny was dismissed. While Penny has clearly been dismissed, it should be stated that unless she has been employed for two years she will not be entitled to a statutory redundancy payment, although Express Deliveries may have its own scheme that gives its employees better rights and Penny may have enough continuity to claim under the private scheme. In order to claim, however, Penny must show that her dismissal was for reasons of redundancy. It has already been stated that one of the redundancy situations in s 139(1)(b) is that the employer's requirements for employees to do work of a particular kind have ceased or diminished. While *North Yorkshire County Council v Fay* (1985) appears to go against this decision, this is in doubt since *Horst*, *Church* and

Murray. Furthermore, in *Fay*, the employee was dismissed to make place for an employee who was redundant. This is not the situation here. In Penny's case, she was taken on to replace another worker who eventually remained. She was also taken on as a trainee, not because of any increase in work. In *O'Hare v Rotaprint* (1980), a company expanded its workforce and anticipated increased production that never materialised. The EAT held that the dismissal of the extra employees was not a dismissal for redundancy because it could hardly have been said that work had diminished if, in fact, it never materialised in the first place. In Penny's case, the amount of work that the employer requires and the number of employees it requires to do that work have remained static. Thus Penny has not been dismissed for reasons of redundancy and is not entitled to a redundancy payment.

Wendy has resigned because her method of work has changed from manual to computerised. Again, it is necessary to establish whether Express Deliveries is in repudiatory breach of contract before turning to the issue of redundancy. While there is no flexibility clause in Wendy's contract, there is an implied term in any contract of employment that the employee must adapt to changes in working methods. In *Cresswell v Board of Inland Revenue* (1984), revenue officers refused to operate a new computerised system of PAYE administration. Walton J refused the employees a declaration that such changes were outside their contractual duties. It was stated, however, that such a change should be accompanied by relevant training, and a failure to provide such training and the dismissal of an employee for incapability could be an unfair dismissal. Wendy has only just been told of the change and it will not be brought in for six months. Provided that Express Deliveries institutes the proper training, it is within its contractual rights to alter working methods and, as such, there has been no breach on its part. Wendy has thus resigned and not been dismissed and is not entitled to a redundancy payment. Even if there had been a dismissal, a change in working methods is not a diminution in the employer's requirements for work of a particular kind (*North Riding Garages v Butterwick* (1967) and *Vaux and Associated Breweries Ltd v Ward* (1968)) and thus there is no redundancy.

QUESTION 43

Fragrancies is a company marketing and selling cosmetics and other beauty products. Due to financial difficulties, Fragrancies went into negotiations with Smashing Smells, a company manufacturing perfume, with the aim of selling off the beauty products side of the business. The cosmetic side of the business was to be wound up. Todd was employed as a technician developing cosmetics. He was given three months' notice of redundancy but, two months before his notice expired, Fragrancies discovered that he had been selling technical details to a rival firm. It sent Todd a letter telling him of its discovery, but stating that, due to the liquidation, he could work his notice.

Ron worked for the cosmetics side as a salesman. When he was given three months' notice of redundancy, because of the liquidation of that part of the company, he went on strike until the company was wound up.

Smashing Smells operates tight security and employs security men. It decided to put out the security operation to tender and Group 8 won the contract. Last week, Group 8 took over the security. Len worked as a security guard. He was dismissed by Smashing Smells two hours before the transfer took place because he is 62 years old and Group 8 refused to take employees over the age of 60.

▶ Advise Ron and Todd of their entitlement to a redundancy payment, and Len of any legal rights he may have under **TUPE 2006**.

Common Pitfalls ✗
❖ This is quite a complex question and again it is important to focus on what the question is asking.
❖ In respect of Len, given his age, it would be easy to get into a discussion of age discrimination but the question asks specifically about **TUPE 2006**

Answer Plan

This is a complex case involving three employers, and it is necessary to establish the claims that lie in relation to each of the employers. Thus, Ron and Todd will be claiming against Fragrancies. Len may have a claim against Smashing Smells or Group 8. Ron and Todd will be claiming under the ERA 1996 and Len may have a claim under the TUPE Regulations. In a question like this, it is important to identify the strands at the beginning, otherwise the answer will not be coherent and logical.

Particular issues to be considered are:

❖ the situation of employees where the employer is wound up under s 136(5) of the Employment Rights Act (ERA) 1996;
❖ the position of the employee whose misconduct is discovered during notice of redundancy under s 140(1);
❖ the exception to the above in s 140(2);
❖ the definition of a transfer of an undertaking in the Transfer of Undertakings (Protection of Employment) (TUPE) Regulations 2006;

❖ the impact of *Watson Rask and Christiansen v ISS Kantineservice A/S* (1993); *Stichting (Dr Sophie Redmond) v Bartol* (1992); *Dines v Initial Health Care Services* (1994); *Suzen v Zehnacker Gebäudereinigung GmbH Krankenhausservice and Leforth GmbH* (1997); *Betts v Brintel Helicopters* (1997);

❖ the meaning of employed 'immediately before the transfer' in *Litster v Forth Dry Dock and Engineering Co Ltd* (1989); and

❖ the interpretation of reg 7 of the TUPE Regulations 2006.

ANSWER

The problem involves a discussion of two different pieces of legislation. In relation to Ron and Todd, the issues to be discussed are whether they can claim a redundancy payment from Fragrancies as there is no transfer of the cosmetics side of the business; rather, it is being wound up. In relation to Len, the question is whether he has been transferred as part of a transfer of an undertaking or not and thus where liability may lie in relation to the dismissal.

Ron and Todd wish to claim a redundancy payment from Fragrancies. An employee is entitled to a redundancy payment if he is dismissed by reason of redundancy. By s 136(5) of the ERA 1996, the liquidation of the employer shall be treated as a dismissal for reasons of redundancy unless the exception in s 140(1) applies. Section 140(1) provides that where the employee is under notice of redundancy, an employee shall not be entitled to a redundancy payment where his employer is entitled to terminate the contract by reason of the employee's conduct and:

❖ terminates without notice;

❖ terminates with shorter notice than the redundancy notice; or

❖ terminates with the same notice as the redundancy notice but accompanies the notice with a written statement that it would be entitled to terminate without notice by reason of the employee's conduct.

Thus, if s 140(1) applies, the reason for the employee's dismissal is his conduct and not redundancy; he is not entitled to a redundancy payment.

Todd was under notice of redundancy when the company discovered that he had been selling technical details to a rival firm. The employee owes a duty of fidelity to his employer and breach of this duty will constitute gross misconduct. Part of this duty is the requirement not to divulge confidential information (*Cranleigh Precision Engineering Ltd v Bryant* (1964)); thus, Todd has broken this duty and committed gross misconduct, which would entitle Fragrancies to dismiss him without notice. The employer must have evidence, however, that the employee is guilty. If the employer merely has a reasonable belief in the employee's guilt, s 140(1) will not operate (*Bonner v Gilbert (H) Ltd (1989)*).

Todd has been guilty of gross misconduct, but to be disentitled to a redundancy payment, s 140(1)(c) must apply. There has been much debate on the meaning of the section. One argument is that the section means that the employee has been dismissed for redundancy, but in circumstances in which the employer could have dismissed for cause, either by giving no or shorter notice or the same notice but expressly stating the dismissal is for cause. The second interpretation is that the cause rebuts the presumption that the dismissal is for reasons of redundancy but the employer must comply with the procedural requirements for the rebuttal to be effective. *Sanders v Ernest A Neale Ltd (1974)* leans towards the first interpretation while stressing the importance of the procedural requirements. In *Simmons v Hoover Ltd (1977)*, the EAT held that if an employee is dismissed but the dismissal is not wholly or mainly attributable to redundancy but to misconduct, then the procedural aspects of s 140 put the employee on notice to that effect and should the employer fail to comply with the procedural requirements, it cannot rely on the section. In Todd's case, although the employer knew about the misconduct, it did not terminate the contract immediately or give shorter notice than the redundancy notice. Fragrancies made Todd aware that the misconduct had been discovered, but said that, given that the liquidation was happening, he could work out his notice. It does not appear that Todd was told that the employer could terminate without notice because of his conduct, and thus could hardly be said to make Todd aware that he was being dismissed for his misconduct. As such, it is submitted that Fragrancies has not satisfied the procedural requirements in s 140(1)(c) and thus Todd is entitled to a redundancy payment.

Ron also appears to fall within the provisions of s 140(1) as he went on strike, which is a breach of contract. There is an exception to s 140(1), however, in s 140(2). This provides that if, after being given notice of redundancy an employee goes on strike, s 140(1) shall not operate to deprive him of a redundancy payment. This section protects the employee who strikes in protest of redundancy but does not protect an employee who is on strike and then is selected for redundancy (*Simmons v Hoover*). Therefore, as Ron has taken strike action in protest at the redundancy, he falls within the provisions of s 140(2) and is entitled to a redundancy payment.

Len was employed by Smashing Smells as a security guard. The security operation has been taken over by Group 8. The first point to establish is whether this is a transfer of an undertaking to which the TUPE Regulations 2006 will apply. The original 1981 Regulations were introduced to bring into operation the Acquired Rights Directive

(77/187/EEC) and, as such, their interpretation is subject to the Directive. Before amendments made by the Trade Union Reform and Employment Rights Act (TURERA) 1993, the TUPE Regulations did not apply to transfers that were not commercial ventures. After the decision of *Stichting (Dr Sophie Richmond) v Bartol* (1992) in the European Court of Justice (ECJ), the Regulations were amended to include non-commercial ventures that were transferred. From *Stirling v Dietsmann Management Systems Ltd* (1991), it appeared, however, that the Regulations would not apply where the transfer did not involve a transfer in the ownership of assets and where a peripheral part of the employer's business was transferred but not the main part.

This interpretation is now incorrect since the ECJ decision of *Watson Rask and Christiansen v ISS Kantineservice A/S* (1993). In this case, the catering service of a company was put out to tender. The company that won the contract took over control of the employees and the existing catering equipment. The ECJ held that the Directive applied where there is a change in the person who is responsible for the business, regardless of whether there was any change in the ownership of the undertaking. This has been followed in *Wren v Eastbourne Borough Council* (1993) and *Dines v Initial Health Care Services* (1994). It is unlikely that Smashing Smells is only employing one employee in security and equally unlikely that, if it employs more than one, only Len is being transferred; therefore, cases like *Suzen v Zehnacker Gebäudereinigung GmbH Krankenhausservice and Leforth GmbH* (1997) and *Betts v Brintel Helicopters* (1997) are not relevant. It should also be noted that reg 3(1)(b) of the 2006 TUPE Regulations makes it clear that a transfer applies when a service provider changes and that there will be a TUPE transfer if the transferor ceases activities that are taken up by the new contractor, as long as there is an organised grouping of employees whose main purpose is to carry out that activity. Given existing case law, the transfer of the security service will be the transfer of an undertaking under the Regulations.

As the transfer does fall within the Regulations, reg 4(2) provides that the transfer operates to transfer all the transferor's rights, powers, duties and responsibilities over to the transferee. This means that, in relation to employees transferred over to Group 8, their contractual terms should remain the same. Regulation 4(2) therefore transfers liability from the transferor to the transferee. Such liability, however, only transfers in relation to employees employed immediately before the transfer (reg 4(3)). Len was dismissed two hours before the transfer took place. Under the old authority of *Secretary of State for Employment v Spence* (1987), 179 employees were dismissed three hours before the transfer took place; they were held not to be employed immediately before the transfer, but this is now subject to the House of Lords' decision in *Litster v Forth Dry Dock and Engineering Co Ltd* (1989). This judgment inserted the words into reg 4(3) 'or would have been so employed had he not been unfairly dismissed by reg 7'. In addition, in *ECM (Vehicle Delivery Service) Ltd v Cox*

(1999), the EAT held that a transferee cannot avoid the TUPE Regulations by refusing to take on the transferor's workforce. Whereas it does not appear that Group 8 is refusing to take on the whole workforce, this decision may help Len.

Thus, Len may have been transferred to Group 8 if his dismissal is unfair by reg 7. That regulation provides that a dismissal of an employee as a result of the transfer will be automatically unfair unless it is for an economic, technical or organisational reason that entailed a change in the workforce (reg 7(2)), in which case there is a fair dismissal for some other substantial reason, although the employer still has to satisfy the requirements of reasonableness. In Wheeler v Patel (1987), it was held that the dismissal of employees as a condition of the transfer taking place did not fall within reg 7(2). In Meikle v McPhail (1983), it was held that a redundancy situation caused by the transfer did fall within reg 7(2).

In Len's case, it appears that the reason for his dismissal was not an economic, technical or organisational reason involving a change in the workforce. Even if such a reason were proved, there has been no warning or consultation and as such the employer has failed to comply with the requirements of reasonableness in s 98(4) of the ERA 1996. As such, Len has been unfairly dismissed and, on the basis of Lister, liability for that dismissal has transferred to Group 8 and it is that employer which he should sue.

QUESTION 44

The implementation of the Acquired Rights Directive in the form of the TUPE Regulations 1981 was meant to alleviate the deficiencies in the statutory protection; however, the original misimplementation of the Directive reduced the protection afforded to employees. The TUPE Regulations 2006 have sought to remedy these deficiencies.

▶ To what extent do you consider the **TUPE Regulations 2006** now provide complete protection for employees who are the subject of a transfer?

Answer Plan

This question requires a fairly detailed knowledge of both the Transfer of Undertakings (Protection of Employment) (TUPE) Regulations 1981 and TUPE Regulations 2006 and to demonstrate whether the 2006 Regulations now provide adequate protection. To answer this question, a student must be aware of the changes made by the 2006 Regulations and analyse whether they provide greater protection for employees.

Particular issues to be considered are:

- the definition of an undertaking pre-2006;
- the interpretation of a transfer within the Regulations and the changes required by ECJ decisions;
- the protection afforded by reg 4 (2);
- the impact of *Litster v Forth Dry Dock and Engineering Co Ltd* (1989);
- the protection in reg 7.

ANSWER

The TUPE Regulations 2006 were brought into force to implement the Acquired Rights Directive (Directive 2001/23/EC). The Directive derives a lot of its provisions from the original Acquired Rights Directive (77/187/EEC), which was subsequently amended by Directive 98/59/EC.

The purpose of the Directive and the Regulations is to preserve the whole of an employee's contractual rights through the transfer and not only his continuity rights. Such protection, however, only occurs where there is a relevant transfer of an undertaking. Thus a tribunal must first consider whether there is an undertaking for the purposes of the Regulations and second whether that undertaking has been transferred.

The 2006 Regulations do not include a definition of what constitutes an undertaking, unlike the 1981 Regulations. However, reg 3, which defines what is meant by a transfer, does have phrases that adopt ECJ jurisprudence in this area. Regulation 3 talks of the transfer of an economic entity that retains its identity and defines an economic entity as an organised grouping of resources that has the objective of pursuing an economic activity, whether or not that activity is central or ancillary (reg 3(2)). It is also contained in reg 3 that the Regulations apply to both public and private undertakings whether operating for gain or not (reg 3(4)(a)).

In *RCO Support Services and Aintree Hospital v UNISON* (2002), the Court of Appeal upheld the finding from the EAT that there could be an undertaking even where neither substantial assets nor the majority of the workforce transfers. In *Cheeseman v Brewer Contracts Ltd* (2001), the EAT stated that to be an economic entity does not entail the undertaking having significant assets and that in certain undertakings, such as cleaning, the assets are the manpower. This gives a wide definition of undertaking and affords protection to those employees in service industries who may be more vulnerable to transfers. Thus in *P&O Trans European Ltd v Initial Transport Services*

Ltd (2003), the EAT held there was a transfer of an undertaking where P&O took over the provision of a back-up delivery service, plus drivers, operated for Shell. There were no assets transferred but the EAT held that there was a discrete economic entity that could be transferred.

Regulation 3 defines a relevant transfer. This applies in two situations. The first is similar to the old definition under the 1981 Regulations – that is, 'the transfer of an undertaking, business or part of an undertaking or business . . . where there is a transfer of an economic entity which retains its identity' (reg 3(1)(a)). However, there is a new second definition of a transfer where there is a 'service provision change'. This is where either activities cease to be carried out by a person and are carried out by another on behalf of that person (a contractor), activities cease to be carried out by a contractor and are carried instead by another on behalf of the person (a subsequent contractor), and activities cease to be carried out by the contractor or subsequent contractor and are carried out by the person on his own behalf (reg 3(1)(b)). However reg 3(3) must also be satisfied for there to be a service provision change. This means that there must be an organised grouping of employees that has the principal purpose of carrying out the activities in question, the activities must be more than the organisation of a single task or of short-term duration, and the activities must not consist wholly or mainly in the supply of goods for a person's use. It is clear that this new provision is intended to cover contracting out, re-contracting out and contracting in, activities that were prevalent in the 1980s with the then government policy of compulsory competitive tendering.

This is a welcome clarification and adopts ECJ jurisprudence. While the 1981 Regulations were amended to include non-commercial ventures, national interpretation of what constituted a transfer left large numbers of employees unprotected.

The EAT in *Stirling v Dietsmann Management Systems Ltd* (1991) said that to have a transfer within the meaning of the Regulations, there had to be some transfer of ownership of assets and the part transferred had to be a major and not peripheral part of the employer's business. On this interpretation, if an employer put out a service to tender, such as catering or security, given that no ownership of assets was transferred, merely employees, this was not a transfer within the Regulations.

In *Watson Rask and Christiansen v ISS Kantineservice A/S* (1993), the ECJ interpreted the Directive. In that case, a company tendered its catering provision that it had previously run itself, employing the catering staff. The company that won the tender merely took over control of the existing employees and equipment. It changed the terms of the employees' contracts and then the employees resigned and claimed constructive dismissal. The transferee claimed that there had not been a transfer within the provisions of the Directive as there was no transfer of assets and the transferee was only providing a service for the transferor. The ECJ held that a relevant transfer had occurred. This happened when there is a change in the legal or natural person who is responsible for carrying out the business and who incurs the obligations of employer vis-à-vis the employees. As such, *Stirling* is now not good law and *Watson Rask* has since been applied in national courts (*Wren v Eastbourne Borough Council* (1993) and *Dines v Initial Health Care Services Ltd* (1994)). However, where an employer loses, for example, one contract that affects only a number of its employees, it is then a matter for the tribunal whether an undertaking has been transferred (that is, an economic entity as opposed to an identifiable activity). This is the result of *Suzen v Zehnacker Gebäudereinigung GmbH Krankenhausservice and Leforth GmbH* (1997), in which the ECJ held that the loss of a one cleaning contract to a competitor did not amount to the transfer of an economic entity, as an entity cannot be reduced to the activity it performs. This was followed in *Betts v Brintel Helicopters* (1997), in which the loss of a contract to provide helicopter services where the new contractor acquired the rights to land on and use oil rig facilities did not amount to the transfer of an economic entity where no staff were transferred. According to Lindsay J, in *Cheesman v R Brewer Contracts Ltd* (2001), the transfer of an economic entity implies a degree of structure and autonomy, which can be concluded by looking at factors such as the identity of the workforce, the management structure, the way work is organised, the operating methods and the resources. If however, the reason that the workforce is not taken on is to avoid TUPE, then, according to the Court of Appeal in *ECM (Vehicle Delivery Service) Ltd v Cox* (1999), there is relevant transfer and the employees can claim from the transferee. This is supported by *RCO Support Servces and Aintree Hospital Trust v UNISON* (above).

The effect of a transfer on an employee's contract is in reg 4. Regulation 4(2) provides that the transferee shall acquire 'all the rights, powers, duties and liabilities' under or in connection with the contract. The regulation also states that any act or omission, before the transfer is complete is treated as an act or omission of the transferee. This merely encapsulates judicial interpretation under the previous Regulations so that, in *DJM International Ltd v Nicholas* (1996), it was held that the transferee became liable for an act of sex discrimination committed by the transferor prior to the transfer. However, in *MITIE Management Service Ltd v French* (2002), the EAT held that it does not extend to the transfer of a profit-sharing scheme but what transferred was the entitlement to participate in an equivalent scheme provided by the transferee.

Regulation 4(4) and (5) specifically spells out protection for an employee against a variation in his terms. Such a variation is void (reg 4(4)) unless the principal reason for the change is an economic, technical or organisational (ETO) reason entailing changes in the workforce. Regulation 4(5) allows an employer and employee to agree a variation where the principal reason is an ETO reason. Similar wording appears in reg 7 covering dismissal discussed below.

Regulation 4(2) gives wide protection. It expands on the wording of its predecessor (reg 5(3)), which only applied to those employees employed immediately before the transfer. In *Secretary of State for Employment v Spence* (1987), the Court of Appeal held that the regulation did not protect employees who were sacked three hours before the transfer took place. In the later case of *Litster v Forth Dry Dock and Engineering Co Ltd* (1989), the House of Lords held that such an interpretation would go against the purpose of the Directive and inserted the phrase in the Regulations 'or would have been so employed had he not been unfairly dismissed by reg 8 (now reg 7)', thus protecting those employees dismissed as a result of the transferee's insistence. This wording is now contained in reg 4(3) so enshrining case principles in legislation. It should be noted, however, that the dismissals are not void; the decision merely establishes that liability for the dismissals rests with the transferee and not the (normally) bankrupt transferor. This appears to go against the ECJ decision of *Bork (P) International A/S v Foreningen af Arbejdsledere i Danmark* (1989), which made it clear that the Directive was intended to prevent dismissals before the transfer. The problem of dismissal is probably the most pertinent for a transferred employee. Under the Regulations, the employee is protected in two ways. First, reg 7(1) provides that a dismissal as a result of a transfer is automatically unfair unless the employer can show that the dismissal is for an economic, technical or organisational reason entailing a change in the workforce (reg 7(2)). Should the dismissal fall within reg 7(2), then it is a fair reason under some other substantial reason, although the employer will have to satisfy the requirements of reasonableness in s 98(4) of the ERA 1996. It has been held that a dismissal as a condition of the sale does not fall within reg 7(2) (*Wheeler v Patel* (1987)), nor does a reduction in salary after the transfer (*Berriman v Delabole Slate Ltd* (1985)), but that a redundancy caused by the transfer does (*Meikle v McPhail* (1983)). However, the Advocate General, in *D'Urso v Ecole Marelli Elettromeccanica Generale SpA* (1992), expressed the opinion that a constructive dismissal caused by a change in terms would only be fair if such a change would have occurred despite the transfer. This raises doubts as to whether reg 7(2) complies with the Directive.

The second protection for the employee in relation to dismissal is found in reg 4(9). This provides that an employee can claim constructive dismissal if the transfer results in a substantial change in his working conditions to his material detriment. This would appear, however, to go against the ECJ decision in *Watson Rask*, in which the change was minor (a change in the pay day) and yet the ECJ held that the employee was protected by the Directive. Furthermore, the protection in regs 4 and 7 is somewhat restricted by reg 4(7). This gives the employee the right to object to his being transferred, but then provides that such an objection terminates his contract on the transfer and there will be no dismissal. While this appears in line with the ECJ decision in *Katsikas v Konstantinidis* (1993), which upheld the German equivalent of the TUPE Regulations giving the employee a right of objection, reg 4(7) leaves an employee in a vulnerable position. He cannot claim redundancy from his old employer because he has not been dismissed and he does not wish to work for the new employer. It is again debatable whether the effect of reg 4(7) is a proper implementation of the Directive.

The 2006 Regulations appear to consolidate previous case law in this area and clarify more specifically an employee's rights in the event of a transfer. In addition, while again adopting existing case law, it is also clear that the Regulations apply in the case of a change in service provider and where the provision being transferred is only ancillary to the main business of the transferor.

There are still gaps, however. It is still left to the discretion of individual courts to determine whether there has been the transfer of an economic entity, and any hope that the Regulations would clarify what such was has not been fulfilled. In reality, the Regulations seem to have done little to improve things for employees, and have merely put on a legislative footing previous decisions of both the ECJ and national courts. It is perhaps debatable whether the Regulations have changed anything. That said, changes to be implemented shortly will include a right for the transferred employee to enjoy equivalent pension rights from the transferee. Pension liability did not transfer under the 1981 Regulations and as such this new right is to be welcomed. In addition, the new Regulations require a transferor to give much more detail about the undertaking being transferred to the transferee. This may make it much clearer for a tribunal to establish whether an economic entity has been transferred. Only case law will tell.

Thus it is inaccurate to say that the 2006 Regulations remove deficiencies apparent in the 1981 Regulations. To a large extent, the new Regulations merely codify existing law and do very little, apart from in the area of pensions, to increase protection. That said, it could be argued that judicial interpretation of the 1981 Regulations had already provided sufficient protection for employees.

Aim Higher ★

❖ Reading articles on **TUPE 1981** will give you a good idea of the problems – for example, Collins (1989) 18 ILJ 144 and McMullen (1992) 21 ILJ 15.

❖ There are a number of authors who write on the **TUPE Regulations** and their insights will improve any answer – for example, McMullen (2006) 35 ILJ 113 and Sargeant (2006) JBL 549.

QUESTION 45

The Nippon Motor Company recently announced that it intended to make 50 or so employees redundant in the next two or three months. In anticipation of this, Arnold volunteered for redundancy and the company agreed to this. Bert, expecting to be made redundant and wishing to protect his interests, accepted a job with a rival firm immediately upon hearing the announcement.

Charles was employed as a paint sprayer. He was ordered to transfer to a job in which he checked the quality of the paint finishes, after Nippon mechanised the entire paint-spraying function at the plant. There is no reduction in his salary or status. Charles felt that he was not using his skills and resigned four weeks after the change took effect.

Den was one of 40 employees subsequently selected for dismissal. His job duties were subsequently allocated between two other staff retained by the company. Although Den was told about his selection 24 hours before his dismissal, his union was not consulted at any time.

▶ Advise Nippon Motor Company.

Answer Plan

This question deals with a variety of issues and brings in procedural requirements and the possibility of an unfair dismissal claim. It is an example, therefore, of the way in which questions can bring together two areas.

Particular issues to be considered are:

❖   the concept of dismissal, mutual agreement to terminate and resignation;
❖   what constitutes redundancy and the offer of suitable alternative employment;
❖   the trial period in new employment under s 138(3) and (4) of the Employment Rights Act (ERA) 1996;
❖   the principles in *Williams v Compair Maxam Ltd* (1982); *Hough v Leyland Daf* (1991); *Rolls Royce Motor Cars Ltd v Price* (1993);
❖   the consultation requirements in s 188 of the Trade Union and Labour Relations (Consolidation) Act (TULR(C)A) 1992;
❖   the protective award;
❖   notification of mass redundancies to the minister under s 193 of the 1992 Act.

ANSWER

The question asks us to advise Nippon Motor Company. Given that all the employees left after the announcement that the firm needed to make some employees redundant, the advice will be in relation to liability in redundancy situations.

In order to claim a redundancy payment, an employee must show that he has been dismissed for reasons of redundancy. Thus, the employee must show that there has been a dismissal within the definition in s 136 of the ERA 1996 and that the reason for that dismissal was a redundancy situation as defined in s 139(1). Should this be established, Nippon will be liable to compensate the employees concerned. In addition, the company must follow a fair procedure when dismissing for redundancy, consult with recognised independent trade unions or elected employee representatives and give notice of mass redundancies to the Department for Work and Pensions. Failure to comply with any of these requirements will increase liability.

Arnold, after hearing the announcement, volunteered for redundancy and this was accepted by the company. A dismissal is defined in s 136(1) as the employer terminating the contract, a fixed-term contract expiring without renewal or the employee resigning in circumstances in which he is entitled to do so by the employer's conduct. On the face of things, it would appear that Arnold and Nippon have mutually agreed to terminate the relationship and thus there is no dismissal within s 136. However, this is a very literal interpretation of the legislative provisions and would mean that if an employer were to call for volunteers for redundancy, all of those volunteering would disentitle themselves to a redundancy payment. What constitutes a mutual agreement to terminate is difficult to establish. Donaldson P in *McAlwane v Broughton Estates* (1973) stated that it would be a rare case in which a tribunal found a mutual agreement to terminate, 'particularly when one realises the financial consequences to the employee involved in such an agreement'.

In *Birch and Humber v University of Liverpool* (1985), the Court of Appeal found a mutual agreement to terminate where two employees had formally applied for early retirement in a situation in which the scheme clearly envisaged that statutory redundancy pay would not be additionally available. This was taken a step further in *Scott v Coalite Fuels and Chemicals Ltd* (1988), in which it was held that there was a mutual agreement to terminate when the employees, while under notice of redundancy, volunteered for early retirement, as such a scheme was seen as an alternative to redundancy. However, in *Gateshead Metropolitan Borough Council v Mills* (1995), on facts similar to *Scott*, the EAT said that volunteering for early retirement did not impliedly withdraw the notice of redundancy and did not indicate that the employee had impliedly consented to the notice being withdrawn. As such, the employee was redundant and entitled to a redundancy payment. By contrast, in *Morley v C T Morley Ltd* (1985), a firm consisting of a father and two sons got into financial difficulty and the father volunteered for redundancy. The firm was later wound up. It was held that there was no agreement to terminate but a dismissal. Additionally, in *Caledonian Mining Co Ltd v Bassett* (1987), an employer who warned of redundancies and actively encouraged his employees to acquire other jobs was held to have dismissed them for redundancy purposes.

Given the authorities, therefore, and the fact that redundancies are inevitable at Nippon and the company has agreed to Arnold volunteering, the employer's act is behind the termination of the contract and there is a dismissal within s 136(1)(a). The dismissal will be for redundancy if Nippon's requirements for employees to do the particular kind of work Arnold is employed to do have ceased or diminished by s 139(1)(b). There are insufficient facts to determine if this is the case.

Bert, on the other hand, does not know that he will be made redundant and has had no discussion with the employer. There appears to be no repudiatory breach by the employer to establish a constructive dismissal, nor have the employer's actions in reality resulted in the termination. In *Morton Sundour Fabrics v Shaw* (1966), a foreman who was warned of impending redundancies left the firm to take up other employment. It was held that he had resigned, Lord Parker CJ saying that there could be no dismissal when the employer stated that it intended to dispense with the employee's services in the coming months but when no date was set for the dismissal. A similar conclusion was reached in *Doble v Firestone Tyre Co Ltd* (1981). Bert has no idea when the terminations may take effect, nor does he know if it will affect him. On the basis of *Morton Sundour* and *Doble*, therefore, Bert has resigned and has not been dismissed for reasons of redundancy. As such, he is not entitled to a redundancy payment.

Charles has been moved to a totally different job because of the mechanisation of the paint-spraying function. Without doubt, there is a redundancy situation under s 139(1) as Nippon's requirements for paint sprayers have now ceased. As a result, Nippon has offered Charles alternative work. If this work constitutes an offer of suitable alternative employment, Charles may find that he has disentitled himself to a redundancy payment if he unreasonably refuses the job (s 141). This means that the tribunal must look to see if the offer is of suitable alternative employment first and, if it is, whether the refusal of the employee is reasonable. This will involve the tribunal in a comparison of the new job with the old and issues such as duties, pay, seniority, status and benefits will all have a bearing on whether there has been a suitable offer (*Carron Co v Robertson* (1967)). Even if the offer is suitable, the tribunal must then look to the employee's refusal. This involves the tribunal looking at a wide range of factors such as health problems and family commitments in relation to the individual employee. Each case is dependent on its own facts and thus precedents are of little use (*Spencer and Griffin v Gloucestershire County Council* (1985)).

This discussion, however, is on the basis that the employee has unequivocally accepted or refused the offer. In Charles's case, it appears that he decided to give the new job a try before resigning. By s 138(3) and (4), an employee is entitled to a statutory trial period in the new employment. By statute, this is four weeks, but this can be extended by written agreement. If, during the trial period, the employee terminates the contract for a reason connected with the change of employment, the employee is treated as having been dismissed on the date the old contract expired and for the reasons that contract was terminated. Charles has now resigned. The reason for this resignation was the change in his job duties, which in the absence of any contractual authority was a repudiatory breach by the employer. At the end of his statutory trial period, he left. His contract therefore terminated four weeks previously for reasons of redundancy and he is entitled to a redundancy payment.

Den has been dismissed for redundancy. While redundancy is a fair reason for dismissal, the employer must still satisfy the requirements of procedural fairness and, in addition, has a statutory duty to consult with recognised independent trade unions. In relation to procedural fairness, *Williams v Compair Maxam Ltd* (1982) has established that the employer should look to see if there is alternative work the employee can do, warn and consult with the employee at the earliest opportunity and use objective criteria for selection rather than subjective criteria. While there are no facts as to the selection criteria adopted in the problem, we are told that Den was given 24 hours' notice of redundancy. In *Polkey v AE Dayton Services Ltd* (1987), lack of warning or consultation with the employee made the redundancy unfair. Williams also emphasised the need to warn and consult with the recognised union in relation to a fair procedure, independent of any other statutory requirements. This means that if there is a recognised trade union, the employer must consult with both the employee and the union to satisfy the reasonableness test (*Walls Meat Co Ltd v Selby* (1989) and *Rolls Royce Motor Cars Ltd v Price* (1993)). Consultation with the union alone will render the dismissal unfair (*Hough v Leyland Daf* (1991)).

In addition to procedural requirements in relation to unfair dismissal, s 188 of the TULR(C)A 1992 requires an employer, where there are at least 20 redundancies, to consult with appropriate employee representatives or a recognised trade union. Section 178(3) of the TULR(C)A 1992 states that recognition means recognition by the employer, to any extent, for collective bargaining purposes. Thus, if Nippon negotiates with the union, it will be recognised for the purposes of the statute.

If there is no independent recognised trade union, Nippon is still required by statute to consult with elected employee representatives. Changes made to the TULR(C)A 1992 by the ERA 1999 now require the employer to make suitable arrangements for the election of such representatives and take reasonable steps to ensure that the election takes place early enough for information to be given and consultation to take place in good time (s 188(7A)). Representatives must be members of the affected workforce and there must be a sufficient number of them to ensure proper representation of the affected employees (s 188(A)(1)(b) and (e)). In the event of a dispute as to the validity of the election, any of the affected employees may complain to a tribunal and the burden is on the employer to show that election conditions listed in the statute were complied with (s 189(1) and (1B)). Affected employees now include any employee who will be affected by the redundancies, not only those who will be dismissed (s 188(1)).

Section 188(1A) requires the employer to consult in good time when it proposes to make redundancies. If, however, there are a substantial number of redundancies, consultation periods are laid down. In relation to the problem, Nippon has made 50 employees redundant. Section 188(1A) requires that, if between 20 and 99 employees are to be made redundant, the consultation period is 30 days. Section 188(4) requires the employer to give the union or employee representatives certain information, such as the numbers and descriptions of those employees affected, and consultation shall include ways of avoiding the dismissals, reducing the number of dismissals and mitigating the consequences of the dismissals. It should take place with a view to obtaining agreement with the union (s 188(2)). The employer may plead the special circumstances defence in s 189(7) – that is, that it was not reasonably practicable to comply with the consultation provisions. The most common argument under this section is that the redundancies were unforeseen, which does not appear to apply to Nippon.

Where the employer has broken the statutory duty to consult, the union or employee representatives can apply to a tribunal for a protective award, which is payable to those employees in respect of whom the union should have been consulted (s 189(3)). This award is compensatory and is paid for the protected period. This period starts from the date of the first dismissals and continues for as long as the tribunal considers just and equitable, but ending, in Nippon's case, 30 days later. Such an award will guarantee Den's salary for the protected period.

In addition, if an employer is intending to make mass redundancies, there is a duty under s 193 to give the appropriate notice to the Secretary of State. The Collective Redundancies (Amendment) Regulations 2006 amend TULR(C)A 1992 and provide that where 20 or more employees are to be made redundant within a 90-day period, the employer must inform the Secretary of State at least 30 days (90 days if over 100 are to be made redundant) before giving notice to terminate the employees' contracts. Previously, the requirement was to give notice before the first dismissal took effect. Failure to do so renders the employer liable to a fine not exceeding level 5 on the standard scale (s 194(1)).

Thus, it would appear that, although Nippon is not liable to Bert, it is liable for an unfair redundancy in relation to Den and, furthermore, must pay him a protective award. In addition, the Secretary of State may take action against the company for a failure to notify, which could result in a criminal prosecution and a fine.

11 Trade Unions and their Members

INTRODUCTION

The law relating to trade unions has been the subject of massive change in the last three decades. It is the area of law that is most subject to the political construction of the government and therefore, when a Conservative government was elected in 1979, a wealth of legislation restricting the power of trade unions was introduced. The change of government in 1997 led to the passing of the Employment Relations Act 1999. This Act introduces rights for all workers and some specific rights for trade union members in addition to recognition rights for trade unions. Further changes were introduced by the Employment Relations Act 2004. This chapter will deal with issues specifically related to the trade union, such as rights to information, rights to consultation and the relationship between the union and its members. Chapter 12 will look at issues in relation to the taking of industrial action.

For questions in this area, general issues that the student needs to understand include:

* the definition of a trade union;
* the status of a trade union;
* issues in relation to independence, listing, recognition;
* trade union elections and amalgamations;
* the right to information;
* the status of the rule book;
* discipline, expulsion and exclusion by a union of its members; and
* rights relating to trade union membership/non-membership.

Questions in this area lend themselves to essay-type questions and may require a discussion of the historical basis for the present legal position. In particular, therefore, students should be familiar with:

* the major pieces of legislation prior to the Employment Act 1980;
* the case of *Taff Vale Railway Co v ASRS* (1901);
* the legal status of a trade union;

* the history of the closed shop;
* the requirements involved with the certificate of independence;
* the consequences of an independence certificate;
* the rules governing trade union elections and amalgamations;
* the rights of trade union members vis-à-vis the union; and
* the enforcement of members' rights against the union.

Finally, while it has been said that questions in this specific area are often essays, the rights of members against the union can come up in the form of problems. In addition, many courses include the rights of an employee not to be victimised on the grounds of membership or non-membership of a trade union at this stage in the course rather than earlier.

Checklist ✔

Students should be familiar with the following areas:

* the regulation by the law of the union constitution, rule book and accounts;
* the rights of a trade union in relation to an employer;
* the statutory rules regarding the activities of a union;
* the rights of union members against the union; and
* the protection of union/non-union membership by the law.

QUESTION 46

'Trade unions are not above the law, but subject to it. Their rules are said to be a contract between the members and the union . . . But the rules are in reality more than a contract. They are a legislative code laid down by the council of the union to be obeyed by the members. This code should be subject to control by the courts just as much as a code laid down by Parliament itself.' (Lord Denning MR in *Breen v AEU* (1971))

▶ What is the basis of judicial intervention in the rule book of a trade union?

Common Pitfalls

❖ It is important to note that the question requires a discussion of the basis of judicial intervention in the rule book and not the statutory control.

❖ Many students do not look at the judgment the quote is from. If this is a coursework question, reading the whole judgment will set the quote in context.

Answer Plan

It is important to note what the question is asking for here. This is a famous quote from Breen and the question requires a discussion of the basis of judicial intervention and not the statutory control of trade unions.

Particular issues to be considered are:

❖ why the common law is still important given the statutory rights;
❖ the grounds for judicial intervention;
❖ problems of interpretation of the rules; and
❖ the rules of natural justice and their relevance to this area.

ANSWER

Since 1980, there have been a series of enactments to protect individual union members. The most important of these rights are arguably the right not to be excluded or expelled from a union in s 174 of the Trade Union and Labour Relations (Consolidation) Act (TULR(C)A) 1992 and the right not to be unjustifiably disciplined in s 64 of the same Act. This does not mean, however, that the common law is no longer relevant, as there may be situations that fall outside the statutory protection or there may be situations in which the common law is more effective in terms of the remedies available. Judicial intervention into trade union rules is based on one of two grounds: lack of compliance with the rules as laid down; or a breach of the rules of natural justice.

The basis of intervention on the first ground is that the rule book is a contract of membership and each member has a right to have the terms of that contract observed. As such, each rule is a term of the contract and non-observance will constitute a breach (*Lee v Showmen's Guild* (1952)). Thus, an aggrieved member may seek to have the rules complied with by seeking a declaration or injunction or may, in some cases, seek damages. Such challenges often come in the form of non-compliance with the rules on elections, or the setting up of industrial action. In *Taylor v NUM (Derbyshire Area)* (1985), a case arising out of the miners' dispute in 1984–85, the court ruled that the calling of a strike without the 55 per cent majority vote in the area, as required by the rules, was illegal and, in *Taylor v NUM (Yorkshire Area)* (1984), it was held that a ballot conducted 30 months earlier was too remote to be capable of justifying a strike in that area. This meant that the members did not have to join the strike and the payment of strike pay from union funds was illegal.

A further important common law protection is that in relation to expulsion and discipline, as expulsion in a closed-shop situation will often result in the loss of a member's livelihood. While the statutory protection is there, the common law protection may be more effective, particularly as a member must show under the statute that he has been 'unjustifiably disciplined'. At common law, the judges will look for a specific power to expel and adherence to the procedure laid down in the rules to effect that expulsion. In addition, the court has the power to interpret the rules and thus a member may challenge the union's interpretation of its own powers.

Particular problems arise, however, with the power of interpretation of the court. First, if the rule is subjective, giving the union a discretion, the courts cannot challenge a valid exercise of that discretion, although Lord Denning expressed the view in *Edwards v SOGAT* (1971) that a vague and subjective rule could be declared invalid. The second problem that arises is whether the claimant must have exhausted all the internal procedures before resorting to the courts. The older cases indicate that the claimant must have exhausted such procedures, but Smith and Baker (*Smith and Wood's Employment Law*, 10th edn, 2010, Oxford) argue that the modern approach is that even an express rule that internal procedures must be exhausted cannot oust the jurisdiction of the courts and they cite the judgment of Goff J in *Leigh v NUR* (1970) to support this contention. In such a case, however, the court will apply the rule, unless the claimant can show good reason why it should not apply. If there is no express rule requiring exhaustion of internal procedures, the courts have a discretion to hear the case, prior to the procedures being adhered to. Section 63(2) of the TULR(C)A 1992 supports this, in that it provides that if a member has applied to the union to have a matter determined, and more than six months have elapsed without such a determination, the court is to ignore any union rule on exhaustion of internal remedies.

A third problem in this area is that the action of the union may be declared void because it is ultra vires. While this will be correct if the union has no power under the rules to take the action, the judges use the phrase in a much narrower sense, in that the action is contrary to the objects of the union. This is a concept common to company law, but seems particularly inappropriate when applied to trade unions because s 10 of the TULR(C)A 1992 states that a trade union is not a body corporate and, as such, will not have an objects clause in the way that a company has. This does not appear to have deterred the judges, however, as can be seen in *Hopkins v National Union of Seamen* (1985), in which a resolution to raise a levy to support the miners strike was held to be ultra vires the rules because the executive under the rules had no power to raise such a levy. However, the payment of funds to the NUM was intra vires the objects of the union because one of the objects was to improve the conditions and protect the interests of the members, which arguably would be achieved, as ensuring the supply of coal, which would be transported by ship, would protect the members' interests.

The fourth problem concerns the application of the rule in *Foss v Harbottle* (1843). This is a rule of company law and provides that:

> . . . where harm is done to a company, the company is the proper claimant; and the court will not restrain an action which the company on a majority vote may later ratify.

An exception to the rule is where the act is ultra vires, in that such an act cannot be ratified by the majority. Whereas the rule has been applied in the past to unions, because of their quasi-corporate status, there are problems in the interpretation of ultra vires, as noted above. The problem is seen in the judgment of Vinelott J in *Taylor v NUM (Derbyshire Area)* (1985), in which he refused to make an order requiring the union to refund money already spent on ultra vires industrial action on the basis that, although the majority could sue, they were unlikely to do so and, thus, such an order would serve no useful purpose. This judgment has been criticised.

A second ground for judicial intervention is that the action of the union is a breach of the rules of natural justice. These rules are briefly that there should be no bias, the member has a right to a fair hearing and no man shall be a judge in his own cause. The importance of this ground of judicial intervention is that a decision made contrary to the rules of natural justice is void. Thus, an expulsion that breaches the rules is invalid and the member is still a member (*Annamunthodo v Oilfield Workers Union* (1961)). Furthermore, any rule of the union that excludes the rules of natural justice is itself void (*Faramus v Film Artistes' Association* (1964)).

It would appear that in spite of problems in relation to interpretation of the rules, the courts have wide grounds on which to intervene. While the problems noted above may restrict this jurisdiction somewhat, two further problems remain. The first is whether the courts have any jurisdiction when a person is refused membership. While there is a statutory right not to be unreasonably excluded by s 174 of the TULR(C)A 1992, it would appear that, on the face of it, there is no common law jurisdiction in this area, since there is no contract of membership in which the courts can intervene. Lord Denning MR put forward an argument in *Nagle v Fielden* (1966) that such a rule would interfere with a person's right to work, and so would be void on public policy grounds. The case, however, did not involve a union. This leads to the second problem: can a rule of the union be struck down on the basis of public policy? It would appear that the only basis on which public policy could be invoked is that the rule is in restraint of trade. While this was the basis of the judgment in *Edwards v SOGAT*, s 11 of the TULR(C)A 1992 now provides that the doctrine of restraint of trade does not apply to the purposes or rules of a trade union. Should the argument of Lord Denning in *Nagle* gain momentum, however (that is, that there is a legally enforceable right to work), it would appear that s 11 could be circumvented and so increase judicial intervention in this area.

QUESTION 47

The rules of the Polo Hole Borers Union (PHBU) contain, inter alia, the following. Rule 1 states:

> A person who is not a member of the Labour Party cannot hold any union office.

Rule 2 states:

> Any official, officer or member of the union who acts in any way detrimental to the interests of the union may be summoned before the Branch Disciplinary Committee and disciplined in any manner considered appropriate by that Committee.

Rule 3 states:

> Decisions of the Branch Committee may be taken on appeal to the Appeals Committee and then on to the Annual General Meeting. No dispute may be taken to a court of law before this appeals procedure has been exhausted.

Footsy was refused as a candidate for the elections to the executive committee on the ground that, having recently left the Labour Party, he was contravening Rule 1. Clarkey was elected. Thatch is summoned to a hearing before the Branch Disciplinary Committee. He is told that he is in breach of Rule 2 by working for an extra-strong mint firm on Saturdays. He is refused representation at the hearing and is not permitted to give evidence himself. While deliberating in private, Steel, a member of the Committee, tells the Committee that Thatch has Tory sympathies. Thatch has persistently obstructed Steel's progress in the PHBU because Steel is a member of the Communist Party. The decision of the Committee was to expel Thatch as a member. Thatch unsuccessfully appealed to the Appeals Committee. The next annual general meeting (AGM) is in three months' time. Thatch wishes to appeal to the courts.

Howe is excluded from membership of the PHBU on the ground that previously, when he was a member of another union, he refused to take part in an official strike.

▶ Advise Footsy, Thatch and Howe.

Answer Plan

This question deals with both the statutory and the common law protection now available to trade union members vis-à-vis the union. As such, students need both a knowledge of the relevant sections of the Trade Union and Labour Relations (Consolidation) Act (TULR(C)A) 1992 and the position at common law.

Particular issues to be considered are:

❖   the provisions relating to trade union elections in ss 46 and 47 of the TULR(C)A 1992;

❖   the right not to be unreasonably excluded or expelled in ss 174–177 of the TULR(C)A 1992;

❖   the application of the rules of natural justice;

❖   the role of the certification officer.

ANSWER

The three parties in the question all wish to take action against the PHBU in respect of its conduct. In Footsy's case, he could not stand as a candidate for the executive committee because the union argued that, as he has left the Labour Party, this is contrary to Rule 1. The statutory provisions relating to elections to trade union office are now contained in ss 46–59 of the TULR(C)A 1992. Section 47 deals specifically with the candidates in such an election. Section 47(1) provides that no member shall be unreasonably excluded from standing as a candidate and s 47(2) provides that no candidate shall be required directly or indirectly to be a member of a political party. As such, Rule 1 infringes s 47 and is thus void.

Footsy has two available courses of action he may pursue. He is a person who by s 54(2) can make an application to the certification officer or the court, in that he was a member of the union at the time the election was held. Section 55 provides that a person with sufficient interest, as defined in s 54(2), can apply to the certification officer for a declaration that the provisions in relation to the election have failed to comply with the Act. The certification officer may make such enquiries as he deems appropriate, give the applicant and the union the right to be heard, and then refuse or grant the declaration. Conversely, Footsy has the right by s 56 to apply to the court for relief. These are alternative remedies. The court or certification officer, when making a declaration, can impose a requirement that a new election is held or any other requirement to remedy the breach of the statutory provisions (ss 55(5A) and 56(4)).

Thatch has been expelled from the union on the basis of Rule 2. The union originally deemed that his extra job is conduct that is detrimental to the union, but it would also appear from the facts that Steel's revelations about Thatch's Tory sympathies may have affected the decision of the Disciplinary Committee. Thatch's situation raises a variety of issues. First, by s 174 of the TULR(C)A 1992, all individuals have a right not to be unreasonably excluded or expelled from a union. Section 174(2) lists the situations in which exclusion or expulsion would be reasonable and includes, inter alia, conduct of the member. Conduct that, by s 65(2), would not justify the member being disciplined by the union cannot justify his expulsion (s 174(4)). The conduct that originally prompted the Disciplinary Committee, however, is not listed in s 174(2) or s 65(2); thus, on the face of it, it would appear that Thatch has no statutory right to take action against the union. It appears that the decision to expel was influenced by Thatch's political sympathies. Section 174(4) states that conduct that does not justify expulsion is the membership of the member of a political party unless membership of that party is contrary to a rule or objective of the union. If Thatch is a member of the Conservative Party, he may have protection under s 174(4), but we have no facts on this, merely an allegation that he has Tory sympathies. Unless the reason for his expulsion was his membership of a political party, therefore, Thatch has no statutory right to take action against the union.

He may, however, have a common law right. Although Rule 3 states that no action may be taken in a court of law until all the union internal procedures have been exhausted, in *Leigh v NUR* (1970), Goff J held that such a rule cannot oust the jurisdiction of the courts. It may also be the case that s 63(2) applies, in that it is now more than six months since he appealed against his expulsion. While the courts are more likely to allow recourse to the common law where there is no express exhaustion provision, they have a discretion in cases like Thatch and may exercise this discretion, given that the AGM is still three months away.

If Thatch persuades the court to hear his case, he may have a problem on interpretation of the rule. The rule is widely drafted and allows the union the discretion to decide what conduct is detrimental to the union. While Lord Denning in *Lee v Showmen's Guild* (1952) stated that a vague and subjective rule could be invalid as contrary to public policy, this has not been followed subsequently, and Thatch may have to challenge his expulsion on the basis of mala fides or that no reasonable tribunal could have reached that decision.

Thatch, however, has a much stronger line of argument. During his hearing, he was not allowed representation, a member of the Committee was biased against him, and it appears that his expulsion may have been for his political sympathies rather than his Saturday work. In relation to any disciplinary hearing, the courts require unions to comply with the rules of natural justice. These provide that there should be a fair hearing, Thatch should know the case against him, he should have an opportunity to put his side of the case and the hearing should be unbiased. In the problem, we are told that Thatch was not allowed representation and was not allowed to put his side of the case. This is a breach of the rules of natural justice (*Stevenson v United Road Transport Union* (1977)). In addition, Steel was biased, as Thatch has impeded his progress in the union and should not have been a member of the Committee (*Annamunthodo v Oilfield Workers' Union* (1961)). It also appears that the decision was influenced by Thatch's political sympathies, a fact he did not know had been raised and one he was not allowed to challenge. As such, the hearing was contrary to the rules of natural justice and thus the decision to expel Thatch is void. He can therefore seek a declaration that he is still a member.

Howe has been excluded from membership of the PHBU on the basis that, when he was a member of another union, he refused to take official industrial action. Howe has a statutory remedy under s 174. As has already been stated, the section provides a right for a member not to be unreasonably expelled from a union but, in addition, it also gives non-union members the right not to be unreasonably excluded from a union. It has already been stated that the statute provides the situations in which such exclusion is lawful by s 174(2) – By s 174(4)(b), a person cannot be excluded from a trade union for conduct falling within s 65(2) – that is, conduct that would not justify discipline. By s 65(2)(a), a union cannot discipline a member for failing to participate in a strike or other industrial action. By s 174(4), therefore, an individual cannot be excluded or expelled from a union for failing to take part in a strike or other employment action. This is the reason for Howe's exclusion and thus, he has been unreasonably excluded by s 174(4). By s 174(5), he may bring an action against the PHBU in the employment tribunal within a period of six months from his exclusion, although the tribunal can extend the time limit if it feels it was not reasonably practicable for the complaint to be brought within the period. The tribunal can make a declaration as to Howe's rights and make an award of compensation that it considers to be just and equitable.

Aim Higher ★

❖ The case of *ASLEF v UK* (2007) led to a change in the law relating to expulsion or exclusion from a union. For a discussion of those changes and the implications, see Ewing (2009) 38 ILJ 38.

INTRODUCTION

The law relating to the capacity of a trade union to take industrial action underwent massive change during the Conservative administration of 1979–97. It is perhaps hardly surprising that the Labour government of 1974–79 gave unions a great deal of freedom to pursue industrial action and operate closed shops. This period of time is seen as a period of trade union strength during which there was high union membership and unions had total immunity from actions in tort. The Conservatives, on the other hand, wanted to curtail trade union power and, some would argue, bring back the provisions of the ill-fated Industrial Relations Act 1971. What is important to note, however, is that, first, the Conservatives did not restrict trade union power by one piece of legislation as previously, but adopted what is known as the 'softly, softly' approach. As such, since 1979, we had the Employment Act 1980, the Employment Act 1982, the Trade Union Act 1984, the Employment Act 1988, the Employment Act 1989, the Employment Act 1990, the Trade Union and Labour Relations (Consolidation) Act (TULR(C)A) 1992, the Trade Union Reform and Employment Rights Act (TURERA 1993) and the Employment Rights Act (ERA) 1996. Not all of these affect trade unions directly. It is, however, wrong to argue that all of these pieces of legislation returned the law to that of 1971. Many would argue that this had been successfully achieved by 1984 and that legislation after that date took the law much further than the Industrial Relations Act. While the Labour government introduced some minor changes by the Employment Relations Acts 1999 and 2004, most particularly in relation to minor breaches of the statutory balloting provisions, major legislative intervention since 1997 has been in the area of recognition (Employment Relations Act 1999) and increasing protection for individual employees against inducements by their employers to join or not to join a union, not to take part in industrial action, or to pull out of collective bargaining (Employment Relations Act 2004). Little has been done legislatively in the area of industrial action.

For questions in this area, general issues that the student needs to understand are:

❖ the changes made by the different statutes;
❖ the effect of those changes on the union's capacity to take industrial action;

❖ the economic torts that can be committed when taking industrial action;

❖ immunity from liability for civil wrongs;

❖ the law relating to picketing; and

❖ criminal liability.

Questions in this area tend to raise four particular topics: the legislative history behind the present statutory position; the economic torts; statutory immunity; and the law relating to picketing. Whereas the first topic would usually be self-contained, the other areas can be either self-contained or mixed.

Therefore, students need to be familiar with:

❖ the changes in the definition of a trade dispute and its implications;

❖ the loss of trade union immunity in relation to civil wrongs;

❖ the loss of the right of a trade union to enforce a closed shop;

❖ the difference between official and unofficial action;

❖ how a union can repudiate official action;

❖ the balloting provisions;

❖ the 'golden formula';

❖ the main economic torts, such as conspiracy, inducement, interference, procurement and intimidation;

❖ when a picket will be lawful; and

❖ criminal liability.

Finally, this is a complex area that needs to be fully understood before a question is tackled. It is no use understanding the 'golden formula' without a knowledge of the economic torts. In other words, it is not an area in which a student can question spot. This area must be an all-or-nothing approach!

Checklist ✔

Students should be familiar with the following areas:

■ liability in tort and the statutory immunities in **s 219** of the **Trade Union and Labour Relations (Consolidation) Act (TULR(C)A) 1992**

■ provisions outside the immunities;

■ the definition of the 'golden formula';

■ restrictions on the statutory immunities in **s 224** of the **TULR(C)A 1992** – that is, secondary action, unlawful picketing, action to enforce membership;

action taken in response to the dismissal of unofficial strikers, pressure to impose union recognition and action without the support of a ballot;

■ lawful picketing;

■ potential civil and criminal liability in relation to picketing;

■ the Code of Practice on Picketing 1992 (Secretary of State);

■ the **Public Order Act 1986**

■ the **Criminal Justice and Public Order Act 1994**

■ the **Protection from Harassment Act 1997**

■ union liability in tort.

QUESTION 48

Legislation since 1980 appeared to be attempting to erode trade union strength. It can be argued that, since 1980, a trade union's power to take industrial action has been so undermined that unions are now impotent and a collective system of industrial relations no longer exists.

▶ To what extent has legislation since 1980 eroded the power of a trade union to take industrial action?

Answer Plan

This is a fairly typical essay question, which asks for an overview of the legislation since 1980 and how it has affected trade union power in relation to industrial action. It therefore requires a detailed knowledge of the situation prior to 1980, the changes made since then and an evaluation of how the changes have affected a trade union's power. This means that the student must deal with the changes that have impacted on trade union power, and thus does not require a discussion of the legislative intervention in relation to the rule book, etc.

Particular issues to be considered are:

❖ the situation under the Trade Union and Labour Relations (Consolidation) Act (TULR(C)A) 1992;

❖ the changes to the immunity for secondary industrial action by s 17 of the Employment Act 1980;

❖ the narrowing of the definition of a trade dispute and the introduction of union liability in the Employment Act 1982;

- ❖ the introduction of balloting for industrial action by the Trade Union Act 1984;
- ❖ the removal of further immunities by the Employment Act 1988;
- ❖ the removal of protection for unofficial industrial action by the Employment Act 1990;
- ❖ the consolidation by the TULR(C)A 1992;
- ❖ the further conditions on balloting and notice introduced by the Trade Union Reform and Employment Rights Act (TURERA) 1993;
- ❖ disregard of small accidental balloting provision failures introduced by the Employment Relations Act 1999;
- ❖ other changes in balloting provisions made by the Employment Relations Act 1999.

ANSWER

Until the last quarter of the 19th century, trade unions were in danger of many of their activities being construed as criminal. Various statutes rendered certain combinations criminal and it was only by the introduction of the Trade Union Act 1871 that the purposes of a trade union were deemed not to be unlawful merely because they were in restraint of trade. Legislation such as the Conspiracy and Protection of Property Act 1875 removed criminal liability for conspiracy for those engaged in a trade dispute, but those aggrieved turned to the civil law for a remedy, and the famous case of Taff Vale Railway Co v ASRS (1901) held that a trade union could be sued in tort, thus putting union funds at risk. This led to the passing of the Trade Disputes Act 1906, which gave unions total immunity from liability in tort, gave immunity from liability in conspiracy and inducement to officers and members of a union acting 'in contemplation or furtherance of a trade dispute' (the 'golden formula'), and provided that an act done under the golden formula was not actionable in tort because it interfered with the legitimate interests of a person, hence giving immunity from liability for the majority of the economic torts. This protection was completed by the Trade Disputes Act 1965, which gave immunity for the tort of intimidation, applied by the House of Lords in Rookes v Barnard (1964).

The system as established was then altered by the Industrial Relations Act 1971, which abolished a trade union's total immunity from civil liability. That Act was short-lived and the position was restored by the Trade Union and Labour Relations Act (TULRA) 1974, as amended by the Trade Union and Labour Relations (Amendment) Act 1976. This Act extended immunity to breaches of commercial contracts as well as to contracts of employment, so giving protection for secondary action, and gave protection for interference with a contract. In reality, this gave total immunity from any likely tort committed while taking industrial action.

When the Conservatives came to power in 1979, it was after the 'winter of discontent', when many felt that the law gave too much protection to trade unions and their members. The Conservatives, however, were wary of the reception that greeted the Industrial Relations Act 1971, and the consequent demise of the government of the time. The government therefore proceeded with a programme of legislative reform that has gradually reduced trade union power to take industrial action.

The first piece of legislation was the Employment Act 1980. This restricted certain secondary action by s 17, whereby action against only the first customer or supplier to the employer in dispute was protected by statutory immunities, so restricting the power of a union to indulge in secondary or tertiary action. The second piece of legislation was perhaps the most damning to a trade union. The Employment Act 1982 redefined a trade dispute. The definition of a trade dispute is part of the golden formula and therefore crucial to the immunities. Prior to 1982, a trade dispute was a dispute between workers and workers, or workers and employers. The Act changed the definition to a dispute between workers and their employer. Thus, the new definition removed from protection all action not protected by s 17 of the Employment Act 1980, and all inter-union disputes. In addition, s 15 of the Act removed the total immunity enjoyed by a trade union. Such immunity had existed since 1906, apart from the time when the Industrial Relations Act 1971 was in force, and, in reality, s 15 resurrected Taff Vale. Thus, if members are liable, so now is the union, and the union is more likely to be sued, given its funds. As Smith and Baker (*Smith and Wood's Employment Law*, 10th edn, 2010, Oxford) point out:

> a litigious employer (not directly involved with the dispute) was given his cause of action by the 1980 Act and his defendant (the union itself) by the 1982 Act.

The process was extended by the Trade Union Act 1984. This Act introduced the requirement of a compulsory ballot before industrial action could be taken. Any action taken without such a ballot lost the protection of the immunities. It has been argued that this step alone has been responsible for the decrease in industrial action in recent years, and a large number of cases taken against trade unions since have been for breach of the balloting provisions rather than economic tort liability per se. It also increases the remedies available to an employer, which can obtain an interim injunction to prevent the threatened action because of the lack of a ballot or because an illegal ballot has been held.

The Employment Act 1988 tightened up on the balloting provisions by requiring separate workplace ballots where the employer operated more than one site. It also removed the immunities from any industrial action taken to enforce a closed shop, so costing trade unions in respect of membership. The Employment Act 1990 repealed s 17 of the Employment Act 1980, thus rendering all secondary action unlawful, distinguishing between official and unofficial action, removing unfair dismissal protection from those members engaged in unofficial action, and greatly increasing the liability of a union for the acts of its officials and committees. Thus, a great many persons can call industrial action that will be thus official and render the union liable, but only the president, the general secretary or the principal executive committee can repudiate such action and thus remove union liability. Furthermore, the legislation lays down the procedure for a valid repudiation (written notice to all those involved and their employers) and failure to comply with the provisions mean that the union is still liable.

By the time the 1990 Act was passed, there were a great many pieces of legislation covering liability in this area. The area was thus consolidated by the TULR(C)A 1992. Unfortunately, the respite from amendments did not last long and the TURERA 1993 introduced further reforms in the area of industrial action. The three principal reforms introduced were: compulsory postal ballots on industrial action, with an independent scrutineer; at least seven days' notice to the employer before the ballot and before the action starts; and, finally, the right of any individual (whether an employer or not) to seek an injunction restraining unlawful industrial action if it affects the supply of goods or services to that individual. This final reform greatly increases the number of potential claimants who can take action against the union.

Some of the effect of the reforms has been mitigated by amendments made by the Employment Relations Act 1999: for example, small accidental failures in complying with balloting provisions will not invalidate the ballot provided that the failures are not on such a scale as to affect the ballot result (s 232B of the TULR(C)A 1992 and P v NAS/UWT (2003)). In addition, a new s 228 and s 228A relieve a union of the requirement to conduct ballots in every workplace in certain circumstances.

The question asked is how far the legislative reforms since 1980 have eroded trade union power in the area of industrial action. It has to be said that the reforms have greatly eroded this power. Prior to 1980, a union could call on members to take industrial action without the union incurring liability for any tortious wrongs that such action may incur. Today, a union is liable for any unlawful tortious wrongs committed by its members, and has vicarious liability in relation to a great number of officials or committees, who may, without the authority of the union, call industrial action. The statutory requirements on repudiation are complex and costly. Furthermore, the union usually must: ballot by post all its members who may be called upon to take industrial action (again, costly); give at least seven days' notice to the employer in dispute before the ballot is taken; and give the employer at least seven days' notice before such action starts, so losing any element of surprise. No customer or supplier of the employer in dispute can be the subject of any action, picketing is limited to the employee's own place of work, and any member of the public who has a contract for the supply of goods or services with the employer in dispute and the action affects that contract can seek an injunction and stop the action.

Many would argue that the law was right to prevent the violence and the mass picketing seen at Grunwick, Wapping and during the miners' strike. Violence, however, has never had protection, since the only immunity has always been in respect of civil, not criminal, liability. The law as it stands at present means that to take industrial action will be costly for the union in terms of the balloting provisions and costly in relation to any unlawful action taken by any member. Furthermore, the action that is lawful has been severely restricted. The union cannot prevent supplies reaching the employer in dispute (which, given that it has notice of the action, has time to make other arrangements anyway) and restrictions on picketing mean that it is possible that only six pickets may be allowed to picket at the entrance or exit of their own place of work (Code of Practice on Picketing (1992) published by the Secretary of State). This almost reduces industrial action to peaceful protest.

While amendments made by the Employment Relations Act 1999 have relieved some of the stringency in the balloting requirements, the Act has done nothing to increase the type of industrial action that will attract immunity from liability in tort. Nor has it resurrected total trade union immunity. Some would argue that peaceful protest is all workers should be able to do. It should be remembered, however, that unions were set up to fight abuses by employers and have done a great deal to improve working conditions and the health and safety of workers. Good industrial relations law should balance the interests of employers and workers. It can be argued that the present legislative provisions, by removing power from the unions, have tipped the balance in favour of employers.

QUESTION 49

Scab Ltd is a private company manufacturing farm machinery and equipment. Last month, a dispute arose with the union represented in the company, the NFU. The union objected to the company obtaining supplies from Scrap Ltd, a company that employed non-union labour. Picket, the union convenor at Scab Ltd, spoke to the managing director and informed him that the union was very perturbed about the situation. In fact, Scab Ltd was already thinking of severing its links with Scrap Ltd on account of the latter failing to honour its obligations last month under its existing

2

contract with Scab Ltd, the third fundamental breach under the present contract. Last week, Scab wrote to Scrap, informing Scrap that it considered that Scrap had repudiated the contract and that it was thus relieved of all further obligations. The NFU was unaware of the breaches by Scrap Ltd. Today, having heard that Scab Ltd has terminated the contract with Scrap Ltd, Picket stated publicly that the union wished Scab Ltd to terminate the contract lawfully by giving one week's notice. In fact, the notice period under the contract was four weeks, which is normal for the industry.

At the time of the start of the first dispute, the union also discovered that Scab Ltd intended to enter into a contract with Hadless Ltd, another company that employs non-union labour. Picket threatened Scab that, unless it abandoned plans to enter into the contract, he would call a strike at the plant. Scab Ltd declined to enter into the contract with Hadless.

▶ Advise Scab Ltd, Scrap Ltd and Hadless Ltd of any torts (if any) that may have been committed by Picket.

Common Pitfalls

- The question is only asking you to advise the companies on the torts that may have been committed by Picket.
- It requires a detailed discussion of the torts, do not go off at a tangent and start discussing liability – this is not what the question is asking for.

Answer Plan

It is important in this question to look at exactly what is being asked. The student is being asked only to discuss any torts committed. As such, a detailed discussion of the torts is required.

Particular issues to be considered are:

- ❖ potential economic torts that may have been committed;
- ❖ the requirements for an actionable direct inducement of a breach of contract;
- ❖ the requirements for actionable causing loss by unlawful means; and
- ❖ the requirements for actionable interference with a trade or business.

ANSWER

The question asks us to advise the companies on the torts that may have been committed by Picket. The first tort to consider is that of a direct inducement of breach of contract. This tort was established by the case of *Lumley v Gye* (1853), in which a theatre owner induced a singer to break her existing contract so that she could sing for him instead. The necessary components of the tort are:

❖ there must have been an unlawful act;
❖ knowledge of the existence of the contract and enough of its contents to realise there could be a potential breach;
❖ an intention to cause a breach of contract;
❖ an actual inducement; and
❖ causation.

We can now apply these components to the first dispute between Scab and the union in relation to Scab's contract with Scrap. The first is that there must have been an unlawful act. In the problem, Picket tells the managing director that the union is concerned about the contract with Scrap. Scrap, however, has committed three fundamental breaches of contract and Scab has treated such breaches as repudiatory. As such, Scab feels no longer bound by its contractual obligations. Should Scab not be in breach, but perfectly entitled to pull out of the contract, no unlawful act has been committed and thus the first component of the tort does not exist. The facts are unclear, however, as to what breaches have occurred and whether a court of law would hold them to be repudiatory. Furthermore, in *Torquay Hotels Ltd v Cousins* (1969), the Court of Appeal held that the tort could be committed even though no liability arose for the breach. In that case, although there was an inducement, there was no liability because of a force majeure clause that excluded liability for breach caused by industrial action. The majority of the Court of Appeal held that the tort had been committed because a breach had occurred, even though no liability arose. Lord Denning MR went much further, however. He stated that the tort had occurred because there had been an interference with the contract. This interpretation is important to the problem. If the majority of the Court of Appeal is followed, then, if Scab is entitled to pull out, there is no breach and thus no inducement. If interference is enough, then potentially the tort may have been committed. It must be noted, however, that the facts are unclear as to whether Scab is entitled to treat the contract as repudiated.

The second element of the tort is knowledge of the existence of the contract and enough of its terms to know a breach may occur. Picket announces that the union wished Scab to terminate the contract lawfully, giving one week's notice, but the facts state that the notice required was four weeks, which is usual for the industry. On the face of it, therefore, it could be argued that Picket had insufficient knowledge of the contract, given that he got the notice period wrong. The law, however, may imply knowledge. In *Bents Brewery v Hogan* (1945), a union official persuaded a brewery manager to divulge information that was a breach of the manager's implied duty of fidelity. It was held that the official must have been aware of such a duty. In *Stratford v Lindley* (1965), Lord Pearce stated that it seemed unlikely that the union would not know terms that were commonplace within the industry. On the basis of these authorities, it is likely that Picket will be deemed to know that the term of notice was four weeks, given that this is usual.

The third element is that of intention. In other words, Picket must have intended to cause a breach of contract. This means that he must have foreseen the possibility of a breach as well as wishing to achieve that end. While in *Emerald Construction v Lowthian* (1966) it was held that recklessness was sufficient to satisfy this element, the House of Lords in *Mainstream Properties Ltd v Young* (2007) has held that, to satisfy the tort, the perpetrator must deliberately induce a breach and that negligence or carelessness is not enough. In the problem, the union was unaware that Scrap had committed fundamental breaches and it is clear that it wished Scab to get out of the contract. It can be argued, therefore, that Picket wanted the contract terminated and foresaw that this may involve a breach, although it may be debatable whether he deliberately induced such a breach given his comments.

The fourth element is that there must have been an inducement – in other words, 'pressure, persuasion or procurement'. In *Allen v Flood* (1898), it was held that communicating the view of employees to the employer was not sufficient to constitute an inducement (see also *Thomson v Deakin* (1952)). However, over the years, the standard has been relaxed and the fact that the party is willing to get out of the contract will not prevent an inducement occurring. Thus, the fact that Scab wished to get out of the contract does not prevent Picket's words constituting an inducement, although it must be asked whether what he said amounted to pressure, persuasion or procurement. It would appear from later authorities that if the statement influenced Scab in any way, then an inducement will have occurred (*British Motor Trade Association v Salvadori* (1949)).

The final element is that the inducement must have caused the breach. It was held in *Stratford* that the breach had to be a reasonable consequence of the inducement; thus, if the words spoken had no effect on the hearer who was going to break the contract anyway, the tort will not be made out. In the problem, if the words spoken by Picket finally induced Scab's decision to get out of the contract, causation is satisfied.

In relation to the second dispute, two potential torts may have been committed. In relation to the threat to Scab, it is possible that Picket has committed the tort of causing loss by unlawful means and it is also possible that he has committed the tort of interference with a trade or business.

Discussing causing loss by unlawful means first: there is no existing contract between Scab and Hadless, and thus the tort of inducement cannot apply. In *Rookes v Barnard* (1964), however, the House of Lords considerably widened the then tort of intimidation. The tort was known as intimidation because it had only previously been committed when there had been a threat of physical injury; however, in *Rookes v Barnard* (1964), the House of Lords extended the operation of the tort. In that case, the branch chairman and two officials of the union told BOAC that if it did not dismiss Rookes, they would call a strike. Rookes was therefore lawfully dismissed with notice. The House of Lords held that this constituted intimidation as there was a threat of an unlawful act (breach of contract) and intimidation covered the threat of any unlawful act, not just the threat of physical violence. However, in the joined appeals of *OBG v Allan, Douglas v Hello! Ltd* and *Mainstream Properties v Young* (2008), Lord Hoffman said that the word 'intimidation' had been wrongly ascribed to the facts in *Rookes*. He felt that the tort of causing loss by unlawful means had existed since the case of *Allen v Flood* (1898) and this was the reason for the decision in *Rookes*. The elements of the tort are that there must be an unlawful threat. Here, Picket has threatened a strike if Scab enters the contract. A strike is a breach of contract but, since *OBG* and *Rookes*, would not be covered by the immunities and thus will be deemed to be an unlawful threat. Second, there must be an intention to harm the plaintiff – in this case, Hadless. If Scab does not enter the contract, Hadless will suffer financial loss and therefore will be harmed. Third, there must be causation – that is, the threat must cause the hearer to act. Looking at the problem, it is unclear whether the threat of a strike caused Scab not to enter the contract but if it did, causation has occurred. Fourth, there must be loss to the plaintiff, and we have already noted that Hadless will suffer financial loss. Lastly, there must be unlawful means. In *OBG*, the House of Lords held that unlawful means included an interference with the freedom of a third party in his dealings with the claimant. Thus, in *Douglas*, *Hello!* magazine was not liable because it obtained the photographs from a freelance photographer and thus it was the actions of the photographer, and not the magazine, which had interfered with the dealings between Douglas and *OK* magazine. In the problem, it was Picket who interfered with the dealings between Scab and Hadless and thus, if causation can be proved, the tort has been committed.

The tort of interference with a trade or business by unlawful means is nebulous. It was declared to exist by the Court of Appeal in *Hadmor Productions Ltd v Hamilton* (1983) and the House of Lords in the appeal in that case appeared tacitly to accept its existence. Again, the essence of the tort is the use of unlawful means, an intention to harm the claimant and the claimant must sustain loss. The tort is a developing one, as seen in *Lonhro v Fayed* (1990), in which the House of Lords stated that it was not necessary to show that the defendant's predominant purpose was to harm the claimant, but it must be shown that the defendant's unlawful act was directed against and intended to harm the claimant. Here, Picket has threatened an unlawful act (a strike) with the intention of persuading Scab not to enter into a contract with Hadless, the result of which has been that the contract has not been entered into. Therefore, it would appear that the necessary elements of the tort have been made out.

In summary, it would appear unlikely that Picket has directly induced a breach of contract: first, because it is unlikely that a breach has occurred between Scab and Scrap; second, because, under *Mainstream Properties*, it is arguable whether he deliberately induced a breach; and third, because, even if a breach has occurred, it is unlikely that there was an inducement or causation. On the other hand, it is likely that Picket has committed the torts of causing loss by unlawful means and interference with a trade or business by unlawful means.

Aim Higher ★

♦ The House of Lords in *OBG v Allan* almost rewrote established law since 1964 and thus a detailed knowledge of the judgments will improve your answer.

♦ Much has been written on the *OBG* case, and reading academic views on the judgments will help you to understand them and enhance your answer. See, for example, Carty (2007) 15 Torts Law Journal 283 and Simpson (2007) 36 ILJ 468.

QUESTION 50

Robinson is a shop steward of the Red Union at Yellow Ltd, and sits on the branch committee of the union. The workers at Yellow Ltd are in dispute with their employer about payment for washing time. Robinson ballots all the workers at Yellow and, after getting a majority vote in favour of strike action, calls the workers out on strike after giving Yellow one week's notice. Because of the strike, Yellow refuses to place any more orders with White Ltd (a major supplier of Yellow Ltd), despite the fact that White has a seven-year contract to supply Yellow with materials. This action causes White to suffer severe financial loss. White Ltd is also in dispute with the Red Union at its factory in relation to payment for washing time and the union has asked Robinson for support.

▶ Advise Yellow Ltd and White Ltd of any actions that might be available to them, and against whom.

Answer Plan

The facts in this problem are vague and, thus, the answer requires a discussion of the possible torts that may have been committed and whether immunity exists in respect of those torts. As stated, the facts are deliberately vague, meaning that the student must discuss an either/or situation.

Particular issues to be considered are:

❖ the tort of direct inducement in relation to the calling of the strike;
❖ the tort of indirect inducement in relation to the contract between Yellow and White;
❖ the 'golden formula';
❖ the immunities in s 219 of the Trade Union and Labour Relations (Consolidation) Act (TULR(C)A) 1992 and whether they apply;
❖ whether the action is official;
❖ whether the balloting and notice provisions have been complied with and the consequences if not.

ANSWER

The question requires us to give advice to the companies involved. The advice will consist of the possible torts that have been committed, the immunity that may exist and whether the immunity applies in the given situations.

In the first part of the problem, there is a strike at Yellow Ltd. Robinson has called the workers out on strike. A strike is a breach of contract and thus, by making the strike call, Robinson is directly inducing the workers to break their contracts of employment. For a direct inducement to occur, there must be: an unlawful act; knowledge of the contract on the part of the inducer; an intention to cause a breach of contract on the part of the inducer; an inducement; and the breach must have been a reasonable consequence of the inducement. It looks likely that, on the facts as set, Robinson did directly induce a breach of contract by the employees.

As a result of the strike, Yellow has refused to place any further orders with White. This action is in breach of contract, given that there is a seven-year contract between the parties. Furthermore, it could be argued that part of the reason for Robinson's actions was to support the workers at White Ltd and that he intended White Ltd harm.

If this can be shown, then it is possible that Robinson has also committed the tort of indirect inducement. In *Stratford v Lindley* (1965), the union officials induced their members to break their contracts of employment, causing their employer to break a commercial contract with the plaintiffs. The elements of the tort of indirect inducement are the same as those for direct inducement, except that there must be the use of unlawful means. This means that if the action for direct inducement is protected by the statutory immunities, there can be no action for indirect inducement.

This leads to a discussion of the immunities. The immunity for both direct and indirect inducement is found in s 219 of the TULR(C)A 1992. Section 219(1)(a) provides that an act done in contemplation or furtherance of a trade dispute is not actionable in tort on the ground only that it induces a person to break a contract. This means that the action by Robinson may have immunity if the actions were in contemplation or furtherance of a trade dispute.

The words 'in contemplation or furtherance of a trade dispute' are known as the 'golden formula'. Thus, the starting point when looking to see if the immunity applies is to ask whether a trade dispute exists. The definition of a trade dispute is found in s 244(1) of the 1992 Act.

This states that a trade dispute is a dispute between workers and their employer that relates wholly or mainly to one or more items listed in the section. The dispute in question is between the employees at Yellow and their employer in relation to payment for washing time. The dispute must be wholly or mainly related to one of the items in the section. Section 244(1)(a) provides that a dispute relating to terms and conditions of employment is a trade dispute, and thus the dispute as to payment for washing time falls within s 244(1)(a). The predominant reason for the action appears to be the dispute, and a secondary reason appears to be that it will also help the employees at White Ltd. Thus, a trade dispute exists within the statutory definition. The next question to be asked is whether the action was in contemplation or furtherance of that trade dispute. Loreburn LC in *Conway v Wade* (1909) said of the phrase:

> I think they (the words) mean that either a dispute is imminent and the act done is in expectation of and with a view to it, or that the dispute is already existing and the act done is in support of one side to it.

In the problem, a dispute exists before the strike. Does the strike further the dispute?

In *Beaverbrook Newspapers v Keys* (1978), a dispute existed at the *Daily Mirror* that resulted in a stoppage of production. As a result, the *Daily Express* decided to print extra copies and the union at the *Express* refused to handle the extra copies, in support of the workers at the *Mirror*. It was held that the blacking was not in furtherance of the dispute at the *Mirror* as it would do nothing to aid it. This introduced an objective test in the area. This went against the judgment of Loreburn LC in *Conway* when he said that the intention behind the action was important – that is, a subjective test. The Court of Appeal, in a series of cases between 1978 and 1980, adopted the objective test, but the House of Lords reaffirmed the subjective test from *Conway* in a series of appeals. In *Express Newspapers Ltd v McShane* (1980), their Lordships said that the test was whether the defendants honestly and genuinely believed that they were furthering the dispute. On the basis of this authority, if Robinson and the members genuinely believe that the dispute will be furthered by the strike, then the action is in furtherance of the dispute. Hence, it falls within s 219(1)(a) and immunity exists in relation to Robinson.

The question remains as to the position of the Red Union. Section 20 of the 1992 Act states that a union will be liable for the torts of its members where the action was authorised or endorsed by the union. Action is taken to be authorised or endorsed if it was authorised or endorsed by one of a statutory list of persons or bodies within the union. Section 20(2)(c) states that an action will be official if it was authorised by an official of the union (whether employed by it or not). Robinson is a shop steward and therefore an official of the union. He called the strike and thus the strike is official action authorised by the union, by virtue of s 20(2)(c).

The reason why the above discussion is important is that the union is required to comply with the statutory balloting and notice provisions contained within the Act. Failure to comply with either the balloting provisions or the notice requirements removes the immunity from the union (ss 226(1) and 234A). There are no details on how the ballot was conducted. It must have been a postal ballot, the voting paper must have been in the statutory form, the employer must have received notice of its occurrence at least seven days before the ballot and a sample ballot paper, and an independent scrutineer must have overseen the ballot. In addition, by ss 231 and 231A, both employees and the employer are to be informed of the result of the ballot as soon as is reasonably practicable. Even if the information has been given and the balloting procedures complied with, s 234 states that the ballot ceases to have effect at the end of a period of four weeks unless the union and employer agree a longer period. There is no evidence of such an agreement, so if the action started more than four weeks after the vote, it will be unprotected.

In addition, s 226A requires the union to give at least seven days' notice of the ballot to the employers of the employees who will be called on to vote, and giving the employer such information 'as would help the employer make plans and bring information to the attention' of such employees. Information should be given about numbers and categories of staff but failing to name relevant staff does not mean that the notice is in breach of the statute. Similar provisions exist in s 234A, which requires the union to give the employer at least seven days' notice before the action begins. In *RMT v London Underground Ltd (2001)*, the union gave the employer notice that it would be calling out 40 per cent of the workforce. The notice stated that the 40 per cent included all categories of workers and all places of work. The Court of Appeal held that this was an infringement of the statute as the union was required to give a breakdown per site of the number of staff in each category who would be involved (now an amended s 226A(2A) and (2B)). Such information should enable an employer to determine the total number of employees concerned, the categories to which those employees belong, the number of employees in those categories, the workplaces where they work and the number who work at each workplace. In addition, the union must also provide a sample voting paper to the employer at least three days before the starting date of the ballot.

The problem states that Robinson gave a week's notice. If this is a working week and thus only five days, Red Union has lost all immunity and thus can be sued for both direct and indirect inducement of a breach of contract. In addition if Red Union failed to give seven days' notice of the ballot, as required under s 226A, and did not give the employer the information required under s 226A(2) or s 234A, this failure will also lead to a loss of immunity.

While both Yellow and White will have suffered financial loss, it will be more important to them that the action is stopped and thus both may seek injunctions to prevent the action continuing. In particular, both may wish to apply for an interim injunction to stop the action pending the trial of the substantive case. An interim injunction, however, is not a trial of the issue, but merely a decision whether to give temporary relief. From *American Cyanamid Co v Ethicon Ltd (1975)*, all that the claimant has to show is that he has an arguable case fit to go to trial and once that has been shown, the decision whether to grant the injunction is made on the 'balance of convenience' test – that is, will the claimant suffer more damage without the injunction than the defendant will suffer if it is granted? If the claimant can show financial loss, this will be greater damage than the union's loss of a tactical advantage and thus the injunctions are usually granted in favour of the employer.

Thus, both White Ltd and Yellow Ltd can take action against Red Union for indirect and direct inducement and, in order to stop the action, either or both should apply for an interim injunction, which, on the balance of convenience test, is likely to be rewarded.

Index